THE
NOVOTNY
PAPERS

THE
NOVOTNY
PAPERS

'A BIT VULTURE, A BIT EAGLE'

LILIAN PIZZICHINI

AMBERLEY

For Duke

OXFORDSHIRE COUNTY COUNCIL	
3303685028	
Askews & Holts	02-Nov-2021
B.NOV	

First published 2021

Amberley Publishing
The Hill, Stroud
Gloucestershire, GL5 4EP

www.amberley-books.com

Copyright © Lilian Pizzichini, 2021

The right of Lilian Pizzichini to be identified as the Author of this work has been asserted in accordance with the Copyright, Designs and Patents Act 1988.

ISBN 978 1 4456 9750 5 (hardback)
ISBN 978 1 4456 9751 2 (ebook)

British Library Cataloguing in Publication Data. A catalogue record for this book is available from the British Library.

1 2 3 4 5 6 7 8 9 10

Typesetting by Aura Technology and Software Services, India. Printed in Malta.

CONTENTS

PART TWO

INTRODUCTION

'I'm Mariella Novotny. Notorious Novotny according to your editor but perhaps I misread him. He may have said "Notornis" and I'd go along with that because according to my *Funk and Wagnall's* that means "a wingless bird" and I'm all of that.'

This is the story of a very strange woman. Mariella Novotny was a twentieth-century call girl who pursued literary fame and political notoriety, and who ended her days an *agent provocateur*. She was calling time's up before time up was a remote possibility. She was a difficult woman before being a difficult woman was allowed. She knew many of the pre-eminent men of her time although they tried their hardest not to admit it. The list of her lovers is too long to type and the implications are too many. More tellingly, she refused to be defined by the shackles of shame that attach themselves to women who work in the sex trade. She is a compelling subject for anyone interested in the networks that govern our society because her attempts to expose the sexual hypocrisy that protected those in power were well ahead of her time.

Mariella was well known as soon as she reached adulthood. She made newspaper headlines both sides of the Atlantic and across Europe several times; the first time in a nebulous case of white-slave trafficking in New York and Washington involving herself as a wayward minor and the most powerful man in the world, the President-elect John F. Kennedy. She was believed to be part of a vice ring set up by an alleged Communist agent who was also a well-known British film producer. FBI officers called their investigation 'The Bow-tie Case'.

Two years later the young 'Monroe lookalike' was receiving rave reviews for a major part in another sex scandal with implications for national security. This imbroglio was set in England: the Profumo Affair. Mariella was the hostess of the Man in the Mask party. She was a close friend of Stephen Ward, the osteopath and pander to high society, who died in murky circumstances. Both the Profumo Affair and the Kennedy call-girl ring were stories that dogged her until her untimely end. Who was the man in the mask? And did she really play nurse and patient with JFK while reporting to the Soviet Union?

Then, in the late 1960s, she encountered a famous safe-cracker-cum-national treasure. Eddie Chapman, aka Agent Zigzag, was England's most successful wartime double agent. He was so successful he claimed that Adolf Hitler himself awarded him the Iron Cross in 1943. (It's more likely he received the War Merit Cross 2nd Class, or *Kriegsverdienstkreuz*, as the Iron Cross was reserved for military personnel.) With Mariella, Eddie lived in a *ménage a trois* that included her voyeuristic elderly husband in a fifteenth-century castle on the outskirts of Rome. In April 1964 Mariella gave birth to Agent Zigzag's illegitimate child.

In the 1970s, she started to chronicle her exploits. In 1971 Leslie Frewin published her *roman-à-clef*, *King's Road*. Written in the Harold Robbins style, it fictionalises 'London's jet set, the high life and low life of London's turned-on, beautiful people'. It reveals details of Black Power enclaves in Notting Hill and an MP's bewilderment in the face of vaginal piercings.

She is bizarre, sometimes grotesque, and she likes to shock.

But I can hear a yearning, edgy, ambitious young woman who wanted to get out of wherever she was, the constraints that kept her in place, the person she was supposed to be. She touches me in a way that her contemporaries, the likes of Germaine Greer and Rosie Boycott, cannot. She rubbed shoulders with them but she lacked the education and emotional resources to shape a clear vision. She was conflicted in what she wanted to achieve, and attempting to use men's language to talk about what women knew. In a time when women were struggling to break free of the virgin/whore mould, she aimed high by using low tactics. Her trump card was sex and she played it to the bitter end, trying to get on in a world in which the pill and women's liberation created an opportunity for men to exploit women.

I know everything about wanting to get out, and the getting out doesn't come easy. She would not put up with marginalisation and she would not shut up. None of the FBI, the CIA or the British secret services could keep this woman quiet. The journalists and historians – the biographer of Agent Zigzag, the reporter who befriended Stephen Ward – refuse to give her credence. They retreat with a *moue* of distaste. Her unabashed sexuality, indecorous and immodest, the social and sexual mores she tore to shreds – this is the real scandal for her critics. They find her distasteful. I like this woman who rips apart the veil.

Hers is a life larger than the woman who led it. Mariella embodies the emergence of a radical sexual politics. Besides this she was a con artiste – a compulsive, recidivist storyteller. She kept company with some of the key figures of twentieth-century history. They went to enormous lengths to cover up the fact of her existence. At times their efforts were so convincing I wondered if I had made her up. At other times I felt there was something inhuman about her.

Some might think she is a strange choice for a biographer. But I have always found the misdeeds of history's vanquished more endearing than the achievements of its victors.

But can she be trusted? Investigative journalists tread carefully when dealing with Mariella's allegations. In his memoir, Tom Mangold describes her as a 'fantasist'. He is referring to her claims of intimate acquaintance with famous names and cover-ups concerning illicit sex. Mariella's need for the spotlight was urgent and relentless. She was capable of saying or doing anything to get it. But in all that she said or did there is a painful truth emerging. Unusually for a woman of her generation, she is quite candid in chronicling the abuse and exploitation that robbed her of her childhood. We are now entering a phase in history in which survivors of child exploitation (or CSA – child sexual abuse) are raising awareness of the collusion that surrounds these offences. We are also more aware of the widespread occurrence of CSA and the psychological implications for survivors.

The debate around repressed memories and false accusations continues to perplex courts of law. This is what makes Mariella's story so relevant to the twenty-first century. We are slowly learning that memories which are fragmented, blurred and distressing carry a light that shines on something dark and disquieting. There is a photograph of Mariella taken on her wedding day by the young photographer David Bailey. The date is 29 January 1960; the beginning of a new decade. The bride's eyes have a lot of light in them and yet they seem curiously blind. They remind me of old photographs I have seen of lunatics kept in an asylum. I have seen many photographs of Mariella – a lot of them taken by Bailey – and the light stays the same.

This is a story about memory. Mariella was carrying the kind of memory that a great many of us (one in four women, one in six men) have repressed. It was the kind of memory for which a framework had not yet been put in place. It profoundly shaped her intimate life without her understanding, her assent or her knowledge. This memory was the expression of a self-induced amnesia, the queen of defences. But memories cannot be held down. They come out sideways, and for Mariella they came out as the need to sexually dominate men. She was a call-girl, yes, but a call-girl who whipped and beat men into submission. She was a vengeful harpy, a woman who came from nowhere and made astonishing advances on patriarchal society. She was bound to attract derision and disbelief.

Not just derision and disbelief but fascination.

'My curiosity to meet them was immense,' Thomas Critchley wrote. Critchley was Lord Denning's private secretary while Denning was conducting his inquiry into the Profumo Scandal.

I share his curiosity. In 1978 my grandfather – the paterfamilias of a clan that abused, exploited and trivialised women and girls as a matter of course – died in circumstances similar to those in which Stephen Ward died. In other words, some people believe it was murder. Some even say my grandfather died at the end of a poisoned umbrella. But it was the woman who was responsible for his downfall who caught my imagination. How did she do it? Where did she get the balls?

Mariella Novotny departed this world leaving scant traces behind her. Based on the historian's premise – absence of evidence is not evidence of absence – I kept trucking on. I discovered that in the mid-1970s, when the world was entrenched in the Cold War, Mariella was laying waste to a Caribbean Prime Minister. Two-way mirrors and microphones were hidden in a room at Brown's Hotel. The call-girl turned novelist was now styling herself an *agent provocateur*. There were bungled attempts on her life. Michael Eddowes, the author and campaigner for miscarriages of justice, tried to ghost her memoir. Masked men came into his home and beat him, giving him a stern warning to back off. So frightened was he that he burnt the manuscript.

Mariella had been trying to tell us what had happened to her, about war crimes and the death of old Europe, childhood trauma and the struggle to earn a living since she was seventeen and a hatcheck girl at the Pigalle Club in Piccadilly. No one believed her. It was too frightening.

Maybe, I hoped, I had the balls to do it for her.

PART ONE

'I have always been a bird. A bit vulture, a bit eagle.
I have looked the sun in its face. Born several times –
dead several times so that I could be reborn from my ashes.'

1

A BIRD FROM BOHEMIA

In the former territories of the Austro-Hungarian Empire, in the aftermath of war, Mariella Novotny's portrait, she claimed, was 'engraved on the [Czechoslovakian] nation's banknotes, and [her] birthday declared the National Day of celebration'.

Accounts of her childhood vary. The primary source I have for the following account is an elderly gentleman living in Sweden who says he met Mariella through the omnipresent Stephen Ward. This is the same Stephen Ward who ran an osteopath practice and dating agency for young, provincial girls and worldly older men. My Swedish correspondent was a model for Stephen Ward in films that he made for his osteopath practice. 'Sven' became Mariella's lover at the age of fifteen, when she was seventeen and married to fifty-six-year-old Hod Dibben. They spent many hours together, he told me, talking and laughing about the old men who were infatuated with her. But she also confided in him as a trusted friend. According to Sven, Mariella's story starts in interwar Bohemia. Her father was from a landowning Czech family. As a young man, during the summer months Novotny *père* raced motorcycles across Europe. He partied, drank, bedded women, and saw the war coming, so he rode a Velocette to England.

Aged thirty-five, Mr Novotny was too old to join the RAF. But he apparently flew night-fighters out of a Lincolnshire airbase. I could find no paper trail to back this story up but it was in the Lincolnshire airbase, Sven told me, that Novotny met Mariella's mother. Here I was on firmer ground. Mariella's mother accompanies her daughter on many of her capers and even features in early newspaper interviews. Her name was Constance Capes, and at the outbreak of war, she was thirty-six years old and single.

Constance is listed on the 1939 register as living at 122 Durham Road in Grimsby, Lincolnshire. She was a shorthand typist, living with her brother, a scaffolder, and their elderly mother, Harriet. So Constance Capes, Mariella's mother, was a single woman living with her widowed mother and younger brother in Grimsby. Constance's family had been shuffling around terraced streets in the centre of Grimsby Town for decades prior to the war. The main distinguishing feature of the Capes is Constance's status as a single woman. This is not part of the story Mariella tells. In an article she wrote for *Club International* in 1973, she focuses on her father. In Prague, she says, the dashing Czech was married. But here in England, on a small cobbled street on the East Anglian coast, he became involved with a shorthand typist called Constance.

Mariella also said that her father was in Intelligence. There is no way of verifying this. Nevertheless, there are rumours that the British government was aware of his presence in this country. At this stage I could go along with Sven's account and Mariella's testament unquestioningly or I could offer some alternatives. For example, during the Second World War, very close to Grimsby Town, in Weelsby Woods, was a camp for Italian prisoners of war. The woods were a short walk from Durham Road which, in the opposite direction, led to the seafront. So it is entirely possible that a thirty-six-year-old woman did meet an exiled young man nine months before Mariella's birth date in May 1941.

The child was born Stella Marie Capes. 'My memory is seared by brutal experiences as a child in refugee camps,' she wrote under the pen name of Mariella. After the war, the same woodland in Grimsby was used to house the Polish Carpathian Lancers. This was the armoured element of the 2nd Polish Corps. They arrived in Grimsby in 1945 and made their camp where the Italians had been. Grimsby was their home until 1947, when their demobilisation was complete. Locals still remember one notable officer who was reputed to hail from Polish aristocracy. Amongst the locals he had the unofficial title of 'Count' and he was always very friendly and polite.

I wondered if this could have been the man who inspired a little girl to flights of fancy. It is easy to understand how a lonely girl born to a single mother in a small town would invent stories of romantic trysts and star-crossed lovers. But Mariella's descriptions of her childhood in Czechoslovakia are detailed and passionate and hard to ignore.

If what she says is true, between 1942 and 1945 her father worked for the Czech government in exile. After the war he returned to Czechoslovakia, as part of the Czech Independence Movement. He took her with him, as well as Constance. He was looking forward to reclaiming his land and his titles. But he was to be disappointed. Edvard Benes, the leader of the independence movement, had put his faith in Soviet policy. Benes believed Stalin when he talked of a Central European federation; a 'Leninist neo-pan-Slavism'. You could hardly blame Benes for trusting the Russians as allies. The West had left his country to face Hitler alone. It was Stalin's army that liberated his country from the Nazis.

Once Czechoslovakia was liberated, Mariella told various media outlets (including Sven, who has his own website) that at four years of age she was living in a grand palace where it was Christmas all year round. There were governesses, parties, lace and velvet dresses, horses, and riding with her father on his Velo.

By 1947 hard currency reserves had dwindled. A shortage of grain and fodder led to a national emergency. Mariella would have been six at this point, sitting in a palace surrounded by guards. Mass meetings were taking place on Wenceslas Square in Prague. In February 1948 five thousand Czechs left for the American zone of Germany; ten thousand entered Austria. Mariella's father left her to join the underground resistance. Constance went with him. Borders to the west were sealed. Frontier police were stalking escapees in synchronised formations. Mariella's parents had vanished.

This is where the details come in that make Mariella's story credible enough to continue listening. The Novotnys' housekeeper, her husband and their small son found a space for Mariella on a cattle truck, and they made their escape from Prague. They didn't get far. The truck was searched. They were discovered and taken to a refugee camp in Germany. Mariella was six years old with no papers and only the housekeeper's family to look after her. For the next two years, she 'never once had a bath or saw a proper lavatory. Sickness spread like wildfire.'

There was so little food that women and girls were selling themselves, and one awful night Mariella 'was snooping round the cookhouse for food' when two soldiers captured her. They took her behind some huts and made her watch while they raped a twelve-year-old girl. Next time they said it would be her. Mariella passed out. When she regained consciousness her vision had shrunk to a nine-inch radius. It is this kind of detail that makes me believe she suffered some trauma from which she never recovered. Whether that trauma took place in Germany or Grimsby we will probably never know.

More horrors were to come. She and Wolfie, the housekeeper's son, found a gap in the barbed wire around the camp and got out to play in a wood, where they stumbled across a dead man hanging from a cherry tree. They were so frightened they ran back into the camp through the official entrance. Soldiers grabbed hold of the two infants and locked them in a tiny dark hut for two days. Every night little Stella heard women's screams coming from behind the huts: she knew what that meant and she could never forget.

According to Sven, Mrs Capes came to rescue her child, and got her home by hitching on lorries. She then had to 'buy' ferry-tickets for herself and the child with 'services rendered', as she had no cash. Mother and child came home to England impoverished.

The stories are harrowing. The background to her story is true enough. Soviet troops did assist in a *coup d'état* in Prague. The Communists moved quickly to consolidate their power. Thousands fled the country to avoid living under Communism.

The documented evidence tells a different tale, however. Mariella's birth certificate states that she was born in Sheffield on 9 May 1941. Her mother was living at 77 Rustlings Road. There is no father on the certificate, but there are some candidates with a suitably exotic back-story. The Sheffield Co-ordinating Committee for Refugees kept house at numbers 75 and 79 Rustlings Road, either side of Constance's abode. After the birth, Constance and her baby slipped under the radar. So it is possible they were overseas. It is possible they returned to England when Mariella was ten. They made their next recorded appearance in London in 1957.

At this point Mariella is best defined by her birth to an unmarried woman with no visible resources in wartime England. This would be hard enough at a time when illegitimacy was a cause of shame. By the end of war, Constance had a little girl who 'couldn't sleep at night and ... spoke to nobody'. Perhaps as an adult Mariella developed the stories she heard from refugees and Polish soldiers into her own lost claim on an ancestral home in Bohemia; a renegade father in a fairy palace. The intrigue of political events added jeopardy to her story. The day after her seventh birthday, on 9 May 1948, Czechoslovakia's Communist Party put forward a new constitution based on the Soviet model. Paper currency was printed to celebrate this fact. Twenty-five years later,

Mariella wrote that her portrait was printed on Czech bank notes to celebrate her birthday.

Again, it is possible that there is a grain of truth in this. Maybe she *was* in Czechoslovakia in 1948 and remembered hearing adults talking about a new regime, a new currency. She might have distorted this memory to serve her own purposes. She would not be alone in doing that. But what is very clear to me is that being Stella Marie Capes, the illegitimate daughter of a shorthand typist from Grimsby, was just not good enough. A little girl's fantasy became a woman's reality. This invention was the foundation stone of her survival.

2

AND HOD CREATED WOMAN

The constant in this account of Mariella's life is the question of how a little girl from Grimsby became an International Woman of Mystery via storytelling and prostitution. These themes – of secrets and revelation – keep surfacing with the obstinacy of an unhealed wound. The themes emerge in the preamble to Mariella's future. This short episode showcases her future husband Hod, and her predecessor Patsy.

Horace 'Hod' Dibben was born on 15 April 1905 in a respectable suburb of Southampton. His family lived in a Victorian villa. The family firm was Dibben & Sons, Ltd, Builders' Merchants and Ironmongers. Hod's parents were prominent members of the Plymouth Brethren, a conservative, Low Church, Nonconformist, evangelical Christian movement whose history can be traced to Dublin in the late 1820s. For a child who would grow into a notorious epicurean this meant that during festivals, any activity that was not religious was forbidden.

Hod's mother died suddenly when he was very young and in 1929, aged twenty-three, he married a girl from Portsmouth. Newly married, he went into business as a radio engineer. Regular wireless broadcasts were moving towards the formation of the

British Broadcasting Corporation. Hod wanted to gain a foothold in an emerging industry. War came, and he took his skills into the RAF where he listened to enemy transmissions. Mariella once said he was based in the Orkneys where he witnessed a death so horrifying she had to summon her 'guardian angel' to rid him of its impact.

On being discharged, Hod opened a firm of radio wholesalers in Southampton. His father had died and the ironmongery business had gone to another branch of Dibbens. By now Hod had a small son to support. But it would seem financial responsibility was not his strong suit. By 1949 he had been made bankrupt, and he had to get a job in an estate agent's office. Hod began to study land management and furniture restoration at evenings and weekends.

In *Honeytrap*, authors Stephen Dorril and Anthony Summers describe an interview they conducted with Hod in 1990. He told them about a formative life event that took him to a world far, far away from the Plymouth Brethren. One night after work at the estate agent's, he followed a female colleague to her home. He had been fascinated by her for a while. So he took this opportunity to hide in her garden and peer through her curtains. The lady in question was in her front room wearing a corset and suspenders. She was whipping a man who was kneeling at her feet.

It was well known throughout Hod's crowd and well reported in Mariella's writings that he was a voyeur. But there was more to him than this. A week after spying on his colleague, Hod had allowed her to tie him to a tree in the woods. She flogged him with briars until the blood flowed. This is just the kind of fruitiness I would expect from a man who would one day marry a woman like Mariella. It soon followed that after the incident in the woods, Hod's first wife did them both a great service. She left him and took their son back to her parents.

In 2016 I approached a relative of Hod who emailed me in return with some information that was more revealing in what it didn't say than what it did:

I have to be slightly careful about this, as I know there are family members who very much want to put the past behind them. I'd prefer it, if anything I say can be uncredited and confidential. That said, I have no great bombshell to drop – and though Hod and I became great friends in his later life, my knowledge of his earlier life is sketchy.

I think the Dibbens were quietly wealthy, with money from engineering businesses in the Southhampton area. There is a village in Hampshire called Dibden, where I think they came from originally. Hod had one son who sadly died ... a good ten years before Hod.

He was obsessed with antiques and made quite a collection, most of which he gave away. He did serve in the army, but details [are] sketchy. He was living [with his son and daughter-in-law] in Eaton Square in 1965, so there was definitely money at some point. He was a famous socialite and one of his best friends was Cipriani, the hotel owner in Venice. He apparently helped invent the Bellini cocktail on a mad night in Harry's Bar, Cipriani's bar in Venice. He seemed to know a lot of famous people. He had a night club in Knightsbridge called Esmeralda's Barn, and another I think, called the Black Sheep. I imagine they were full of celebrity/socialite types and probably fairly racy.

Hod, right to the end, was a very charming, funny person, a brilliant raconteur and lover of life. And he had a brilliant life, not regretting a single thing. I was with him when he died [in 1990] and he told me that.

After his first marriage dissolved, Hod Dibben put an advert in the papers: 'Intelligent young girl required for antique business. Must have knowledge of art.'

By now he had become an estate manager and an 'expert' on eighteenth-century furniture. He needed a Girl Friday.

3

THE EARRING GIRL

Before Mariella, there was Patsy, the sixteen-year-old daughter of a Hampshire grocer. From what I have discovered about Patsy Morgan, her parents lived in a modest red-brick house in the New Forest. Hod provided her with the opportunity to leave it.

As far as he was concerned, Patsy had the right look – Roman nose, dark hair and eyes, graceful bearing. He needed a girl to soften up the punters, deflect creditors and host parties. He didn't want another wife. He didn't want dependents. He wanted an accomplice.

The story goes that Hod sent Patsy to a finishing school run by the Duchess of Devon. The self-styled Duchess of Devon (she had once been a chamber maid and was later a variety artiste) rented a boarding house in Exeter and taught her gels how to balance an invisible tray and how to do their make-up. Having learnt how to walk, chat, dance, play bridge and ride side-saddle, Patsy joined Hod at Lytes Cary Manor in Somerset. (He had rented a manor house from Sir Walter Fitzjenner on the condition that he spruce it up.) Patsy changed her manners, her deportment and her name to Morgan-Dibben.

'All parts blend to perfection with one another,' said Nikolaus Pevsner of Lytes Cary. The parts he was referring to were the chapel, which was built around 1343; the Great Hall, added in the fifteenth century; and the Oriel Room, which came one hundred years later. Hod invited his friends to weekend shoots. Patsy made her entrance like a ballerina who had strolled in after a season at Salzburg. In 1949 *Tatler*'s diarist attended one of their parties and declared, 'The sweet life has begun.'

But behind the scenes all was not well. In a self-scribed article for the *People* in 1961 Hod revealed a dark and terrible secret. During the war, whilst stationed on the Orkney Islands, he had been engaged in occult activities. On leaving the coven he had been cursed. The curse had followed him to Lytes Cary. A guest at the manor house (the art connoisseur Reginald Warren) was attacked by an unknown hand in the night. Hod's son from his annulled marriage refused to stay in a haunted house. Hod himself was too scared to sleep for fear of a voice in the night telling him he was doomed. Meanwhile he'd sunk a lot of money into the place, not to mention all the cash and effort he had put into Patsy's clothes, which came from the most expensive couturiers of Paris.

'She was tutored in foreign languages and the social graces,' he told the *People*. 'She travelled extensively and in the end became the toast of five countries.' It was time for London.

This was where a small-time gangster called Ronnie Dice was running a casino in a Knightsbridge club. Esmeralda's Barn was a pokey little dive down the road from Buckingham Palace. Originally named after the woman who had run it as a lesbian's club, it eventually became known as the Kray twins' entry point into high society. Ronnie wanted to run it as a gambling club, and he put a lot of thought into the decor. At street-level, the patron entered a tiny, low-ceilinged lobby. He or she then climbed a dark and narrow staircase up to a long room with a bar and a side room with a chemmy (*chemin de fer*) table. Ronnie had the adaptability to keep going and overcome the odds but he couldn't catch a break. On the club's opening night, Esmeralda was found dead of an overdose in the Baker Street flat of her accountant. Then, just as the club was beginning to make a profit, Ronnie had to run for cover.

In order to pay for croupiers and waitresses, Ronnie had stolen money from Billy Hill. My story now infringes on the annals of organised crime. In the aftermath of the Second World War Billy was the *soi-disant* boss of London's underworld. Imagine a small, compact figure, bristling with energy, a ringer for Humphrey Bogart, with diamond rings on his fingers. Not only was he the mastermind of an organised crime gang, but he was the author of an autobiography. *Boss of Britain's Underworld* was published by Naldrett Press in 1955. The book's launch party was at Gennaro's restaurant in Dean Street. It was attended by Lord and Lady Docker, and some heavy-set fellows in drape suits. Spoof telegrams were read out: 'Hope you have a topping time – Britain's No. 1 Hangman'; 'Will you send us back our mail van? We miss it – Postmaster General.'

It did not surprise me that Billy fetched up in Hod's story. If Hod was on the raffish side then he would have encountered gangsters. They were the lifeblood of London's social life in the post-war years.

Billy had people running games for him all over London. One of these people was my grandfather Charlie, whose downfall, as I mentioned previously, was heralded by Mariella. At this point in her story Stella Marie, as she was still called, was living in digs with her mother in Sheffield (or Grimsby), whilst dreaming of the beautiful people of London (or Prague). Charlie, whose beginnings were similarly shabby, was rubbing shoulders with West London's beautiful people, playing cards for Billy in a flat on Moscow Road. Bayswater was Billy's gambling HQ. Hill had learnt to play baccarat and its variant *chemin de fer* at Monte Carlo. There he met the swells of the gaming elite: John Aspinall, who founded the Clermont Club, and Tom Holland of Crockford's. Illicit gambling was the cornerstone of crime in the fifties, and Billy was on to Ronnie Dice and his rival game at Esmeralda's. Plus Ronnie owed him money. Billy called Teddy Machin, a man who much later on acted as minder to my grandfather. Teddy was about six foot one. He had black hair and black eyes. He knew how to dress and he had the walk of gangsters back then. You'd think he was Sicilian. But his mates in North London called him Terrible Ted and as king of the Upton Park mob he was making a splash in the West End. It was Teddy who told Dice he'd better get out of London quickly and leave the lease to Esmeralda's in Billy's name.

No doubt through Hod's connections with Stephen Ward's set, he had by now become a player on the London club scene. So Hod took over management of Esmeralda's Barn. Billy ran the chemmy tables and protection, and twenty-seven-year-old Patsy was *maitresse d'*. All parts came together perfectly.

Patsy was glamorous, lively, and pretty, with a head for business. No records exist charting her birth, life or death. But during her tenure as Hod's model of a perfect woman, various reporters gleaned some nuggets. Her father, Harry Morgan, had founded a chain of grocery shops in Hampshire after starting as a shop boy behind the counter. Patsy was daddy's golden girl. He sent her to a private school. She had the charisma to ensure that schoolfriends were flattered to be invited for tea. Charisma and business acumen are a powerful combination. The launch of Esmeralda's Barn in 1955, with interior design by Annigoni and carefully contrived marketing, soon brought the young Guards officers, the debutantes and the celebrities. It became the favoured night spot for the Duke of Kent. Lord Astor turned up with Stephen Ward. Hollywood actress Leslie Caron popped in, as did other stars of stage and screen. Patsy renamed it the Torch Theatre Club, but Esmeralda's stuck.

Now begins Patsy's stellar career. Her first newspaper cutting comes from *Tatler*. On 19 October 1953 she attended the opening night of the Vienna Ballet at the Prince's Theatre. She was photographed wearing gold and garnet earrings, originally part of an eighteenth-century head-dress, with a boldly striped gown. Patsy was a fast learner. Everyone needs a gimmick to stand out, and earrings were going to be hers. By the next issue, she had earned herself the soubriquet 'The Earring Girl'. She was forever in the newspapers, attending first nights, being photographed, and borrowing jewels from Asprey's.

In 1953 Mariella was twelve years old, and Constance was struggling to get the girl educated. Whether the brother with whom Constance had been living or her other siblings helped out is unclear. My guess is that she and her child were alone. They have the feel of abandonment about them, of being outside the social mores of the northern heartlands. Like Patsy, Mariella was a studious child. She was well spoken. From her writings it is clear she read widely if superficially and that she held education in high regard. There is no mention of friends – apart from Wolfie – and there are no revelations from former schoolmates. It is as though she and Constance, and Patsy for that matter, materialised on the stage fully formed, like Athena from Zeus's wild imaginings.

It was a remarkable period in twentieth-century history. Massive social change was taking place from the stodgy fifties through to the permissive seventies. Sheffield and Grimsby lay largely untouched by this earthquake. Further south, London was the epicentre of this cultural revolution. At the same time, there were no computer records and there was no electronic surveillance. Confidence tricksters could invent and re-invent themselves at will. Aristocrats could go underground with gangsters and *parvenus*. *Demi-mondaines* could disappear and reappear at will. There was a frisson in the air. Esmeralda's bottled that frisson. Not only was Esmeralda's prescient in its permissiveness but it was exotic too. Hod had managed to acquire a board member of superlative Continental pedigree: the Spanish jockey, bobsledder, polo player and racing driver, a nobleman-*conquistador* who had competed in the Grand National, Formula One and the Winter Olympics, Alfonso Cabeza de Vaca, the Marquis de Portago. He had a stake in Esmeralda's. More intriguingly, Portago – Fon for short – would provide Patsy with one of the strangest episodes in her short career. From the opening in '53, with Hod and Fon as her backers, Esmeralda's was where Patsy learned her craft.

In October 1956 the journalist Patrick Skene-Catling described the Barn as 'London's most attractive and beguiling night club'. In his column, 'From a Window in Fleet Street', he marvelled at the attitude of Patsy's staff. Patsy chose them with care. The hatcheck girl was 'Olga Peniakoff, daughter of "Popski", the commando who led Popski's Private Army in the Middle East during WW2'. Olga, 'an intriguingly temperamental brunette', took her lead from Patsy. If she was too busy to 'take your hat and coat', it was because 'she was reading a novel or playing with Busta, a long-haired dachshund, named after Alexander Bustamante, former PM of Jamaica'.

The waitresses had two characteristics in common: they wore tight sweaters and they were all 'astonishingly good-looking, ranging from the Audrey Hepburn gamine type to the blond and substantial'. Waitressing was apparently avocational as these girls, of all nationalities, preferred to discuss Rubinstein's rendition of Chopin, acrostics or Russian history.

The folk artist Cy Grant was singing Calypso the night of Skene-Catling's visit. As for Patsy herself, Skene-Catling described her as a 'patrician Ava Gardner'. Everyone assumed she was Hod's daughter. He let it out he was her legal guardian. She welcomed the punters with a painted smile and a catchphrase, 'Hello sweetie'. Her *savoir faire* and marketing strategies were hitting the spot. Gracious informality hid a steely ambition. Patsy described the membership policy to Skene-Catling: 'We just take the people we like the look of. It's too bad, in a way, I suppose. So often the people we don't want are so rich.'

Patsy had found her *metier*. Her methods were ostensibly haphazard but the results, 'amusing to her friends', were profitable. Amusement is the keyword in Skene-Catling's article. Esmeralda's turnover was averaging £500 a week. In a country still struggling from shortages and rationing, Patsy coolly admitted she had recently visited the United States for 'the skiing at Aspen and the gambling at Las Vegas'. The skiing was 'fabulous and the gambling, without *chemin de fer*, was a bit dull'. At any rate, she concluded, they were a change from the usual Bavarian Alps and Riviera.

She was cool and amusing but there was more to her travels than she was prepared to reveal to Skene-Catling. Four months before the interview, in July 1956, Patsy had left the club. She had told Hod she was going to the continent for a long holiday and to look for 'certain work'. If she found it she would stay on indefinitely. One month later, on 20 August, the *Daily Mail* reported that Hod was 'terribly worried'. The antique connoisseur plucked anxiously at his 'miniature Dundreary whiskers' and told the reporter that Patsy had disappeared six weeks previously, and that he urgently wanted her back. He had no idea where she was, and was desperate to hear from her. The reporter informed Hod that Patsy had been spotted on a yacht in the French Riviera. The yacht belonged to the Earl of Warwick who was holidaying there with his brother, the Hon. Richard Maynard Greville.

'But the burly ex-RAF officer who became Patsy's guardian when she was in her teens said: "I don't want to add to any of this talk in the papers. Is Patsy in Zurich? – That's just one of the things which are being said."'

The following day, again in the *Daily Mail*, Patsy's biological father put his views forward. Harry Morgan told a door-stepping reporter: 'This is a storm in a tea cup. I know where my daugher is: and, believe me, I am not worried in the slightest. That is all I am saying. Now I would like you gone from here.'

'Here' was a garden gate in the New Forest.

In the same article, the Earl of Warwick was quoted from his Riviera abode. 'She was here for a little while,' he said, 'but she left last week. I don't know exactly where she is.' He thought she might be with friends in Germany, perhaps trying to avoid a man who was 'pestering' her.

None of this would matter if Patsy did not eventually disappear for good. But she did. If this was her attempt at escape, from whom or what was she escaping?

4

ON THE ROAD

Who was the man who was pestering Patsy? A clue emerges in the letters pages of the *Daily Mail*:

> I agree with H. Christopher Gill. The Carol Day strip has been an important part of my life. But there the mutual sympathy ends. My sleepless nights are spent worrying about that absolutely delicious man Lance, who is obviously going to land himself into trouble with an irate guardian very shortly.
> Patsy Morgan-Dibben. Garmisch-Partenkirchen, Germany.

Garmish-Partenkirchen is a famous bobsleigh resort in the Bavarian Alps. It was where the bobsleigh enthusiast Fon and his best friend, Eddy Nelson, were staying at the time of Patsy's disappearance. In the same year that Patsy was writing a letter to the *Daily Mail* from Garmisch-Partenkirchen, Fon had taken up the bobsleigh (he came fourth in the Winter Olympics). So it is possible that Patsy had deserted Hod and Esmeralda's for Fon and his friend Eddy.

Fon was descended from a long line of distinguished Spaniards. His father, Antonio Dabeza de Vaca, was well known throughout

Europe and England as the man who won $2 million, and therefore broke the bank, at Monte Carlo. Fon was very proud of his father, and emulated his lifestyle. A spanner in the lotus-eating works was his mother, Olga, who kept a tight hold on the money. She was an Irish girl who had married rich before she met Fon's father. Once widowed, Olga had become the most sought-after woman in Europe. Fon's father snapped her up. Then he died in the middle of a polo match.

Patsy was running with a character who ran through his trust fund as though it were sand running through his fingers on the beach at Cannes. Fon was always trying to think up schemes to make more money. According to his one-time lover and America's first supermodel, Dorian Leigh, smuggling gold coins to Paris from Switzerland was just one of his scams.

'Fon was a liar.' So says Dorian, Revlon's 'Fire and Ice' Girl, the 'Girl who had Everything', the It Girl of the 1950s. She didn't need a Hod to help her sashay her way into the headlines. Dorian was in a different class. Nevertheless, Patsy and Dorian got to know each other through the auspices of Fon and Eddy.

It seems they made a foursome because Dorian recalls the four of them having dinner in Paris. Fon first introduced her to Eddy by describing him as his *homme d'affaires*. According to Dorian, Eddy was a 'thoroughly evil, thoroughly amoral man who had a terrible influence on Fon'.

As for Patsy, well, Dorian wrote that her family surname 'Morgan Dibbyn' and that she 'was well known in Wales'. It's true that Morgan is a Welsh name. It's also one of the most common names in the world. Patsy, Dorian says

> ... was an education in herself. She wasn't pretty, but she was one of those tall, slim, horse-faced Englishwomen who had an inexplicable allure of their own, and she had a marvellous sense of humour. She ran a bar for a living. At first I thought she was Eddy's girl, but Fon told me that the two of them had met each other only that evening.

Later that evening in 1956, the four decided to go to Crete for the rest of the summer.

The cartoon strip 'Carol Day' was created by David Wright, and was accepted by the *Daily Express* before being hi-jacked by its circulation rival, the *Daily Mail*, that same year. Carol was a tall and attractive blonde, a fashion model who got into scrapes with unavailable men. The very first episode finds our heroine on the Riviera with a handsome American hunk desperate to marry her. The storylines derive mainly from Carol's work as a fashion model, her romantic entanglements and her dysfunctional circle of acquaintances, including a conman. But Carol has a secret. She has another man in her life: a possessive, needy and demanding man, her 'guardian – poor uncle Marcus'. 'I had to take this holiday,' Carol tells her suitor, 'because I needed it so badly. You see ... he can't bear me to be out of his sight.'

'He sounds like an old bloodsucker to me,' says the hunk. The illustration for uncle Marcus bears out the hunk's hypothesis. An elderly, withered man in a wheelchair, uncle Marcus collects African tribal artefacts and has tantrums on a daily basis. The strip was published on a daily basis and echoes the plotline of Patsy Morgan-Dibben's life. The hunk even comments: 'Say, who is this guardian of hers? Sounds like a cross between Svengali and a full-time hypochondriac!'

It sounds like Hod. Meanwhile his Girl Friday, Patsy, was in cahoots with an American hunk, probably married, definitely unavailable, called Eddy Nelson. One rumour has it that he was working as a lift-man in the Plaza Hotel in New York when Fon met him. Edmond Nelson, a native of South Dakota and an Air Force veteran, was then forty-two years of age. His first automobile race was in 1953 when he participated in the Carrera Panamericana as co-driver to Luigi Chinetti. But his main outlet was the bobsleigh, and it was he who introduced the sport to Fon.

So Patsy was high-footing it with two of the most dazzling playboys in the world. Reading through their exploits, they sound like the sort of men who could turn a girl's head. Let us start with the Marquis de Portago. At seventeen, he won a $500 bet by flying a plane under London Bridge. Edmond Nelson, meanwhile, was athletic, well-built, a champion bobsledder. He was also a nobody from America, riding the tails of a marquis.

Think Jack Kerouac and the Beat Generation. Instead of taking Route 66, we are skiing down the slopes of St Moritz, into the casino at Monaco and racing round the great European circuits, stopping in Paris to spend evenings at *L'Elephant Blanc*. It's *On the Road* for rich people and their wannabes. But the idea is the same: in Eddy Nelson, Fon found his Dean Moriarty, completely broke, a chequered past, eager for experience and sensations. For Kerouac and Moriarty, the adventure came in literature and poetry; for Fon and Eddy, it was the competition, challenge, and danger. Their goals were no different: to go to the end of what they had decided to be and do, regardless of the judgment of others and *completely true to themselves and their friends.*

Judging from the company she kept, this was Patsy's philosophy. In July 1956, she accompanied Fon, Dorian Leigh and Eddy to Crete. The two men had ulterior motives. They were posing as tourists, and the two women were posing as their wives. These roles were a cover. The real reason they were touring the island of Crete was to search for Nazi gold worth £1.5 million.

It was Eddy's idea. After the war he had met a British officer engaged in cleaning up post-war Germany. The really intriguing nugget is that, according to Dorian, he met this officer through Patsy. Anyway, this officer had arrested an ex-Gestapo agent who had been on a special mission to Crete in advance of the German airborne invasion. Put ashore by a U-boat with six men, it had been his task to hide three-quarters of a ton of gold. The hiding place was a bulge at the bottom of a well in the grounds of a whitewashed villa a few hundred yards inland.

Patsy's officer friend gave Eddy the map, and Eddy showed it to Fon. X marked the spot on the map where the treasure was hidden. For a month the lotus-eaters searched in vain. They had overlooked the fact that whitewashed villas are ubiquitous in Crete, and most of them have wells.

But at last they found a villa that looked likely. One problem: a large new building had recently been constructed on the site. It was occupied by NATO personnel. Worse still, barbed wire ringed the area. But faint heart never won a fortune. Fon and Patsy crawled under the fence, climbed a rope down the well and began their search. Eddy and Dorian kept watch. Dorian relates that a curious goatherd came to join them. At the bottom of the well Fon and Patsy waited out the long, weary hour as the goatherd chatted amiably with the glamorous couple. Unable to move, silenced by the goatherd and at the mercy of fleas, lice and centipedes, they could find no hidden gold.

Perhaps she tired of the madcap adventures and thrill-seeking escapades. Perhaps Eddy could not offer her a viable future. Patsy's alter ego, Carol Day, eventually drops her hunk, and Patsy came back to London. But never fear, for she soon had another unavailable man in her life: Philip Ridgeway. So let's allow Eddy and Fon to fade into the background momentarily.

5

LA MILLE MIGLIA

In April 1955, Patsy mad a brief return to London. She was interviewed by *Photoplay* as a rising star in the fast-growing industry of publicity. It looks like she had outgrown Hod altogether. But her new man was just as luridly fashioned. He was the son of a radio impresario, a demobbed army major with a gammy leg and a swagger stick. Like Patsy, Philip Ridgeway liked to be noticed. When he sat down, his trouser leg would ride up to reveal a curved dagger in a jewelled sheath attached to the top of his sock.

On a tour of Iceland for the Armed Forces in 1941, the comedian Frank Muir asked Ridgeway if the knife was strictly necessary.

'One of our undercover chaps in Cairo gave it to me when I managed to get him out of a spot of bother in a cellar,' Ridgeway said, quietly. 'I've only had to use it once.'

As Muir says, this was 'preposterous, B-picture stuff', but with the characters who populated London's entertainment industry, 'it could just be true'. Ridgeway led Patsy away from Knightsbridge towards the West End. She was working now as a PR Girl. She got a pair of Viennese ballerinas to wear miniature bottles as earrings for wine-tastings; for Derby Day, a little horse on each ear. She had also cottoned on to the fact that a brand identity was crucial too.

The singer David Hughes became Mr Heart-throb. The starlet Zena Marshall was 'the girl who put the V in TV'.

Under Hod's tutelage, Patsy had become Patsy Morgan-Dibben, a Somerset farmer and erstwhile hostess of a nightclub. With the Earl of Warwick she was part of the Riviera set. With Fon and Eddy, she was literally a gold-digger. She was now chancing her arm as an agent to the stars.

Where does this bravado come from? This disdain for convention? What is this grocer's daughter from the New Forest, this little backwater girl, doing in a story that's too big for her? And this competitive spirit, this taste for challenge, where did this come from? Was it a trick of genetic coding? Put simply, she was not a pure creature of Hod Dibben, just as Eliza Doolittle is not created from clay by Henry Higgins. There is no doubt that Hod recognised from the beginning all this potential in the young girl who answered his ad. It was probably not too difficult to detect it. But to extract the ore, you have to remove the soul. And maybe hers was too persistent, too far-reaching. Maybe Hod had to wait for Mariella.

Nothing precedes Patsy's meeting with Hod, Portago, Skene-Catling, Ridgeway or Nelson and nothing comes after these men have departed. Apart from one more man, another hound. He would be Patsy's nemesis. But first she witnesses the downfall of her one-time associate Eddy Nelson, who found his own nemesis in Fon.

'I doubt that he will live beyond thirty years. Every time he returns from a race, the front of his car is scratched, from pushing the other competitors out of the way at 200 miles per hour.' And then comes the *Mille Miglia*. Fon insists that he wants Eddy as his teammate.

On 12 May 1957, an uncharacteristically nervous Fon admits he is worried about taking part in the *Mille Miglia*, an Italian open-road endurance race over one thousand miles. Even with his trusty navigator and co-driver Eddy Nelson by his side, he is worried that he does not know the course well enough.

His latest girlfriend sees him off at the start-up. Her name is Linda Christian – another American supermodel. She watches Fon and Eddy set off. They gain ground to third place. They are travelling at 150mph on a straight road in Lombardy between Cerlongo and Guidizzolo when a tyre explodes on their Ferrari 335 S. The car cannons over a canal, ricochets back and kills nine spectators, and both men.

In England, Patsy is asked to comment by the *Daily Mail*: 'Fon was gay, but dangerous.'

That same year, she met the nephew of Lord Oranmore and Browne. Michael Mordaunt-Smith was the London stringer for Hollywood scandal sheet *Confidential*. A thirty-year-old former subaltern in the Black Watch, he had the classic tweedy style that inspires confidence. He carved himself a role arranging nights out for visiting Hollywood stars, laying on some 'entertainment' and then appearing with a notepad and a photographer. 'Mr Whisper' was his byline. Patsy began to get publicity that she had not engineered.

This was around the time she disappeared for good. On 27 August 1957, it was the *Daily Express*'s tipster William Hickey who was reporting on her movements. Patsy Morgan-Dibben, he revealed, fiancée of *Confidential*'s London agent, had been dropped as the manager of Esmeralda's Barn. 'A spokesman for the club says patrons had become wary of coming round since disclosure of the magazine's London operations.'

On 4 August the following year Hickey spotted her again. This time she is no longer affianced to Mordaunt-Smith and she is back on a yacht on the Riviera. 'Patsy Morgan-Dibben, the ex-fiancée of London magazine tipster Michael Mordaunt-Smith, is yachting on the Riviera with the 47-year-old Earl of Warwick,' her old friend.

'I'm tired of the London life,' she said.

By Christmas that year, a tipster traced her to the home of an Argentine millionaire in the Bavarian Alps. She said she was hiding from someone, and that her lawyer had told her not to say any more. But she had left behind a diary containing 'notes about love affairs with high-placed personalities, the names and peculiarities of so-called refined people, and tales of narcotics and degenerate impulses'.

And so ends the story of Patsy. Perhaps she married or changed her name again. Perhaps she opened that gate to a garden in the New Forest and returned to her father's shop where she can be found behind the counter poised to greet us with her trademark, 'Hello Sweetie.'

Why am I so intent on chasing Patsy down to her lair? She interests me because, in her own way, she tried to break the bank at Monte Carlo. However, unlike Signor de Vaca Senior, the bank made no exception for her and did what it always does: it broke her. Patsy was Hod's prototype, and she started a trend. Forever in the gossip columns, trying to write her own story, by the end of the decade she was a ghost. What's the lesson here? At this point in the long and tortuous history of sexual politics, we find that when women start writing their version of events they disappear.

6

THE BLACK SHEEP

In Prague in 1956, Antonin Novotny was admitted to the Politburo. No sign of his renegade, anti-Communist younger brother – the man Mariella claims as her father. In Sheffield in 1956, Mariella's mother was struggling to find the money to buy a pair of spectacles for her child. The NHS refused to treat Stella Marie Capes, saying she was a foreign alien. In her memoir, Christine Keeler says it was because Constance had not 'paid-in'. But Constance was still dreaming. She wanted her daughter to be a ballerina.

Keeler is the woman who slept with a war minister and a Russian naval attaché concurrently. She is the most prominent of Stephen Ward's female protégées. In one of her many books, she claimed that Constance walked the streets to pay for private tutors for her child.

In November 1957, after the death of Antonín Zápotocký, Uncle Novotny assumed the presidency of Czechoslovakia. Constance and Stella, aged sixteen, took a bold step and moved to 50 Holmdale Road in Hampstead, London. At first they had no luck. Despite speaking a smattering of many languages and having had some basic tuition in ballet, Stella Marie could not get a job because she was 'foreign'.

There is only one place that accepts foreigners and doesn't ask interviewees pesky questions. The young girl from Grimsby or Sheffield or Communist Czechoslovakia got a job in the Latin Quarter. She must have impressed because the Pigalle Club in Piccadilly was the palladium of striptease. Shirley Bassey performed here and Stella Marie took your hat. You were part of a wealthy and loyal clientele. She led you through a tunnel cluttered with topless girls smoking cigarettes. This was the way to the dance floor. The space opened up. Chandeliers glittered and men stared. You looked at the sixteen-year-old in front of you and found a pocket-sized Venus in fishnets.

A reporter looking for colourful characters in the capital featured the hatcheck girl and her mother in a series on London's nightlife. Mrs Capes showed him a photograph of her infant daughter standing in a breadline at the displaced persons' camp. According to Mrs Capes, who was part Spanish, she said, Mariella's birth was the result of a relationship with a Czech pilot. (Sven, my Swedish correspondent, swears that Mrs Capes was a Spanish Jew and that Mariella spoke Hebrew.) So Mrs Capes started the ball rolling with hints of exotica and Stella pitched in, saying her father was 'first cousin' to President Antonin Novotny. The authors Dorril and Summers have confirmation of her parentage from a reliable source: the Czech journalist and human rights advocate Josef Josten came to the West after the war, and in *Honeytrap* he confirms Mariella's bloodline. Dorril and Summers also assert that the British government knew about Mr Novotny's presence in England, and that the Home Office was sensitive about him entering the country. A document in the National Archives shows he was refused a visa to enter Britain in 1948.

But, Mrs Capes told the reporter, he *did* arrive in England, and when he did, he 'acted very strangely. He was asked to leave by the Home Office...'

She goes on to say, 'Mariella has grown up in an atmosphere of intrigue. She is very nervous. What my husband's secrets were I don't know – but we still get frightening echoes here in London...'

Mariella told the reporter her childhood was 'idyllic' until the Communist *putsch*. 'I was never quite sure what my father did for a living, but we were well off. What I am certain of is that almost alone of his family he was not a Communist. He was, if you like, a political black sheep of the family ... [He] was tipped off that the Communists were about to seize power, and it would be best if he got out of the country...'

When Dorrill and Summers traced Mrs Capes in 1985 she refused to discuss her daughter. 'What does it matter?' she asked. 'They won't believe the truth.'

A man who didn't care about the truth was waiting in the wings. No regrets, no concerns, Hod put Patsy's disappearance down to the curse that had chased him out of Lytes Cary. This was the same curse that kept making him bankrupt and lovelorn. Shortly after Patsy was found in the Bavarian Alps, and teenaged Mariella started working in the Pigalle, Hod tried to marry a sixteen-year-old called Maureen. He offered her wealth beyond her dreams and a three-month trip round Europe. But she was having none of it. Maureen sold her story to the papers and got engaged to the twenty-year-old assistant catering manager at the Dorchester Hotel.

Hod was at a low point in his life. In 1961, he wrote an article on the occult for the *People*. At the start of the fifties, he said, he had consulted a sorceress. 'She foretold business disasters, the sudden death of my father, my banishment from his will, the death of a great friend in a car crash and desertion by a person to whom I was devoted.'

Rejected and ridiculed by Maureen, he was about to meet his Iron Maiden.

From the Pigalle, at her mother's suggestion, Mariella graduated to topless dancing at the Windmill Theatre in Soho. Throughout the Second World War the Windmill had staged *Mrs Henderson Presents*, exhibiting near-naked women in the 'most artistic of lighting and poses for gentlemen audiences'. Nudity may be traced to the Windmill Theatre, which for an age held the monopoly on Soho's flesh. In that famous hall Mariella's tinselled torso stood still or twirled like a cake in a *patisserie* window.

Aged seventeen, she visited The Black Sheep, a nightclub on White Horse Street in Mayfair. Hod had been helping to manage this club since the Krays had taken over Esmeralda's. The Black Sheep catered for 'black sheep from the titled families, because they are the rarest'. Mariella, the daughter of a black sheep, was quick to realise that a club by the same name would be an entree into London's bohemia. First she tried to get a job as a dancer, but there were no vacancies. She had to settle for waitressing. The problem was she was so short-sighted she was continually bumping into diners. When she spilt goulash on a customer's lap the *maitre d'* sacked her. She rushed up to Hod in floods of tears. Within moments they were engaged to be married.

A reporter from the *Daily Mirror* recorded the scene: 'Hod, of course, was an antique compared to Mariella, but when he put a pair of black-rimmed glasses on her, she said, "I still love you. And I can't wait. Let's get married right away."'[1]

On 29 January 1960 Stella Marie Capes, aged eighteen, married H. R. Dibben, fifty-four, at Caxton Hall. The groom was a 'Dealer in Historic Houses'. The bride was a 'Dancer'. The bride's father was 'Ernest Capes, Architect'. Ernest was in fact the bride's grandfather. He had been a construction worker.

The reception was at The Black Sheep, and photographed by up-and-coming David Bailey. How she loved the attention. She came alive in the flash of a camera.

'I've met a lot of rich men in my time as a dancer, but none has shown me the care, love and attention that Hod (Dibben) has.' As one hundred guests drank champagne, Dibben announced that he had given Mariella a twenty-room sixteenth-century mansion in Sussex and a luxury flat in Eaton Place for a wedding present. Her engagement ring was a 200-year-old diamond and sapphire antique. The wedding cake, however, with several spectacular tiers coated in marzipan icing, proved to be stuffed with sawdust.

---

1. Summers and Dorril

The bride was mortified. No matter. She was in the embrace of London's clubland, mixing with the Swingers who liked the sound of a switch slicing through muscle and flesh. Her whiplash career had begun. Hod's best man was Dr Teddy Sugden, a friend of Stephen Ward and member of the Thursday Club. This elite group of rakish, high-profile men met once a week at Wheeler's oyster shop on Old Compton Street. Their number included Miles Kington, a cub journalist. He gives an account that captures the goings-on:

Lord Louis Mountbatten burst into tears and started cradling his head on his arm. 'Nobody understands me,' he said. 'Nobody loves me anymore. Especially in India.'

'Oh, knock it off, Louis!' [Prince] Philip would say. 'OK, so you slaughtered a couple of million Indians during Partition. OK, so you made a mistake. But don't let it get you down! Don't spoil the party! And no pictures please, Cecil!' This to Cecil Beaton, who had already got his little Brownie out.[2]

It was at the Thursday Club, it was alleged, that Philip was photographed with two women in a compromising position. The women who attended these gatherings were barmaids rounded up from the Soho pubs.

'Sugden,' Mariella wrote, 'was a 150-guinea man.' His illegal abortion clinic specialised in society ladies, actresses and whores pimped by the gangsters who ran Soho. He guaranteed he could get them back to work within the day.

Dr Sugden was quite unlike Mariella. He positively shrank from attention. Instead he enjoyed sex games with reptiles in his surgery on Half Moon Street. The night before her wedding, he asked Mariella if he could watch while she simulated sex with a python. She could not tell if he was enjoying her antics, because one side of his face was paralysed. This meant that he was always smiling.

---

2. Miles Kington, *The Independent*, 16 January 1996

7

ALL THE PRESIDENT'S MEN

In an interview with the *News of the World*, Mariella described herself before her marriage. Alienated from her surroundings and her companions, she sits in the dressing room of a strip club, surrounded by other young women.

> All their talk, it seemed, was of sex and boyfriends. After my experiences I couldn't bear a man near me and this they couldn't understand. They thought I was out of my mind when I tore up the dozens of notes that came backstage from admirers. They would never have believed that I spent most of my spare time with London's mediums.

It turns out that Mrs Capes was interested in spiritualism. Mariella and her mother spent most of her nights off in large halls waiting for a message from the other side. One night she got one. The medium told her: 'You must leave the movement. You are too involved. You are ruining your life. Your preoccupation is dangerous.'

Other than this cryptic reference to some mysterious 'movement', she described herself as a dancer who never went out dancing, who never drank, and who rarely went to the cinema.

Hod and Mariella spent their wedding night in the country pile at Sussex. After the disappointment over the wedding cake, Mariella describes herself as being in a 'nasty mood'. Nevertheless, she got into Hod's car and they drove through London towards the coast. She describes a sombre evening. 'We ate a large meal sitting under a canopy of Xmas puds all made prior to 1900... Dibs put away a fair amount of champagne and Chateau d'Y Quem but he got a little piqued when he found he couldn't soften up his bride with a few glasses.'[3]

Bored, Mariella could not stop thinking of

... the luxurious four-poster bridal bed. After eating too much cream-sodden pudding, Dibs thoughtfully suggested I went up to the suite which comprised a number of Tudor rooms on the first floor. I needed no urging. I jumped from my seat and hurried up the old staircase, put a stack of LPs on the player, brushed my teeth, brushed my hair and tugged my pyjamas on. Feeling whacked out I chose a piece of lightweight reading before sleeping – Bertrand Russell's latest tome – then I curled up in the mighty bed. Ten minutes of mathematical philosophy and a Beethoven Piano Sonata was my idea of the best way to round off the long day.

A picture of innocence. Hod's manservant laid a fire so the tapestried master bedroom was warm. But what is this? A young girl who had no idea of her marital obligations. A husband immersed in London's fetish scene. While Dibs divulged the ABC of sexual reproduction, Mariella forgot about the wedding cake and 'drifted on clouds of exciting promise'.

From here on in, for Mariella, sex would become a game. The game centred on the male member: 'Presidential class or the plumber's. Attached to Dukes or dustmen I don't care.' However, Mariella's game had a twist to it. The twist in her psyche that

---

3. *Club International*, July 1973

came from fear made her instil fear in others. Mariella's goal was to shock people, as she had been shocked as a child. She would play out this scene over and again, and she married the right man to play with her.

Hod was a man with tendencies towards paedophilia and an avowed interest in sado-masochism. On the plus side, he shopped in all the best places. Hod got his leather gear from John Sutcliffe at Atomage, the outfitters who supplied Honor Blackman's cat suit for the *Avengers*. He had three suits, two in black and one in a faded red. According to Billy Hill's lieutenant, Bobby Mckew, leather added to Hod's pleasure when Mariella whipped him. 'She ties me to a chair in my leather suit, whips me and then makes me watch her screwing someone else.'[4]

'Go to your own kipology,' Mariella said, when Hod climbed into the bed next to her.[5] He laughed and touched her between her legs. She removed his hand and told him she would rather read her book. She was crazy about Plato. But Hod persisted. Eventually he won her over, and her 'first time' took place on the chaise longue with Hod's manservant doing the honours. Hod was watching from the four-poster. He was wearing his leather gear and sniffing from an ampoule of amyl nitrate. From here on in, events came thick and fast, and she never got past the chapter on Plato.

In February 1960, the newly-weds attended a party given by American grocery millionaire Huntingdon Hartford. In 1960 there were many projects that Hartford was spending his fortune on – an automatic parking garage, a shale-oil company, a handwriting institute, and a table-tennis game called Ten-Net.[6] Hartford's other interest was running a modelling agency. He was in the right place, Swinging London; and amongst his guests were modelling enthusiasts Stephen Ward, and Harry Alan Towers, a well-known

---

4. Douglas Thompson, *Stephen Ward: Scapegoat*
5. *Club International*, July 1973
6. After squandering his vast A&P grocery inheritance, Huntington Hartford turned to drugs and retired to his island in the Bahamas. He named the island Paradise.

TV and radio producer who also ran a modelling agency. (Towers would go on to score major cinematic hits including *Bullet to Beijing, Treasure Island, Cry, the Beloved Country* and the Fu Manchu series.)

Four days after Towers met Mariella at Hartford's party a letter arrived at the Hyde Park Square flat she shared with Hod. It suggested a meeting at Claridge's to discuss some possible modelling work in the States. The letter was signed by Towers' mother, Margaret. This was very reassuring. Towers and his mother offered Mariella a contract as a television model making commercials in America. The fee was $50,000. Harry produced his portable typewriter and punched out a contract, *tout suite*. She signed the contract. Its contents vary according to whom you consult. According to Harry, it was simply about TV work, and if Mariella wanted to make a little bit of money on the side that was her business – 'It's what makes the world go round.'[7]

Over the next few days, Harry introduced Mariella to some of his friends, one of whom tried to have sex with her. This was a new decade, with a new politics of labour, but the sexual politics were still *seigneurial*. Nubile women were fair game so Mariella shrugged it off. Besides, she knew what side her bread was buttered, and she wanted jam.

On 10 December 1960 Mariella got a cable from Harry saying that her plane ticket had been booked. He also told her that his firm, Towers of America, would provide her with the necessary letter to the American Embassy in London, explaining that the firm would be entirely responsible for her. When she went to collect her Pan Am Economy ticket she was told that Harry's cheque had bounced. She paid for the ticket herself, knowing that he had paid a $70 deposit in New York. On 15 December she went to a party at which Stephen Ward was present. She excitedly told him she was off to the States with Harry. He made some sketches of Hod's new bride, newly christened Mariella.

---

7. Douglas Thompson

It was Hod who told Mariella to drop the 'Stella Marie'. It was Towers who insisted she sign herself into the hotel register as Miss M. Novotny. On 14 December 1960 Towers installed the newly minted Mariella in 'a small, seedy, third-rate hotel' on West 57th Street called The Great Northern. Fifteen years later, the garage from which Robert De Niro sallies forth in *Taxi Driver* is located on the same street. The garage has since been demolished but the hotel is still there. Now it has the Art Deco patina of history. In 1960 it was down at heel in a part of town that boasted warehouses and a short-cut to the Hudson River waterfront.

On 16 December 1960 Harry Alan Towers and Miss Novotny listed a telephone answering service at the address. On the following afternoon Towers brought a man to meet the nineteen-year-old model. His name is redacted from the relevant FBI documents. He paid Mariella $40 to 'commit a sexual act'. This was her first 'date'.

'Thereafter I entertained prostitution dates regularly and earned approximately $400 a week. I gave Towers about $300 of this money.'

Furthermore, 'Towers was present when prostitution acts were committed.' She provided lists of madams and prostitutes who had arranged dates or gone on threesomes with her. She named some of her customers who, she said, paid for the British speciality: 'They desired to be whipped with cat-o'-nine-tails.'

Not so, said Harry. 'I know it sounds corny but I was typing up my TV shows when she was arrested ... I tried to stay out of the way, but they arrested me too.'[8]

To this day Harry Alan Towers' role in Mariella's prostitution is up for grabs. But she was making no secret of it. One night she would be in New York on a 'date', the next in Washington. In the capital, she was entertaining VIPs at the Quorum Club. The Quorum was located in the Hotel Carroll Arms, next to the Senate building on Capitol Hill. The Quorum's owner was Bobby

8. Douglas Thompson

Baker. His nickname was 'Little Lyndon'. He was a political aide to Lyndon B. Johnson, and secretary to the Senate Majority. By the time Mariella left the United States, Baker was the former Senate Majority secretary whose business activities were under Senate scrutiny.

The Quorum was a private club requiring annual membership dues from lawmakers and other influential men. In Baker's words: 'The Quorum Club was a place where a guy wanted to get away from, you know, being at the bar downstairs at the Carroll Arms, where there were too many reporters or too many gawkers. It was an easy place for a lobbyist to get together with a Senator, or a Senator's girlfriend – but it was not a whore house.'[9]

At the same hearing he went on to say:

Yeah, it was a social club. One time I was in there and Ellen Romesch was at my table. She was as pretty as Elizabeth Taylor. She was married to a Sergeant in the German Army but stationed at their embassy in Washington. She was sort of like me. She was ambitious. She'd come from Germany broke. She really loved oral sex. So any time – 90 per cent of the people who give you money want to know if you can get them a date. I don't give a damn who they are. They're away from mama and their wives and they have a tremendous desire to party. One of my friends on the board of directors of the Dallas Cowboys gave her $5,000.

When he got off the bus in Washington, Bobby Baker was a fourteen-year-old hillbilly from south California. A few weeks later he was a page in the Capitol. As he said, Ellen Rometsch was just like him, and so was Mariella. Both women were ambitious. They were broke. So what could they do? Fellatio.

---

9. The full transcript of interviews between Bobby Baker and Donald Ritchie of the Senate Historical Office

'[Ellen] went to the White House several times. And President Kennedy called me and said it's the best head job he'd ever had and he thanked me. When, I guess Senator [Carl] Curtis was demanding that she be called as a witness, Bobby Kennedy knew that if she testified before the Senate Rules Committee, President Kennedy would be destroyed. So he kidnapped her.'

At the Quorum, Mariella met the actor Peter Lawford, smooth-talking brother-in-law of the Kennedys and member of Frank Sinatra's Rat Pack. Towers claimed that it would boost her career potential if she got to know Kennedy. Lawford took Mariella to New York for lunch at Luchnow's. This magnificent German restaurant, a landmark on 14th Street since it opened in 1882, was a step up from the dingy Great Northern or even the Quorum with its portraits of female nudes and plaid bar stools. Luchnow's had polished and carved wood panelling, stained glass, oil paintings and mounted stag heads.

'Then I was shot into the whirl of parties and was introduced to JFK, President-elect. I heard several stories of his escapades, and met some of the girls he had had affairs with ... the first time I met JFK was at a large party held at Hampshire House. Vic Damone, the singer, was the host.'

Unbeknownst to Mariella, she was being lined up as a replacement for Simone McQueen, a TV weather forecaster, who had just finished with Kennedy. She was invited to a party. The Italian American crooner Vic Damone was celebrating his move to Capitol Records. All the gang was there, including 'Jack'. The handsome young square-jawed man invited the young English girl wielding a lorgnette and a cut-glass accent into Vic's bedroom.

'JFK was simply called the Senator ... it seemed quite natural to be taken aside for a quiet talk. He talked about England briefly, but locked the door and undressed as he chatted.'

Mariella decided to follow suit. But Damone's Asian girlfriend interrupted the disrobing by cutting her wrists in the en-suite bathroom. 'I have never known a party finish so quickly.

JFK disappeared with a group of close associates – I was bustled out among a crowd of nervous guests.'[10]

Kennedy was elected President in November 1960. The inauguration was on 20 January 1961. He stayed at the Carlyle Hotel during the first week of January. The Carlyle was equipped with underground tunnels that connected the hotel with nearby apartment houses. It was not long before 'the Senator' was telephoning the new girl in town every other day. They met several times in an apartment reached by a tunnel. Peter Lawford supplied two other women, 'an attractive blonde with a stern face ... and a younger girl with a kind, fresh look'. One of these women had studied medicine at the University of California. All the women wore nurses' uniforms for the 'dates'. JFK was their patient. Sometimes a Chinese *émigrée* called Suzy Chang joined Mariella. So he had Mariella, who boasted Czech antecedents, the German Ellen Rometsch and the Chinese Suzy Chang. No surprise that all three women were raising eyebrows at J. Edgar Hoover's FBI.

The notion that a network of agents might be operating beneath the surface of American life was certainly not original to Hoover. Nervousness about the supposedly extraordinary powers and dangerous motives of large organizations has long been a feature of US political culture. In its classic form, the paranoid style in American politics insists that important events are controlled by a vast and sinister conspiracy. Mariella was custom made to exploit this way of thinking.

On a cultural level, Towers was trying to tap into the zeitgeist. He was intent on buying TV rights to *The Saint* from Leslie Charteris. In an attempt to seduce Charteris, he sent Mariella to Los Angeles to negotiate on his behalf. She was too late. The rights had gone to Lew Grade at ITV in London. *The Saint* ran from 1962 to 1969 starring Roger Moore. But there were other fish to fry. Mariella claimed she met the actor Steve McQueen. She had an affair with the jazz drummer Buddy Rich ('the best lover

---

10. MN's 'memoir' as seen by Dorrill and Summers. *Honeytrap*.

I ever had,' she told her readers at *Club International*.) Rich had a reputation for violence towards women. But Mariella was a match for any man, however impossible the odds.

Where was Towers in this high-octane networking? According to his account, he stayed in New York with his mother writing his scripts. Mariella had to pitch in with the rent on their apartment on West 56th Street. On two occasions, she gave him $300, he admitted to Thompson. 'That looked terrible but it was simply that: when she had a little money, she pitched in – she was not a mean girl with anything.'

He maintained cracks started to appear in their relations when Mariella's promised career in television did not materialise. She and Harry had 'a nasty argument' during which she threatened to get him deported through her 'government contacts'.

Who was running the vice ring in New York? Who was using whom? Well, in December 1960 Hod arrived in New York supposedly to buy antiques at the Parke Bernet gallery. Mariella moved into his apartment at Essex House, near the UN building. They started arranging 'evenings for swingers' with sadomasochist specialities. They received a special delivery letter from the actor Douglas Fairbanks Jr.

'Stephen Ward had told him to get in touch when he was in New York. Hod and I went to see him and were amused at his prominent display of photographs of the Royal Family. I found him almost a caricature of himself, but he was fun for a while.'

What happened to Towers? What actually happened between Towers and Mariella? The six counts against the hustling TV producer carried a maximum of eighty-two years' imprisonment. The police alleged that he had arranged for a wayward minor to meet men for prostitution and induced her to give money to various women and that he took the proceeds of prostitution from her. Towers claimed to friends, Douglas Thompson and family (and possibly his mother) that Mariella was just a friend, and that he was horrified when his apartment was raided and he was arrested for white-slave trafficking.

Over a period of eight weeks from April to June 1961, Mariella sold her version of the story to the *News of the World*. On a Friday night in March 1961, she sobbed, she was in a room in Harry's suite with another man. She called him 'Crew-Cut'. Little did she know, 'Crew-Cut' was a cop, and he was about to find out she was a minor. Harry, the big-shot TV producer, was under the sofa in the foetal position. When the cop pulled out his warrant card Harry was screaming so hard he had to stuff her nylons into his mouth. The cop fetched him from beneath the sofa and laughed. Mariella joined in. Harry turned white.

The cop said to Harry, 'I'm arresting you for keeping a disorderly house!'

Harry said, 'What are you talking about? You can't arrest me. I've never seen this girl before.'

At 11.45 p.m. Mariella was booked in a New York police station. Harry was standing next to her, shaking.

'Don't say anything without a lawyer,' he told her. 'I'll fix it all up later.'

But she never saw him again. Plainclothes detectives questioned her in semi-darkness. The questioning went on until 6 a.m. Her fingerprints were taken in the morning. Her mink coat, which Hod had bought for her in London, drew crude comments. The horsewhip in her handbag caused smirks. It didn't help when she told the Brooklyn police that she had carried a whip since she was nine years old. One of the cops tried to caress her ankle but she jabbed her elbow in his face.

'She'll learn,' he laughed to the others.

Two sturdy female police officers shoved our heroine into a cell with rowdy drunken women. She almost fainted in the unventilated atmosphere, heavy with stale sweat and cigarette smoke. Then the same two stony-faced officers took her to Brooklyn Girls' Court. Here the judge placed her on probation for three years for alleged loitering for the purpose of prostitution. At her wits' end, events took a turn for the better. Because of her 'international flavour', Assistant District Attorney Alfred Donati stepped in. She was hauled out of her cell and interviewed by him.

At last she was faced with a polite investigator. She gave him an address book, listing names of her New York clients from the world of politics, law and business. He realised quite quickly that this was not just a prostitution case. 'I knew it would be high profile. I thought celebrity names would be brought in.'[11]

Donati told Summers and Dorrill that he remembered Mariella well: 'Confident, pretty, with a sense of humour ... she looked like a model, not like a whore ... she made no great denial of the charges.'

This sounds like Mariella. No shame, no remorse, no hypocrisy. Just a sense of ruffled politesse and wry amusement. Mariella's bail was set at $500 (approximately $4,000 in today's money), which Hod paid. Bail for Towers was set at $10,000 (about $80,000).

'If I am not allowed to return to England for a short holiday I shall almost certainly have a nervous breakdown. It isn't human,' she said.

Mariella was under house arrest in a huge, sparsely furnished $40-a-week eighteenth-floor penthouse apartment in Manhattan. This was Hod's place. She was talking to the Special Correspondent of the *News of the World*. The date was 30 April 1961. 'I've been in a state of unbearable tension since I first arrived here in December. I take strong sleeping tablets but even they don't work.'

Under the headline 'My Tortured Life' Mariella told her readers about the refugee camps, the Communist takeover of Czechoslovakia, the rape, the dead man, the barbed wire and playing in a wood with Wolfie. How she came back to England in a state of shock; how her first job was as a dancer, and how she met Hod when she was in her uniform of tight black pants, white shirt, gold cummerbund and gold sandals. How Hod, with his mutton chop whiskers and hair so long it curled up at the ends, married her, how he had a monocle but his eyes were young and hazel and he let her live her own life. Finally, how her experience of spiritualism broke Hod's last link with black magic, that she never drank and, unlike some girls, she never wore earrings, because they were vulgar.

---

11. *Honeytrap*

As for Harry, he had cajoled and bullied her into sleeping with his friends. She was frightened of him. She was taken in by him. Hod had forgiven her, but she could never forgive Harry. When Harry skipped bail on 24 April, Mariella was in an even graver position. She was named as chief witness at his trial and her term of probation was extended indefinitely.

Six days after Harry disappeared, guess where he turned up? Moscow.

8

MRS R. TYSON

On 10 May 1961 an agent from the FBI telephoned Bill Taylor at the London desk of the *News of the World*. He asked him if he had had any news of the fugitive from justice and TV impresario Harry Alan Towers. The reporter revealed that he had received messages from Harry through a third party.

'From the tone of these I'm convinced he is in Moscow where the Kremlin could use a man with his talents.'

The G-man told Bill to tell Harry he was due to appear in a New York court the following day to answer grave vice allegations. This conversation took place in the same week as the *News of the World* was reporting the testimony of a GRU agent, Igor Gouzenko, who had defected to the West from the office of the Soviet Military Attaché in Ottawa. 'Throughout Britain and the West there is at work today a vast army of Russian agents and paid Westerners. And the reason that the Red Army lieutenant-colonel and George Blake, both the leaders of their respective cells, went to their long sentences with a smile on their lips, is because they know there are many hundreds, at least, of other agents still at work in Britain.'

Unfortunately for the readers of the *News of the World* Harry's lawyers advised him that it might be against his own interests to reveal the facts that had led to the erroneous charges made against him by the Americans. Over a series of exclusives that ran alongside Mariella's, the man who had worked with Noel Coward, Orson Welles, John Mills and Gracie Fields to name but a few refused to say where he was, what he was doing, or how he got there. With righteous indignation, he maintained his innocence to the end.

I have never taken money from any woman and I repeat that the charges which have been made against me are untrue. Let me make this clear. I am not a man on the run [although he was in an undisclosed location]. I am not running away from justice [although there was a warrant for his arrest lodged in the United States]. I am not afraid of justice [although he had admitted to leaving the States incognito]. Eventually I will tell the story of my reasons for all this.

He never did.

On 31 May 1961 Mariella made her own escape. Some say it was agents from the FBI who smuggled her aboard the *Queen Mary*. She herself said it was associates of the Chinese call-girl and street-smart operator Suzy Chang, the best friend Mariella ever had. For the duration of the Atlantic crossing she stuck to her cover, Mrs R. Tyson. She ate her meals at the captain's table under the supervision of a CIA agent, Jennifer S., who had given her the ticket in the first place. They just wanted her to shut up and keep the President's name away from hers or any others that had a Communist ring to them.

Hod and her mother were waiting at Southampton alongside the senior crime reporter from the *News of the World*. Peter Earle rushed Mariella to the Fleet Street offices. She gave him the lowdown on the Kennedy brothers; that Towers had successfully manoeuvred her into the bed of the man about to be inaugurated as President of the United States, and that his brother Robert, shortly to become Attorney-General, had also succumbed to her charms. Earle believed her story but the newspaper refrained from printing her allegations. The British Secret Services, alerted by the FBI, put paid to that. The details that emerge are mostly about Harry. How he told her about the female impersonator he met in Paris who made him run back to his mother. How he cried when Mariella refused to have dinner with him. How he leapt at her like a tiger because she taunted him about his lack of breeding.

'And I personally shall be very happy to go back, tell my story in the witness-box, and help the American authorities.'

This begs the question: why didn't she?

Perhaps Towers was telling the truth, and her activity was independent of him. Perhaps Mariella was being manoeuvred by some other pander for the Soviet state. Michael Eddowes thought so. He was Hod's friend and part of Stephen Ward's circle. Eddowes was a fierce and indefatigable seeker after the truth. In 1955 he had published *The Man on Your Conscience*, an investigation into the trial and execution of Timothy Evans. The semi-literate alcoholic painter and decorator Timothy Evans had been hanged for the murder of his wife and child. The murders were later ascribed to Reginald Christie, the serial killer played by Richard Attenborough in *10 Rillington Place*.

Eddowes was instrumental in obtaining a posthumous pardon for Evans. He also believed that Mariella was the link to a Soviet plot to discredit Western leaders. Eddowes got a lot of his information from Christine Keeler. He was a married man in his late fifties, small and rotund with thin hair brushed back, neatly dressed in a striped suit, tie and pearl tiepin. He tried to set up Keeler in a flat in Regent's Park. He was too old for her, she said. Maybe he bore a grudge but he suspected that her mentor, Stephen Ward, was playing a dangerous game.

'I had discovered that the group in London who had destroyed Profumo had sent a young woman, Maria [*sic*] Novotny, to destroy the character of President Kennedy. She was the cousin [*sic*] of President Novotny of Czechoslovakia. This is fact.'[12]

---

12. Radio interview: Chicago WGN 1977 / Stephen Dorrill, *Lobster* magazine

The simplest way to look at the Kennedy affair is that Mariella was selling herself and that her hook was her exoticism. What else was a girl to do? Suzy Chang was her friend, and she employed the same strategy. Chang's story is yet another revelatory chapter in this history of twentieth-century sexual shenanigans. She achieves an aura of notoriety simply because she is pretty and poor, and because the line between poverty and prostitution is blurry.

Chang was also deported back to England in the summer of 1961. Like Mariella, she ended up headlining in a *News of the World* feature. Like Mariella, she kept on selling this sexed-up version of herself. Suzy's feature was called *Nudes of the World*. An early English pornographer and cinematographer, Stanley Long, made a film inspired by his favourite Sunday tabloid. He shot the film at a boys' prep school in Dorset during the long vac. A cast of thirteen naked women moved into the 90-guineas-a-term school.

'They were all glamour models and strippers from Soho. The hardest part was getting them to say their lines.'[13] The lead role of 'Miss England' was given to a redheaded Spaniard. 'Miss Hong Kong' was Suzy Chang. Word reached Fleet Street, and the *News of the World* obliged with a headline: 'Top Prep School Bares Its Secret.' The pupils' parents were furious. Perhaps the most extraordinary aspect of this piece of soft porn is that Valerie Singleton narrated the voice-over. A few months later she joined the children's TV show *Blue Peter*.

'She denied being the voice in that film,' Stanley Long said. 'I just couldn't understand that. She only did a bloody voice-over for God's sake.' *Nudes of the World* became a huge hit when it was released in November 1961.

For me, the sadness is palpable. Suzy and the other young women are children with the bodies of women: innocent and playful, the storyline goes to enormous lengths to get them naked. There is no empowerment here, just exploitation.

---

13. Simon Sheridan, *Keeping the British End Up*

Girls, girls, girls. Until her death Mariella would be known as the underage call-girl who bedded JFK. Every time the assassination was re-investigated her name would come up. In the late seventies she was ramping up the intrigue. 'It turned out hidden cameras had been recording my love-making sessions with the President-Elect in the UN HQ.' And finally: 'I kept a diary of all my appointments in the UN building. I still keep diaries to this day.'

How else could she keep the newspapers interested?

Hod had his own line on the story. He told Eddowes that he had seen immigration files on Towers that showed Towers' links with Eastern Europe. When Eddowes became obsessed with the assassination of JFK, he went to New York and met John Malone, head of the FBI. Malone showed him FBI, Immigration and even CIA files on Towers and Mariella. These proved to Eddowes' satisfaction that Towers *was* working for the Soviets, that Mariella *had* been used to get close to JFK for possible blackmailing and that Kennedy *himself* intervened to drop the charges against her.

When Towers, who had been busy making films all over Europe, finally made US bail in 1982 the hot topic was his address book. Mariella said it was full of VIPs' names. 'Their names didn't mean all that much back then. But now many of them are big shots, in very high places.' A reporter from the *NoTW* backed her claim. He quoted the Assistant DA from Washington: 'Towers' address book will never be opened in a court of law.'

The officer who questioned Mariella, the plainclothed Donati, was also approached by journalists. He refused to comment on the espionage connection. If it were just a vice case, he said, he would be able to comment. 'You understand what I'm saying? I cannot be more specific...'[14]

Any story to do with Mariella tends to end like this.

By the beginning of June 1961, Mariella Novotny, the niece of the Czech Communist president and former 'girlfriend' of the

---

14. *Honeytrap*

President of the United States, was the talk of London town. On the back of her notoriety, she was hosting scandalous dinner parties in Hyde Park Square, W1.

'Stephen Ward was the first to contact me,' she confided to her diary. Through Stephen, she was about to meet a Soviet naval attaché at Lord Astor's mansion in Cliveden.

9

HONEYTRAP

I first became aware of this wingless bird when researching a book about my grandfather. Charlie Taylor was what is known as a face: a shyster whose anti-social tendencies flowered against the backdrop of a scabbed and peeling city. Wartime found him deserting ranks and spivving in the dens of London. Fast forward to the end of his career and he hit the headlines for *nearly* breaking the Bank of England. His lowlife story is as colourful as the high life of Fon and his father; it even has some glamour, and it shows a weakness for pretty women. During his trial at the Old Bailey in 1978, Charlie alleged he had been set up by a double agent called Mariella Novotny, codenamed Henry. In court, he claimed: 'She is the woman who arranged for the war minister Mr Profumo to be dropped from the cabinet. She gave evidence to the Lord Denning inquiry but that evidence never appeared.'

The judge told him to stand down and stop being silly.

A few days later, just as things were beginning to look lively, and names were about to be divulged, Charlie died. Some say in mysterious circumstances. This is what regularly happens to the whistleblowers of the twentieth century.

The Denning Inquiry was an investigation into the security aspects of an affair between War Minister Jack Profumo and

Stephen Ward's young friend Christine Keeler. This affair took place against a backdrop of the Cold War and led to fears of a national security breach, ultimately contributing to the fall of Prime Minister Harold Macmillan and his government. Keeler was a model and topless showgirl who worked at Murray's Cabaret Club in Soho, where she met Ward, an English osteopath and portraitist who moved in fashionable circles and had many important friends. Ward took her under his wing and introduced her to one of Macmillan's government ministers – John Profumo. The married Profumo and the nubile Keeler had a brief sexual relationship.

Ward also introduced Keeler to Captain Yevgeny Ivanov, a Soviet naval attaché. When the story exploded onto the front pages of British newspapers there were reports that Keeler had been simultaneously involved with Profumo and Ivanov, and readers wondered: had there been a security risk? Had any vital information been passed to a Cold War rival?

In March 1963, in response to the proliferation of rumours, Profumo made a personal statement to the House of Commons and denied any impropriety. Prime Minister Macmillan backed him. Just a few weeks later, Profumo refuted his own statement, admitted the truth and resigned as an MP. Politically, the impact was huge: Macmillan resigned as PM in October, and the Conservative Party lost the 1964 general election. For the individuals involved, the consequences were equally disastrous. Ward was prosecuted on a number of vice charges, including 'living off immoral earnings' from Keeler and her friend Mandy Rice-Davies. He was convicted but, just before he could be sentenced, died of a fatal overdose.

The fallout for Keeler was more of a slow burn. Having first caught the media's attention after a shooting incident between two of her lovers, she was subject to intense scrutiny as the Profumo Affair mushroomed. She then faded into obscurity and died in poverty.

The repercussions are still reverberating in the twenty-first century. But in the accounts I read there was no reference to Mariella Novotny. In a book called *Honeytrap* I found my first lead: a quote from paperwork surrounding the Denning Inquiry that was secreted in the diaries of Denning's private secretary. Thomas Critchley mentioned both Mariella and her husband, Hod.

Rifling through what records are left of Horace 'Hod' Dibben, the dealer in antiques, it appears he was frequently in the bankruptcy courts. As we have seen, when he met Mariella, he was a nightclub owner in London mixing with the night owls of the *demi-monde*. What I read in the private secretary's diary and in Hod's records had major implications for the Profumo story, pointing to a network of politicians and gangsters, prostitutes and policemen that would make an enemy of the state's mouth water. The descriptions of Mariella and her husband Hod were the starting point for investigating this weird parade of misfits.

'Hod Dibben was allegedly a man of fathomless depravity in whose hands Stephen Ward was clay ... in addition to his interests in black magic he had a tremendous appetite for sex, so long as it was perverted enough.'

This was the opinion of Critchley, a Home Office bureaucrat who became obsessed with Mariella and Hod: 'Mariella Novotny was a beautiful blonde of Czech origin. She had grown up witness to the horrors of the turbulent post-war years in central Europe and [her] experience of rape and torture twisted her nature into something vile and deformed.'

Critchley's response is indicative of the unease that Mariella evokes in her middle-class male audience. It is as though she reflects the dark mass of desires that remained unspoken in twentieth-century Britain. In reference to Critchley's impression of Mariella I found another disturbing mention in another book. In his 2016 memoir, the investigative journalist Tom Mangold described Mariella as a 'common prostitute'.

The term 'common prostitute' was first used in the Vagrancy Act of 1824. In the twenty-first century the term has largely fallen out of use as understanding of the relationship between poverty, alienation, addiction, coercion and prostitution has increased. In his account Tom Mangold was referring to the framework of prostitution that was set out in the Sexual Offences Act of 1956. This reflected the findings of the Wolfenden investigation into prostitution and homosexuality. Prostitution and its status in the law was a moral issue. It was of course the woman's morality that was questionable, rather than her male client's.

In 1973 Mariella herself took issue with this terminology.

> Whenever I see the words 'common prostitute' I'm puzzled, does it indicate that she belongs to the general public? ... Is the common prostitute a chick who takes cash for it so that she can give her widowed mother a nourishing meal while another who stuffs her own belly at Club Dell'Aretusa as a prelude to opening her legs, remains a righteous amateur?[15]

In November 2008 the Home Office published the findings of a six-month review into how the demand for prostitution could be reduced. Home Secretary Jacqui Smith, in a foreword to the review, stated: 'So far, little attention has been focused on the sex *buyer* [my italics], the person responsible for creating the demand for prostitution markets. And it is time for that to change.'

The Labour chair of the Home Affairs Select Committee, Keith Vaz, expressed his concern that he was 'not convinced that the best course of action is to prosecute in the proposed way *men* who go into situations where they wish to buy sex from prostitutes'. Again, these are my italics. Ten years later a tabloid reported that Vaz had hired 'male escorts' – in other words, common prostitutes – for sex. He retired from politics. The Policing and Crime Bill, introduced to the Commons in December 2008 and ratified in 2009, created a new offence of paying for sex with a person of either sex who is controlled for gain. It also introduced new powers to close brothels and modified the law on soliciting. How does this tie in to Mariella's story? It is a question of shame. For her generation of sex workers, they carried that load on behalf of the rest of society. These women were silenced; we simply do not hear from them.

---

15. *Club International*, 1973

GOVERNMENT CHIEF WHIP

On 4 June 1961 Mariella docked at Southampton. She was twenty years old and married to a man born in 1905. Although just out of her troublesome teens, she had jeopardised the presidency of the United States. She had escaped the clutches of the FBI – and possibly been aided by the CIA – as she disembarked in Southampton on the *Queen Mary*. She was ready to meet her public. Mariella Novotny smoothed down her skirt and fluffed up her hair, ready to take the Smoke by storm.

'I was determined to be the best hostess of my age,' she confided to her diary.[16] Her guests flocked to meet the girl who had had such an impact on the most powerful man in the world, John F. Kennedy. The address she gave was 13 Hyde Park Square, W2. Eight floors of brown brick look onto a classic Victorian square with wrought-iron railings, hydrangeas and plinths. At number 15, her neighbours provided some showbiz glitz. Fenella Fielding and Albert Finney were flatmates and young theatrical stars making names for themselves on stage and screen. Finney had just triumphed in the landmark British 'kitchen sink' film *Saturday Night and Sunday Morning*. This was a radical departure

16. 'The Government Chief Whip (Retired)'. Novotny manuscript.

from films featuring the stiff upper lip of classic Brits. Volatile or truculent working-class men were beginning to articulate their anger. Women, especially if they were educated, would have to wait another decade or so. Finney's flatmate, Fenella Fielding, is best known for her husky *double entendres* in *Carry On* films. But she had a subversive sense of humour and more ambition than her film career would suggest. At the time of Mariella's *soirées*, she was starring in a satire on theatrical vanity called *So Much to Remember: The Life Story of a Very Great Lady*. She had written it herself. She kept a copy of Plato's *Republic* next to her bed.

Mariella's bedtime reading was Bertrand Russell and Somerset Maugham. She had been reading Russell's chapter on Plato on her wedding night, when Hod so rudely interrupted her. Mariella had aspirations, too. She wanted to develop her intellect and foster an appreciation for the finer things in life.

> Since my name was linked with extremely erotic activities, I decided to entertain on a large scale ... I chose to concentrate on exotic food and fascinating personalities, and served about seven or eight courses. This combination stunned my friends when my sexual games completed the dinner parties. Within weeks my parties became the subject of gossip among the elite in London.

Stephen Ward was in touch with her within days of her return. 'He pestered me almost daily to meet Eugene Ivanov.'[17]

Ward had missed the boat. The other 'friend' to greet her on her return was Michael Eddowes, who warned her against mixing it up with politicians. So she rejected Ward's invitations to attend Soviet Embassy parties. However, she did go to an intimate after-party:

> Following one reception at the [Russian] Embassy shortly after my return from New York, I agreed to meet Dibs [Hod],

---

17. Memoir as quoted in *Honeytrap*

Stephen and the late controversial writer and broadcaster, Gilbert Harding, at the Turk's Head pub in Belgravia. Gilbert was a great character but I think Dibs was probably one of the few people able to get on with him. They became very close friends. I timed my appearance at the pub to avoid Ivanov. Gilbert was a heavy drinker and often fell asleep, even during broadcasts.

Mariella arrived in time to see the slum landlord Peter Rachman enter the pub with one of Stephen's girls in a blue mink bolero. Stephen explained that the girl, called 'Sally' by Mariella, was on her way to Cliveden for the weekend. He was in boastful form: 'I had a hand in bringing Bronwen and Bill [Astor] together, and Maureen Swanson and Viscount Ednam. I hope I can do as well for Sally.'

Gilbert said something gruff about Ward's introductions service. Rachman took offence at his new girlfriend's non-exclusivity, and promptly left, taking 'Sally' in tow. Stephen admitted that there was more than just marriage guidance counselling going on.

Sally's certainly made a hit with Peter. I'll soon start steering her towards more worthwhile men. She's no fool. Rachman has this two-way looking glass. Sally noticed the thin lines and guessed the score. She got Rachman to admit he enjoyed watching her make love in the next room with a man who had no idea they were being viewed. She'd even heard a rumour that he tape-recorded and photographed them and later he or Michael de Freitas [of whom more later] would apply a little pressure to the unsuspecting fornicator.

It is quite likely that 'Sally' was Mandy Rice-Davies, the showgirl who got out of the Profumo Affair still standing. In fact, she thrived on the backlash and reinvented herself as a chanteuse before trying out the nighlife in Israel. Here she set up a night club with, guess who? Ronnie Dice.

Despite, or perhaps because of, everything she heard, Mariella could not resist an invitation to Sunday lunch at Cliveden. She motored down in the Mercedes sports car she had purchased. Ward had told her to get there before the other guests so that he could show her the grounds.

'He took me straight into the cottage. A man stood with his back to us, looking from the window onto the river ... It was Ivanov – Ward introduced us quickly and rushed from the room ... Ivanov talked well, and said that he was aware I had avoided meeting him ... His manner was so nice it was difficult to fault. Ward brought drinks in, explained he had no idea Ivanov was coming, and left us alone.'

In the idyllic setting of English country-house wealth and ease, Ivanov put the screws on. He had done his homework. He mentioned her missing Czech father; he hinted that he could assist in arranging a visa to Prague, bypassing the difficulties such a trip presented.

'The temptation was great, exactly what I had hoped for one day.' But she was suspicious and cut him short 'before he could tell me what was expected on my part'. Hod joined the party shortly afterwards and told Dorrill and Summers, 'She realised she was being set up.'

'My controversial American involvement was of special interest, I was later informed.' She also gained the impression 'that Bill Astor had a hand in the matter. From evidence I later saw, it was obvious Astor gave Ward his orders and controlled him to a great extent.'

Next, Ward tried to interest her in the Minister for War, John Profumo.

'His tireless endeavours to introduce me succeeded after dozens of refusals from me ... Profumo was another friend of Ward's I did not take to.' As the authors of *Honeytrap* note, it was uncharacteristic of Mariella to be so fussy. However, if she had learnt one thing from her brush with power, it was that she needed to be in charge. For her, this meant literally holding the whip hand.

At this point, Hod and Mariella were occupants of Upper Wyke House, St Mary's Bourne in Hampshire. At least this was the address Mariella gave in court. In the summer of 1964 she appeared before the magistrates in Andover to answer a case brought by a motorist into whom she had crashed. Mariella was a notoriously reckless and short-sighted driver. The motorist's complaint was that she had backed her 'van' into his car and then used a four-letter word when he asked her name and address. (The van may have been used in Hod's furniture-dealing business.)

'Mrs Dibben, also known as Mariella Capes, wife of antique dealer Mr Hod Dibben, admitted careless driving, failing to report an accident and failing to give her name and address. She was fined £75 with £3 1s 9d costs. Her address was given as Upper Wyke House, St Mary Bourne, Hants, and Hyde Park-square, Paddington.'

In an article in *Club International* Mariella mused on the possibility of naming some of her victims and regretfully decided against it. But she did describe what she did to them. On one particular Sunday in the country, after lunch in the Great Hall, Mariella and her guests were strolling in the old walled garden at Upper Wyke House. In the shaded seclusion of mulberry trees, they were all nude. The servants had been dismissed and had left drinks on the Malacca tables in the shade. After some aimless chitchat Mariella ordered 'Sir A' to stand with his back to the trunk of a 200-year-old mulberry. She secured him to the tree and shackled him with handcuffs.

'Let your lunch settle and watch,' she said, ever the showgirl. 'I'm not going to use whips or anything that will damage the flesh.' (The lack of visual evidence such as bruising or cuts was appreciated 'by those who are married to suspicious partners and perhaps even refuse to discuss disgusting perversions'.)

Safely ensconced in the walled garden, she pulled a perforated polythene bag out from behind a rose bush.

'This contains about thirty or forty wasps,' she told the crowd gathered around Sir A. 'I'm going to open it quickly, pop it over his erection and tie it securely at the base of A's penis.'

The onlookers reportedly gasped and Sir A groaned. Mariella showed no mercy. When she had released the victim and left him to deal with his swollen member as best he could, she suggested he try her grandmother's remedy for wasp stings, Reckitt's Blue. Or Daz.

Another guest, 'Lord B.', jumped to his feet and raised his glass of Pimm's Number 1. 'Here's to our hostess, Mariella, the masochist's dream.'

Lord B., 'noted for his snobbish and pompous manner', was next to be punished. Naked and upright, he faced Mariella and her guests 'with some of whom he was wont to negotiate big business – and without a murmur he surrendered his aura of superiority, allowing those present to witness the collapse of his power image'. Suede gloves, the fingers and palms of which were studded with fine metal spikes, were brought into play. Blood, steel, shrieks and humiliation.

Not all Mariella's dinner parties involved sex games. They all, however, involved a desperate kind of narcissism. Mariella needed to feel important and for this to happen she had to surround herself with prominent people. She and Hod entertained on the grand scale: 'Lavish dinner parties in London, and weekend parties in Hampshire. I normally arranged for twenty-four to dine, and served about seven or eight courses ... The sort of friends I invited were not dumb.'

Some of her invitations were addressed to leading figures in the arts world so that Hod could sell precious objects to them. Thus Sir William Emrys-Williams, as Secretary of the Arts Council and Trustee of the National Gallery, was on the list. As were flying ace Sheila Scott and Chikie Moss, the stepdaughter of the golfer Henry Cotton. Beecher Moore was a regular. He eventually donated his collection of pornography to the British Museum. Lord Spencer was a member of the advisory Council of the V&A. There was no question of any 'funny business' when the art elite congregated to dine. But when some parties did descend into orgy, 'some strange incidents developed'.

'The bizarre became normal for me. Nothing surprised me at my parties ... My sadistic nature was no secret. I became humorously known as the Government Chief Whip.'

Sex was cool and calculated. As a young woman, she had resisted, but now she simply became detached, as if what was happening to her was not of any interest. Those who disliked her or disapproved of her saw her lack of warmth as symptomatic of a frigid and unlovable personality. But Mariella did not lack warmth – ask 'Sven', or 'Jackie', the Soho stripper who features later. Mariella's fellow travellers attest to her humour and concern for others. What Mariella lacked was the ability to appeal for love from people who did not care about her.

(WO)MAN IN THE MASK

In La Vie quotidienne dans les maisons closes, 1830–1930, the French writer and biographer Laure Adler records the extent to which voyeurism usurped more traditional pleasures in the nineteenth-century high-end brothel. In her eyes, the sexual demands of the rich were transformed from consumption of the act itself to a more finicky, visual orgasm. Certainly voyeurism is an essential component of desire, but the *maisons closes* began to offer *tableaux vivants*. In the interiors of the grand salons of Paris, the organising genius of the *madame* dreamt up a kind of erotic machinery to delight her customers' senses. For example, on a large black carpet the white bodies of naked women were seated in suggestive poses. Lit from behind by candelabras, the women emerged from behind curtains and choreographed themselves on a rotating floor, like wax dolls fixed for eternity in voluptuous poses. To satisfy the voyeurs, the habitual holes pierced in the shafts of walls or inside closets no longer sufficed: through the skillful arrangement of pinned sheets or wall hangings or thanks to tubes stuck into partition walls and used by some as listening trumpets, by others as magnifying glasses, the spectator could watch in a private peep show. The inventiveness and ingenuity were part of the show.

One evening in December 1961, Stephen Ward, osteopath and portraitist, descended the basement steps of 13 Hyde Park Square. Ahead of him was Juno in a silver mask, and behind him, a Viking in a bronze helmet with horns. The door to Mariella's flat was open and in the large first room was a crowd from another world: a Crusader in a tunic with a large red cross; a pair of female savages painted black, in straw skirts; couples in evening clothes wearing sequinned masks; and Helen of Troy in a golden gown with crossed straps over a bare back. This was Mariella, unmistakable because of her slight frame (she was four foot seven in bare feet) and her Fabergé lorgnette. Hod did not like her wearing spectacles in company. His costume was a pair of hussar's sideburns and a leer.

Their home was filled with TV personalities, embassy officials, a famous one-armed barrister, and a clutch of MPs. They gossiped and buzzed with anticipation among Hod's collection of fine art and antique furniture. Ward, the connoisseur of orgies, was in his element.

'It would be humbug if I did not confess that I looked forward to the sex orgies,' he wrote in his unpublished memoir. 'I have been to every type of that party – those specialising in certain perversions and those given in an elaborate setting where all the formalities were observed.'[18]

Full-scale orgies were taking place all over London. This was how Ward's friendship with Hod had developed in the first place. Hod had been practising masochistic sexual acts since the thirties. He drew on the tradition of erotomania that developed in Second Empire Paris. His appetite for collecting and an increasingly *recherché* bric-a-bracomania, combined with Mariella's penchant for tableau-mania, are echoes of the wily *madame*'s dramatic representations of the temple of love. Together they invited their guests to partake in a tour of the courtesan's boudoir and, ultimately, the house of prostitution. Hod definitely had

---

18. Dr Stephen Ward, 'Notes for an Autobiography'. Unpublished MS.

the practical experience and epicurean refinement to bring this decadence to life. But he could never quite place himself firmly in the *beau monde*. His disregard for discretion made him a fringe figure amongst the people whose approval he craved most of all. Nevertheless they came to Hod and Mariella's parties as though to the opening night of a new show.

To a twenty-first-century enlightened readership it is astonishing how insensible our predecessors were. Alcohol contributed to the narcoleptic fug. Drugs, too. At one party, Ward noted he came across the host 'grinding up pills in a bowl which he put into everything we drank, whether it was gin, whisky, or just coffee. Benzedrine or Methedrine was used.' It is no surprise that inhibitions were loosened. Yet in the midst of craving sensations it is chilling to observe how little they felt.

'I really was curious in a sort of detached way,' Ward wrote. 'Looking back one sees how easy it is to be drawn into a situation out of simple weakness, to be horrified to start with and later to accept it all as normal behaviour or nearly so.'

It is as though the object was to achieve numbness in the midst of extreme pain or pleasure. Sleeping pills, appetite suppressants and amphetamines were widely prescribed by doctors. As a matter of course, Mariella, Ward and their contemporaries swallowed pills to avoid distressing or uncomfortable feelings. If Bertrand Russell could not get her to sleep, Mariella used barbiturates. She had already told the *News of the World* she was using sleeping pills. The numbness seems to have taken the place of her heart. Pills also helped close Mariella's mind to what she was doing. To retiterate her own phrase, 'The bizarre became normal for me,' is to underline that what was unacceptable became acceptable.

So it was that with her emotional life suitably deadened, Mariella developed an appetite for extreme and intricate acts of sadism. Lord Astor was a regular at her country weekends.[19] The rake and gambler Lord Longford, the flying ace Count Manfred Czernin (an SOE operative and one of 'The Few'), and the psychiatrist

---

19. *Club International*, vol. 2, no. 7, 1973

Dr Eustace Chesser (author of the 1940 sex manual *Love Without Fear*, which led to him being arrested for obscenity) were just a few who indulged their curiosity. Some became her lovers. During the period of the Man in in the Mask Party and the Profumo Affair, her lover was Billy Rees-Davies, the one-armed barrister and MP for Thanet.

But the identity of the titular party guest remains a mystery. He was a man wearing a masonic apron and leather mask. He was strapped between two wooden pillars in front of the fireplace.

'A flail or whip was in front of his naked figure. As each guest arrived they gave him one stroke, then left the man to join the party. When he was released before dining, he was ordered to remain beneath the long table, out of sight.'

Once the man in the mask had taken his place under the table, dinner was served. This was Mariella's moment of culinary triumph. For the main course she had cooked a pair of young peacocks. She had 'skewered their necks and heads in position and added the colourful tail feathers of older birds'.

'The Feast of the Peacocks,' Mariella announced. This was the stuff of Roman Emperors or Tudor monarchs, but not everyone was impressed. 'A girl became hysterical and screamed that [the peacocks] signified death,' Mariella wrote. 'She created havoc and had to be sent home, before she ruined the party.'

Ten years almost to the day of the Feast of the Peacocks, Mariella was interviewed for the *Sarasota Herald Tribune* in the United States.[20] She recalled the party, and in particular referred to the girl who had screamed.

'We laughed at her, but five of the guests at the party – two of them titled – died within a short time.' (This was the heightened atmosphere in which Mariella was cooking.) Meanwhile, 'under the table [the man in the mask] obeyed any order I gave him to please my guests'.

Two guests arrived late. They were a pair of seventeen-year-old showgirls called Mandy and Christine. They came fresh from Ward's

---

20. 12 December 1971

Wimpole Mews stable of young women. But not even Stephen had met a girl like Mariella. Christine wrote in her memoir that Mariella fascinated Stephen.[21] Unlike his provincial popsies, Mariella was cultured, had intellectual leanings and was mysteriously 'Eurasian' in appearance. The inscrutable air she cultivated amplified her slanting eyes and haughty bearing. And she wasn't just a pretty face. She spoke of art and antiques; she had flawless taste and manners.

Both Hod and Ward saw themselves as Svengalis. But how much Hod contributed to the finished article of Mariella remains, like everything about her, a mystery.

The party was virtually over by the time the two girls arrived. Stephen had telephoned them to suggest they come along after he had been caught in the bedroom on his knees. In fact, Mariella almost fell over him as she was groping around in her shoe cupboard. On closer inspection she saw that Stephen was holding one of her stilettos over his nose and mouth, leaving his other hand free. Normally, she observed, Stephen was a watcher rather than a doer. On this occasion he was 'huffing and puffing with excitement'.[22] He asked Mariella to put her highest heels on and stand on his scrotum.

Once he had recovered, he made the phone call. In an interview, Mandy recalled: 'Stephen met us at the door, wearing nothing but a sock. I thought it was a joke. Everyone was *déshabillé*, and Mariella had exchanged her gold lame backless frock for a black corset and a whip. Naked people were everywhere, draped over chairs, or standing around laughing and joking.

'I didn't know where to look. After all, I was only seventeen, even if I had been around. I remember spotting this plate of tangerines – they were a rarity in winter in those days – and I attacked those tangerines and some chocolates until I felt sick.'[23]

While she devoured the rare treats, Mandy could not help noticing that her hostess was in bed with six men. Christine got

---

21. Christine Keeler, *Secrets and Lies*
22. *Club International*, vol. 2, no. 7, 1973
23. *Honeytrap* p. 117

up close to investigate. Mariella 'had a tiny waist that exaggerated her ample figure. She was a siren, a sexual athlete of Olympian proportions – she could do it all. She knew all the strange pleasures that were wanted and could deliver them.'[24]

And then there was the man in the mask still cowering under the table.

'The man in the mask was a masochist,' wrote Mariella, 'and asked me to treat him as my "slave". I willingly agreed, and caused him mental and physical pain. This was what he wanted – I did nothing against his wishes. The humiliation he underwent was extreme but was the dream of his life.'

It was not until 1987, four years after Mariella's death, that Hod indicated that the man in the mask might be the Honourable Anthony Asquith, youngest son of a Liberal Prime Minister, the First Earl of Oxford and Asquith. Anthony Asquith had the added distinction of being one of Britain's most successful film directors. His films included a 1938 adaptation of *Pygmalion*, a storyline that occupied the imaginations of Hod and Stephen Ward. Other films were *The Winslow Boy*, *The Browning Version* and *The Yellow Rolls-Royce*. Asquith's cinematic successes were stellar. He was a fellow of the British Academy and Governor of the British Film Institute. To his overbearing mother, he was simply 'Puffin'.

Margot Asquith was known within the family to be highly demanding and critical. Poor health frequently made her 'difficult'. There were rumours she was a 'sapphist'. She made terrible scenes. People become masochistic, Freud said, as a way of suppressing their desire to sexually dominate others and their feelings of guilt about the impulse. Anthony Asquith was 61 years old when he is rumoured to have paid for Mariella's services. He was unmarried and his friends wondered if he was homosexual. They puzzled over his weekend hobby of serving tea at a lorry drivers' café near Catterick, in Yorkshire. They wondered if it signified an escape into anonymity[25] à la T. E. Lawrence. Mariella, the dominatrix,

24. *Secrets and Lies*
25. *Honeytrap* p. 119

had an unerring instinct for the weaknesses of men. She had the wit to create confections of odours, sumptuous sets, multiple mirrors, a profusion of Turkish carpets and an orgy of electricity to set alight an arsenal of pleasure. But did her client list include the son of the Home Secretary who signed the 'gross indecency' arrest warrant against Oscar Wilde?

A writer of my acquaintance told me he thought not. My friend mixed in circles that included the movers and shakers of the cultural establishment and the Kray twins. He was very close to both men, attending their 'parties', befriending Violet, their mother, and visiting them both in prison. He also knew Asquith, who, my friend told me, was committed to a relationship with a working-class East End lorry driver. 'This chap was married to a most accommodating lady, with whom Asquith had an affectionate bond. He was almost part of the family.' It is unlikely that Asquith was Mariella's sex slave.

With each addition of pain or restraint, the man in the mask would stiffen slightly. The descent into deep calm, waiting only to obey his mistress, was his reward.

The strange thing about the Man in the Mask Party was that it happened at a time in English history when the ruling classes collaborated in maintaining a fiction that this sort of thing did not happen at all, and that if and when it did happen, it was out of the ordinary, deeply regrettable and entirely wicked. For generations desire had been twisted into strange, unbidden shapes. Furtive conniving ensured that consummation remained hidden, unspoken and ultimately condemned. Mariella understood this manifestation of shame very well. She spent a lifetime trying to capitalise on it.

12

'EVERYONE WENT HOME
WELL SATISFIED'

These were the last words the 'Government Chief Whip' had to say about her party. In December 1961 she was at the top of her game. The next two years would see the exposure of a British Empire in decay and a government perceived to be run by elderly degenerates. Mariella's client base evaporated. She should have listened to that dapper little man Michael Eddowes. So let me take up the story from his perspective.

On a December morning in 1962, Christine Keeler got into a spot of bother with her two boyfriends from Notting Hill. Like cowboys from Dodge City they enacted a Wild West shoot-out in the soon-to-be notorious Wimpole Mews. With the police on her case, Christine turned to Eddowes for legal advice. She told him about her boyfriends, Lucky Gordon and Johnny Edgecombe, and how they were jealous of each other. She told him about her other boyfriends John Profumo and Eugene Ivanov, and how one had asked her to extract secrets from the other to pass back to him. At this point, she had his attention. Eddowes was a man with an over-active conscience and he told her to steer clear of Profumo. This was not the advice she wanted, and Eddowes was left to wonder about the security implications of what she had confided.

On 14 June 1963 Eddowes held a chummy, confiding conversation with a reporter at his chambers in Yeomans Road, off Knightsbridge. They sat on a low sofa in the lounge of the first floor. The conversation was reported in the *Evening Standard* the following day:

> She [Christine] was in an excited state and I thought it was a good opportunity to put my questions to her about the possibility of espionage. I asked her if Ivanov and Profumo were friends of hers, and she said, 'Oh, yes.'
>
> She added that one used to go out of one door while the other came in the other door. I judged the moment propitious to ask if Ivanov had asked her to get information. She said 'Yes.' I said, 'Anything in particular?' and she replied, 'The date of delivery of nuclear warheads to Germany.'
>
> I asked her if she had tried to get information, and she said, 'No.'

During this meeting, Eddowes told the reporter that he was 'given to understand' that the security police were watching both Ivanov and Profumo in relation to Keeler from November 1962. He obviously enjoyed creating intrigue because he went on to say that he had met Ivanov at Ward's clinic.

> I had an appointment with Dr. Ward for treatment at four o'clock on the day that the American warships were within sinking distance of the Russian ships approaching Cuba. Dr. Ward's receptionist told me he was having coffee in the Coffee Bean Bar in Marylebone High Street, and would I like to go round there. I did.
>
> At a table in the far right-hand corner were sitting Dr Ward and Capt. Eugene Ivanov. I had about an hour's conversation with Ivanov. During this conversation I formed the impression that he was a desperately worried man.

Eddowes explained that he had become concerned about Christine's information on 22 March 1963, when the War Minister,

John Profumo, denied impropriety with Keeler. After further cogitation, on 28 March Eddowes had sent a letter to Special Branch. In this letter, addressed to Admiralty House, he told the Prime Minister to examine closely five specific individuals in the Ward–Profumo nexus. However, he told the reporter, it was now June and he still had not heard back from Macmillan or his minions. On 15 June, a few hours after Eddowes's interview appeared in the *Evening Standard*, Christine's solicitors issued a statement:

> With reference to a letter reported in this evening's *Evening Standard* – from Mr M. Eddowes to the Prime Minister, we are instructed by Miss Christine Keeler to state that Eugene Ivanov on no occasion asked her to obtain from Mr John Profumo any military information of any kind whatsoever, and she has never made any statement to that effect to anyone.

The government's press office spun into action. The official line was that the Prime Minister had a complete answer to questions posed by the letter from Eddowes. Furthermore, no security risk was involved, and conflicting accounts (from Eddowes and Keeler) were adding nothing to a clouded and complex issue. But the story was gathering momentum. After a late-night telephone call, the Home Secretary, Henry Brooke, boarded the naval frigate *Wakeful* at 1 a.m. The frigate was to take him from Guernsey in the Channel Islands to London in time for a meeting at Admiralty House. The Prime Minister and the Lord Chancellor joined him. The main question under debate seemed to be whether the government should send the Profumo Affair to a tribunal. At the same time, leader of the opposition Harold Wilson broke off a trip to Moscow to meet with his deputy, George Brown. The Labour Deputy Leader had spoken to reporters after conferring for almost an hour with President Kennedy in Washington. He said that he and Wilson had had two telephone conversations to discuss developments. The shadow cabinet had concluded that the security aspects of the affair had 'serious overtones'.

'They [the government] have not yet given anything like an adequate explanation.' Wilson made a public request for a full-scale enquiry. Two days later came the Commons confidence debate on the affair. Granada Television had planned to broadcast a clinching interview pre-recorded with Eddowes before the vote. But the plan ended in farce. All Granada put out was a brief statement: 'Early today, Mr Eddowes asked us for this allegation (about warhead information) to be withdrawn from his statement in the programme. Granada agreed, but told Mr Eddowes that the facts (of the withdrawal) would be published. The whole of Mr Eddowes's statement has now been dropped from tonight's *World In Action*.'

That very day Eddowes boarded a plane to New York. 'I don't know how long I'll be away,' he told reporters. And with that, he vanished from the headlines.

As a consequence of his allegations, and the confusion surrounding Profumo's denial and recantation of that denial, the government commissioned the report mentioned earlier to be compiled by Lord Denning, helped by his secretary, Thomas Critchley. The friend and biographer of Ward, Tom Mangold, highlights the prurience of Lord Denning and his secretary when confronted with accounts of Mariella. It was not just the guest lists to her dinner parties, which were stellar, it was what they got up to for afters. Lord Denning was horror-struck. He decided to deliver his invitation to Hod and Mariella to appear before his enquiry *by hand*. For what purpose if not to satisfy his curiosity? His secretary, Critchley, would not allow this act of indiscretion. Instead he would enter the lion's den on Denning's behalf. In preparation for this noble sacrifice, he took advice from the Commissioner of Scotland Yard:

'You'll have to be careful,' said the Commissioner. 'They're a rum lot. He, Hod, practices black magic. Only two days ago, on Thursday morning, one of my young PCs was standing outside the house when the cleaner came out, white and trembling all over. The constable asked her what the matter was. She pointed down to the basement of No. 13. 'There's a coffin in there, a black cloth with lilies on it.'

Such was the potential for devilry and danger, the commissioner arranged for Critchley to be driven from Whitehall to Hod's address in Hyde Park Square by a plainclothes officer. When the intrepid Critchley got to number 13, he knocked on the door. When no one answered, he put his missive through the letterbox. Unharmed and uncontaminated, he returned to his office.

The Denning Report was eagerly awaited by newshounds and the British public alike. Published on 24 October 1963, his lordship's findings were that no security breaches had occurred. To this day, Ward's relationship with Ivanov still has the whiff of sulphur surrounding it. His sudden death was convenient in the way these deaths are. Whistleblowers, procurers and scapegoats have a handy trick of expiring before revealing the contents of their address books. Profumo was ultimately judged to have been careless in his extramarital activities and as penance took to charity work in the East End of London. He was awarded an MBE in 1975. Mariella was piqued that there was nary a word about her in the best-selling Denning Report.

'I lied to Lord Denning, but not about a politician' she wrote. 'My lies were to protect someone from ruin and a criminal charge. A Member of Parliament was present, William Rees-Davies, MP for Thanet, but he was not in the disguise.'

'Jackie', a future colleague of Mariella, said that she never talked about the Man in the Mask because she wanted to protect Billy Rees-Davies, who was a popular figure in the social calendar of the sixties. Of all her elderly lovers, he was Mariella's favourite. He also had a high-profile wife who graced the pages of *Tatler* with appearances at Ascot and Henley. Mariella was loyal and if she liked someone she would not capitalise on their indiscretions. She must have liked the Man in the Mask immensely because his identity remains unknown.

13

THE *JOURNAL-AMERICAN*

In June 1963, Mariella's erstwhile sparring partner Harry Alan Towers emerged from behind the Iron Curtain. He was in South Africa producing his first feature film, *Death Drums along the River*. Over in the States, reporters had not forgotten him. The New York *Journal-American* had been asking Mariella's solicitor friend, Michael Eddowes, what he could tell them about Harry. Eddowes passed on the strange circumstances of Mariella's escape and the flight of her alleged pimp to the Soviet bloc. Leaks from law enforcement sources confirmed Eddowes' story of Mariella and an unnamed Hungarian woman who went on dates with her and reported to a Soviet contact.

Throughout June the *Journal-American* was hot on the heels of what it called the 'Novotny Case'. So while the English were feasting on the Profumo Affair, American readers were lapping up a vice ring that that had existed two years earlier within the United Nations HQ in New York, with diplomats as customers. On 24 June 1963, Congressman Harold Gross called for an enquiry into the UN revelations. He was a Republican member of Congress often used as a mouthpiece by FBI Director Hoover. U Thant, the Secretary-General to the UN, then called for further investigation.

A woman called Evelyn Davis was arrested on vice charges. Then three women – one English, one American, and one Hungarian – were reported to have run away to Prague. The conclusion was that the Czechs had been using the honey-trap technique in New York.

'With the case of the British War Minister and the call girls building up,' said the *Washington News*, 'we can think of no better time for an American President to stay as far as possible away from England.' Strong pressure was exerted to postpone a planned visit to London 'for fear President Kennedy might become in some way involved'. The State Department, however, was keen that Kennedy should visit in order to show that the 'special relationship' was still special. He went first to Germany, where he made his famous speech on visiting the Berlin Wall. He got some great press for being a Berliner but Mariella was raining on the parade. Rumours continued to surface during and in the wake of John F. Kennedy's European trip.

'Now,' she said to a London reporter, 'they are trying to put up a smokescreen ... in case they blundered over two years ago.' On 28 June, John F. Kennedy was visiting the home of his ancestors when the *Washington Post* ran a story by Dorothy Kilgallen, an influential columnist. 'The Novotny story,' she wrote, 'may challenge Christine Keeler's saga before the international call girl scandals become history.' Kilgallen suspected that the British counterpart of the CIA 'knew a whole lot more than it was telling about the international ramifications of the case'.

The next day, just as he arrived at Harold Macmillan's country residence, the *Post* followed up with a story about skeletons floating free from the president's closet. These skeletons were a reference to the latest reports of the *Journal-American* concerning the President, a screen goddess and a 'beautiful Chinese-American girl now in London'. Suzy Chang was that girl, and she was living in Nell Gwynn House, a serviced apartment block in Chelsea.

'I suppose the Americans will want to interview me,' Mariella told an English reporter wearily. Not so; they were on the trail of Esther Sue Yan Chang.

Born in New York City in 1934, Chang was the daughter of two Chinese immigrants. She adopted the name Suzy. UK immigration files show that she came to England in 1954 as a nursing student. She worked at a hospital in Birmingham. By the late fifties she was working in London as a 'model and actress'. In 1960 she was back in the States and met Mariella at the Quorum Club. Newly released FBI files claim that Stephen Ward was involved in supplying these two young women for prostitution. The FBI investigation also suggested that a 'Hungarian madam in New York' was involved in what was called the 'Bowtie' case.

Suzy Chang was refused permission to stay in the US but FBI documents show that she returned over the Christmas period at the end of 1962. In the early 1980s, three husbands later, living in America under the name Suzy Diamond, she told the authors of *Honeytrap* that she had indeed known Stephen Ward and JFK.

'Stephen was a good, good, good friend … I knew him a long time. He used to come to my house to eat … I loved Stephen … I knew all the people Stephen knew … I really cared about him.'

As for Kennedy: 'Well, John – John was the President of the United States … well, we'd meet in the 21 Club. You know, everybody saw me eating with him. It wasn't behind anybody's back. I knew Stash Radziwill, but I didn't know Lee very well, you know what I mean?'[26]

When Summers and Dorrill asked Suzy if she had had an affair with the man who told Harold Macmillan and Rab Butler, 'if I go too long without a woman I get a headache', she said, 'I think the President was a nice guy, very charming. What else am I going to say?'

With Kennedy still at Macmillan's pile in the country, the columnist Dorothy Kilgallen was fact-checking a new article:

---

26. Stash was Prince Stanislas Radziwill, married to the sister of the President's wife. The President did visit the 21 Club between his election and his inauguration. *Honeytrap*.

One of Novotny's closest girl chums was involved with a very big man on the other side of the Atlantic. As Kennedy was dining with Macmillan, FBI man Charles Bates was sending coded telegram 861 to FBI headquarters. It was rated VERY URGENT, and concerned the President. Of twenty lines, seventeen have been redacted.

What remains read: '[NAME CENSORED] TALKED ABOUT PRESIDENT KENNEDY AND REPEATED A RUMOUR THAT WAS GOING AROUND NEW YORK...' Another report provides more clues. This one is addressed to the FBI's Assistant Director in charge of Counter-Intelligence, William Sullivan. It reads, 'ONE OF [NAME CENSORED] CLIENTS WAS JOHN KENNEDY, THEN PRESIDENTIAL CANDIDATE. [NAME] STATED THAT MARIE NOVOTNY, BRITISH PROSTITUTE, WENT TO NEW YORK TO TAKE [NAME]'S PLACE, SINCE SHE WAS GOING ON PRE-ELECTION ROUNDS WITH KENNEDY.'

According to Summers and Dorril, Charles Bates later dropped some more clues. His information came from Assistant Commissioner for Crime Joe Jackson, at Scotland Yard. 'They had questioned a woman,' said Bates, 'apparently Mariella Novotny. She had taken the place of another woman, who had looked after Kennedy during the campaign.'

Who was the woman Mariella replaced?

Dorothy Kilgallen had written of a 'girl who could tell all ... reported to have committed suicide not long ago'. There are many candidates fitting this description – there was a high suicide rate amongst Kennedy's lovers. The girl most likely to tell all, according to the reporters from *Journal-American*, was Suzy Chang.

Charles Bates, the FBI man in London during the President's visit, remembers being shown Scotland Yard reports on the way Kennedy's name came up in the Profumo case.

'I saw something about a couple of girls who went over to the US in 1960, during the JFK campaign. They went to New York, they were in a hotel there. One or both later rode the campaign train to furnish her wares to those who wanted it. Also, one of them was given an assignment to meet a man in a certain hotel room. Then the other girl was sent over to take her place. That's vivid in my mind – the business about the hotel in New York, and the report referring to the man by the initials JFK.'

As fast as JFK's brother, the attorney-general, acted to clear the family name, leaks were dripping through to the press. On 31 July, Robert Kennedy summoned the journalists responsible for the Novotny story to his office in Washington. He sent the Kennedys' private plane, the *Caroline*, to fly them in from their homes in New York. The two journalists were the *J-A*'s managing editor James Horan, winner of the Pulitzer Prize, and a cub reporter named Dom Frasca.

According to an internal memo that survives, Robert Kennedy asked the newsmen to name the 'huge US aide' who was being linked to the the Profumo Affair. Horan replied that the reference was to the President, and that, according to the newspaper's information, he had 'been involved with a woman' – not Mariella – shortly before his election.

Horan and his cub refused to reveal their sources and the meeting ended in frosty silence.

Summers and Dorrill conclude that it was J. Edgar Hoover who saw to it that the *Journal-American* got its stories on Novotny and Chang. Hoover considered Kennedy a Red Menace and the *J-A* was an outlet for anti-Kennedy smears. Throughout the fifties Hoover had been using the Hearst-owned paper to fan the flames of a Communist witch-hunt that destroyed any left-leaning liberals in America. There were former FBI men on the paper's staff. The star writer, Walter Winchell, was a personal friend of Hoover.

In 1963 Robert Kennedy threatened the *Journal-American* with a government anti-trust suit if it did not cease to pursue the Novotny story. The *Journal-American* did not pursue the story. Four years later it folded. The managing editor, James Horan, responded to his redundancy by writing a novel, *The Right Image: A Novel of the Men who 'Make' Candidates for the Presidency*. The characters include a barely disguised Mariella, an Oriental girl called 'Suzy Chu' and a 'German madam whose brothel caters to the perverse whims of jaded politicians'.[27] Of the politicos, the most intriguing is 'an incredible madman who lives in the maze of tunnels under Manhattan, is an expert with mechanical eavesdropping equipment, and is insanely certain that Communists are taking over the country'.

In 1980, Michael Eddowes published *The Oswald Files*, on the assassination of John F. Kennedy by Lee Harvey Oswald. According to Eddowes, the real assassin was a Soviet agent. He went so far as to call for an exhumation of Oswald's grave in order to verify the corpse's identity.

Eddowes was back in England in time for the question of his letter to Admiralty House to re-surface. On 16 August the *Guardian* reported that the FBI had spirited him out of England and into their New York offices. It was here that he collaborated with the agency's alleged mouthpiece, *Journal-American*. With their help he was able to establish subversive activity undertaken by five members of the 'the Ward-Ivanov spy ring' in the United States.

'Those were the most staggering days of my life,' Eddowes said. When Kennedy was killed on 22 November 1963, he embarked on intensive research into the killing. As for the Profumo Affair: 'I stick by what I said in 1963. The reason I withdrew the Granada statement was because my lawyers advised it was defamatory – not because it wasn't true. I have never publicly named the five people.'

Many, including the brother of Lee Harvey Oswald, have accused Eddowes of seeking publicity. It is true that as a former Wimbledon tennis ace he knew how to play the game. But he saw himself as a serious investigator who had discovered 'colossal

---

27. *The Scranton Times*, 15 July 1967

ramifications' concerning the Profumo Affair and the Kennedy assassination. His parting shot to the *Guardian* was one 'amazing' item of evidence that pointed to an organisation behind the presidential shooting. A CIA document had been compiled soon after that fateful day. It had recently been released. It mentioned an anonymous call to the *Cambridge Evening News*. The caller supposedly told a reporter to ring the US Embassy in London for 'some big news'. The call was timed twenty-five minutes before the assassination occurred.

14

AGENT ZIGZAG AND
THE FOURTH LADY

Mariella liked men who were in a position of power or men with a powerful presence. After the Profumo debacle, her next lover was Billy Hill's enforcer, 'Italian' Albert Dimes. Dimes was the inspiration behind the terrifying mobster in Stanley Baker's 1960 film *Criminal*. Mariella liked to match herself against men like Dimes, and he was enjoying all she had to offer according to his colleague Bobby McKew. With one caveat: she had told him of an incident involving a window cleaner that had involved a needle landing in the window-cleaner's testicles when he tried to seduce her. The window cleaner, an associate of the British security services, according to the author Douglas Thompson, affirmed that it hurt but that it had been well worth the pain.[28]

In a stifling smog of tobacco smoke and harsh male voices, I felt like I was in an episode of *The Sweeney*. I was in fact in the Green Man pub on Berwick Street, Soho, with an elderly friend of my uncle called Tricky Dicky. He had started coming to Soho when he was seventeen. It was 1963 and he was a Mod. For 'modernists' outside the un-square mile, a weekend 'up west' was a pilgrimage.

'The fing about being up west on a Saturday night: in one sense you were a nobody; just another one of Soho's lost souls – but at

---

28. Douglas Thompson, *Hustlers*

the same time, you're standing at the pedestrian crossing in the middle of a mob of tourists and you're there. Bloody Mod from head to toe.'

Tricky claimed to have met Mariella many times and to have stolen her diaries at the behest of my uncle James. Both men were to play significant if faceless roles in Mariella's clandestine career. Their accounts are examined in some detail towards the end of her story. For now, Tricky, a retired burglar, was showing me his archive in the saloon bar of the Green Man. I picked up what looked like a letter. It was blue onion-skin Air Mail paper. On closer inspection it wasn't a letter – it was a scribbled fragment, with many crossings-out. The writing was Mariella's and it looked like she was working out a passage in her memoir: 'The air was dense with the noise from the band, the chatter of bohemians running up a tab … At first we prowled around each other like two predators. It wasn't long before we pounced, dancing and reading extracts from accounts of our lives.'

Her style was florid, her tone portentous, but this was good news. With all the Kennedy-related attention, a disgraced cabinet minister and a dead Stephen Ward, Madame Novotny's VIP boyfriends had run for cover. Mariella herself had been caught squinting in the headlights and did not like coverage that left her besmirched or, worse, ignored. Understandably, she needed to lick her wounds. As I pored over Dicky's collage of letters, scraps and cuttings I was building a picture of a woman with chameleon tendencies but her one striking feature was a loyalty to certain types of people. They all sought refuge in the comforting anonymity of Soho. The flimsiness of the paper added to the allure of the past. Mariella was taking full advantage of London's Swinging Sixties.

It was against the backdrop of coffee bars and skiffle clubs that she caught up with her old flame Billy Hill, his lieutenants and her lovers, Albert Dimes and Bobby McKew. Mariella and her men embody collapsing empires, a subsiding, war-torn Europe, but at the same time a flourishing new growth of opportunists. Hill was about to induct another villain into Mariella's hall of fame. For it was in a Soho night club that Mariella Novotny, the Government Chief Whip, collided with Eddie Chapman, Agent Zigzag.

Eddie had been coming to Soho since the twenties when he was a trapeze artist, wrestler and masseur. Then he became a member of a 'jelly gang', which specialised in robbing safes by blowing them open using gelignite. His skill as a thief made him a good deal of money and allowed him to live the life of a playboy. The Second World War saw him imprisoned in Jersey, where he sweet-talked the occupying Germans into using him as a spy on the English mainland. Once parachuted into England he handed himself into the nearest cop shop, told them he'd been recruited by the Germans, and so began his role as double agent. Since the war he had been coasting a bit. It is worth mentioning that Eddie was also a friend of Stephen Ward, who had been his osteopath since the late 1940s. Eddie's last parachute drop into England for the Germans had left him with severe back injuries. With the death of his osteopath, Eddie started taking things easy until he bumped into London's self-appointed Napoleon.

In late 1953 Billy had boated across the Channel to the Riviera. Here he bumped into Eddie, who was messing about on *The Fourth Lady*, a Royal Navy launch powered by a diesel engine. Eddie was not part of Hill's gang, but they were friends – friends who egged each other on. In a fit of *folie à deux*, Billy and Eddie became involved in a plot to restore Sultan Mohammed V of Morocco to power. The French General Augustin Guillaume, who had been resident-general of Morocco since 1951, had clashed with Mohammed V because of the latter's support for the Moroccan independence movement. Guillaume led a campaign to overthrow him and replace him with his cousin Sultan Mohammed Ben Arafa who was more malleable. The *putsch* was supported by the French colonists and even some Moroccan leaders, such as Thami El Glaoui, the Pasha of Marrakesh. Eventually, the sultan was arrested, loaded onto an aeroplane and sent into exile, first in Corsica and later in Madagascar.

Before he had left Soho, Hill had been approached by a 'French Soho spiv' with an offer of $50,000 to take on the hare-brained scheme of kidnapping the exiled sultan. He was up for it. He demanded, and was promised, $100,000, plus $25,000 in expenses. He persuaded Eddie to change the name of his launch from *The Fourth Lady* to *Flamingo* and transfer the registration from British to Costa Rican. With their incognito boat afloat, in February 1954, *Flamingo* sailed to Tangier. Hill took a plane and got there first. He used his time wisely, spreading the word that *Flamingo* was in the smuggling business.

With this as a cover, Hill and his gang made their way along the Mediterranean, through the Suez Canal and down the coast of East Africa to Madagascar to pick up the sultan and transport him back to Tangier. The skipper and Eddie were the only ones who knew anything about boats and engines; the rest of the crew were a collection of hardened criminals, described as a 'broken-nosed, chiv-scarred bunch'.

Tangier was an international area at the time. Here Eddie and Billy met two leading members of the Arab Nationalist movement. The four men fine-tuned the plan put together by the daring duo. They would use the fully armed *Flamingo* to stave off any French objections to the plot. The crew would land on Madagascar and surround the police headquarters with the help of twelve Arab gunmen while Eddie went solo to extricate the sultan. From then on, it would be plain sailing. An Egyptian co-conspirator from the Arab League flew to Tangier to confirm the *Flamingo*'s position by radio from the Indian Ocean. The League was on standby ready to send a seaplane to pick up the sultan and help him get to Morocco. From here, he would lead the Arab Nationalist movement in an attempt to defeat the French.

In preparation for the kidnapping, the crew of the *Flamingo* did a trial run smuggling contraband cigarettes. They made a profit of £18,000 in the process. With all the will in the world, however, the best-laid plans will founder if your crew is a gang of roughnecks intent on drinking and partying with the women of Tangier.

Some entrepreneurial types lured the men to their bars or brothels. The crew became so notorious for the ensuing fist fights that large crowds gathered each night at the harbour to watch the wild goings-on. Inevitably, the *Flamingo* caught the attention of the police. A few months after the trial run, French authorities managed to unveil the real plans of the British gang. On the run now, the *Flamingo* sailed to Savona, a small town in Italy. Via Interpol, the French police had accessed the criminal records of Hill and Chapman and every other member of the *Flamingo*'s crew. The plot was revealed and the ship's cargo of guns was flagged as a potential concern. Eddie hot-footed it back to England to visit his wife who had given birth to their child. Billy Hill abandoned ship and flew back to London before the French authorities impounded the vessel.

Eddie, Billy, Ron and Reg. We know about the men of the underworld. They wrote their memoirs or were written about. What about the women? The emphasis on sex makes Mariella's story harder to tell. One person's distaste will be another person's moment of insight. This problem is compounded by the ambience in which she moved. It is full of passers-by and time-travellers who might be stars, or gifted con men, or a bit of both. So no one really knows what's going on. But in February 1965, she stalked down the gangway of a Boeing 707. This time she was a Venus in tweeds, an old-school cosmopolitan: this was how she planned to conquer Rome.

'A woman's day clothes must look equally good at Salisbury Station as the Ritz bar,' said Hardy Amies, her favourite English designer. Mariella Novotny was not to be confused with the *Inglese* dolly bird. She was on her way to the film premiere of a World War Two biopic, *Triple Cross*. And the man on her arm was Agent Zigzag.

15

MODERNISTS

But it started in Soho. Wherever there was a basement there was a nightclub. Wherever there was a dilapidated garret or first-floor drawing room there was a nightclub. Wherever there was a nightclub there were hostesses – Murray's Cabaret Club in Beak Street was employing Stephen Ward's popsies, Christine Keeler and Mandy Rice-Davies – at £8 6s a week. There were nightclubs with strippers, where Mariella's friend Jackie plied her trade. There were nightclubs for various branches of the entertainment industry, just as there were clubs for various branches of the criminal justice system. There were clubs for blacks, clubs for whites, drinkers, spielers and gambling joints.

From what Dicky told me, I am assuming Eddie met Mariella at the Mazurka on Denman Street, west of Great Windmill Street. 'We used to call it "Ginnie's" after the ex-Windmill girl who ran it', Dicky told me. The Mazurka had an interesting clientele drawn from the surrounding streets. There was the Billiard Hall and next to that Solomon's Gym belonging to one of England's greatest boxing promoters. In Solomon's basement was Mac's Rehearsal Room. By night, it was one of the earliest jazz clubs in the UK, run by Cy Laurie, the bandleader. At all hours of the day and night there would be dozens of musicians and showgirls crossing and re-crossing the street on their way to gigs. Late night strollers, pushers and street walkers added their specific frisson of exoticism and menace. Nightshift workers like musicians and waiters were there to take their pleasures by day.

One night in 1964, around Christmas time, he reckoned, Dicky was at Ginnie's and got his first glimpse of a 'crazy girl' in a twin set. He was on his nightly patrol of Soho's all-nighters. These clubs were down dark passages where Mods listened to Trax and Motown from America, gyrating in time to the vinyl on the latest Duke Vin sound system. He was on his way to The Scene on 16 Great Windmill Street, the buzziest night-club ever. This was where he met my uncle James, who at fifteen was two years younger.

Back to Dicky and the sound of Britpop on the jukebox in the Green Man. Dicky's eyes gleamed as he described the showgirls popping in for a drink in their nylons and feathers. Ginnie's female clientele did not disappoint. Leggy and drinking Remy on the rocks, they smoked cheroots like they were Princess Margaret. The crazy girl in tweed was throwing Dicky sideways glances. He didn't know what to do. She had minders on either side; one was an old guy with sideburns who kept turning to her and kissing her hand. This, I would guess, was Hod. The other was his old pal, the abortionist Dr Teddy Sugden, the man with the frozen face.

Eddie came along at just the right time. Physically, he excited her more than the MPs and toffs she had been dating. He was tall and rangy, old enough to be her father, with thin lips, mean eyes, and a scar. For Eddie, it was very simple.

As his friend Bobby McKew explained to Douglas Thompson:

> Usually they were in bed. Eddie saw a lot of her; Eddie liked to fuck her. Eddie would ask me to pick him up and they'd still be in bed having breakfast. Hod had served them – he'd be in bed with them or in his 'viewing' chair, reading the paper. She'd have her hat on in bed. And then she had the cheek to whimper at me: 'I'm Henrietta.'

Mariella, Henrietta, Stella Marie, Mrs Tyson, call her what you will, she was a smouldering girl whose appetite for Eddie's brand of modernity was explosive. Eddie liked explosions. He was the Gelignite Man. Straightaway, she introduced Eddie to Hod, the disreputable dealer and restorer of stately homes. He had a contacts book that read like *Burke's Peerage* and *Photoplay*. Eddie saw the potential straightaway. The patina of history combined with the patter of provenance was a perfect front for money-making activities that he would rather not discuss. It was love at first sight for all three. The fact that all three were married – two of them to each other – added to the romance. As for the practicalities: Eddie was living off £4,000 a year working for a firm on the Gold Coast. He had received £46,000 for the film rights to his book. He was doing all right.

'Eddie is a crook and will always be one,' said Terence Young, the director of *Triple Cross*.

'I mixed with all types of tricky people,' Eddie wrote in his autobiography. Mariella must have loved his stories of 'racecourse crooks, thieves, prostitutes, and the flotsam of the night-life of a great city'. It was a great yarn.

And then there was the greatest yarn of all. Eddie had first offered his services to the invading German army whilst imprisoned at His Majesty's pleasure in Jersey. After extensive training in SS tactics, he was parachuted into England, where he promptly offered his services to the Brits. Terence Young wanted to bring Eddie's deviousness to the screen. He declared to a lawyer friend, 'He probably has more principles and honesty of character than either of us.' Young's film had a stellar cast including Yul Brynner, Christopher Plummer and Romy Schneider. It was premiering in Rome, arguably the cinematic centre of the world.

16

TRIPLE CROSS

London had Soho. Italy had Rome. The Sixties were the years of Hollywood *sul Tevere*. Day after day they filed into the city, the actors, extras, troupes of dancers, clowns and make-up girls. Cinecittà welcomed them all – the foreigners with hard currency, the friends and relations of foreigners with hard currency, the friends and relations of the friends and relations of foreigners with hard currency, the fly-by-nights, the terminally curious and the ne'er-do-wells. With the greatest of ease, Eddie Chapman, Hod Dibben and Mariella Novotny took their places in the parade.

Above all, the newspapers were exploding with news of deals made and broken, alliances forged and dissolved. The star of *Triple Cross*, Christopher Plummer, gave an interview. He said that Eddie was to have been a technical adviser on the film but the French authorities would not admit him entry where they shot the film because he was still wanted over an alleged plot to kidnap the Sultan of Morocco. Every night there was a screening and a competition to see who could flush out the gossip *il più piccante*. The story under their noses went as follows.

Mariella Novotny was no mere adjunct to Eddie Chapman's antihero. Together with her husband, the notorious voyeur and sado-masochist, she had been under investigation at the highest level on both sides of the pond already. Her most famous lover, the most powerful man in the world, had been shot dead. The others were running for the hills. She was now the central axis of an unlikely *ménage a trois*.

Either Eddie or Hod used their European contacts to find a suite of rooms in a castle fifty kilometres outside Rome in the wooded mountaintop village of Caprarola. In January 1966, Villa Farnese, originally conceived in 1504 by the future Pope Paul III as a symbol of his family's power, was home to a domestic setup straight out of Fellini. Mariella spent most of the daylight hours writing a book and hunting small birds. She was a crack shot. Now Eddie showed her how to make timed incendiary devices.

She describes their bomb-making exploits in some detail:

One night, shortly after moving into the Castello which was to be home for several months, I was lying awake in bed. A scene in the book I was writing called for a description of how to make bombs. My knowledge of this was nil and, even though I considered myself an avid and enthusiastic researcher, I couldn't come up with where to get such specialised info. There was always uncle's army but the little obstacle of the Iron Curtain blew that source. The IRA, Black September, the Black Panthers? No, these jolly outfits didn't make me jump with wild abandon. I needed to be well clued up before I poked my mug into their lawless camps. As I lay there in the early hours, I mentally wrestled with the problem then the answer hit me – via my ears. Deep snores shook the massive bed and reverberated off the high ceiling. A person I once respected, I've forgotten who, told me always to go to the experts for in-depth clue-up sessions. Lying half on top of me was the very person to teach me the art of explosive making ... I didn't need many lessons from [Chapman] to reach proficiency. My bombs and timing devices were pretty hot. They reminded me of king-size fireworks. And since I was a crack shot I felt nothing unusual in handling explosives for real.[29]

Her novel, by the way, related the story of a distinguished Czech family cut off from their inheritance and chased out of their homeland by evil Communists.

She drove round the city nightly; Eddie refused to allow her out of his sight. In her convertible sports car she 'freaked out a good few lorry drivers' whilst performing her party trick: masturbating whilst driving at high speed.

When the premiere of *Triple X* came to Rome, so did Yul Brynner, who played Eddie's wartime Nazi chief, Trevor Howard, who played the British Intelligence chief, and Romy Schneider – who received short shrift from Mariella.

'[Romy Schneider] had been written into the script for a bit of lustology. Even [Eddie] argued against *that* blatant inaccuracy.'[30]

Where to start?

Christopher Plummer, who played Eddie, also turned up for the premiere. Mariella attended as Eddie's girlfriend. Unfortunately, the event was 'fraught with dangers'. Eddie's wife Betty had flown in from England especially. The press agent guided her to her seat next to Mariella. They did not actually come to blows, but it was 'touch and go'.[31]

The reviews did not flatter Eddie's *amour propre*. The *Times* concluded: 'It is the sort of story that could hardly go wrong on screen. But it does ... Chapman is played by Christopher Plummer with a continuous self-congratulating smirk – perhaps justified considering how things turned out for the hero.'

Betty went home the following day storing up her resentment until she wrote her memoir in 2013. Eddie paid no mind.

---

29. *Club International*, July 1973
30. Ibid.
31. Ibid.

The American film director John Huston had invited him to visit the set of his new film, *Reflections in a Golden Eye*.

In her Mercedes, Mariella drove Eddie from their rural retreat through the centre of Rome to the famous Cinecittà. On set Huston introduced them to Marlon Brando. He didn't look much to Mariella, who said he appeared 'overweight and undistinguished'. Nevertheless, he 'came on strong with the superstar attitude'. But Mariella was no *ingénue*, and she made sure he knew it. Her lorgnette in place, she swept her gaze down to the screen god's crotch and, travelled back up to his face. He was not used to young women who took the bull by the horn. When Brando's leading lady, Elizabeth Taylor, arrived on set, she was late and disgruntled. Liz took one look at Mariella and ordered her off the lot. Mariella drove herself and Eddie home in a filthy mood.

17

L'INTERVIEW

On 6 January 1967 there was an interview for French TV. 'Eddie Chapman: Ex-Gangster, Ex-*Espion*' was about the former gangster, hero, and double agent who had reinvented himself as an antiques dealer. The French journalist Pierre Dumayet was a well-known figure in the French TV establishment. Throughout his long career he distinguished himself by interviewing important cultural figures such as Eugène Ionesco, Claude Levi-Strauss, Jean Cocteau, Jorge Luis Borges, and Louis Ferdinand Céline. Political and religious leaders were also held to account by his sinuous, probing questions. Most notable of these were Dagpo Rinpoche and Thoupten Phuntshog, the first llamas who came to France following the Tibetan uprising in 1959.

Dumayet's interview with Eddie and Mariella is a masterclass in incredulity. Eddie, smirking like Christopher Plummer in *Triple Cross*, is seated on a throne, with his young companion to his left, and her elderly husband lurking in the background, all three 'creating a strange atmosphere'.

Eddie started on familiar territory.

The last time I was in the Med, I was on my yacht, *The Flamingo*. Billy Hill and I got friendly with some Arab nationalist group doing the rounds off the north African coast. They were offering £100,000 for the kidnap of the Sultan of Morocco. We took them on, got an advance, and put into Tangier to revictual. Before we could leave harbour, though, some bastard rival of Billy's set fire to the *Flamingo*, crippling her engine. Game over. Still, it was a nice idea. The time before that led to the biggest dope bust in Spanish history.

It would be hard to guess who was more infatuated with whom: Hod with Mariella or Mariella with Eddie or Eddie with Hod or Hod with Eddie. But Mariella kept both men in hand with a successful combination of deference and knowingness. She knew how men worked. She was compliant.

She appears in Dumayet's report wearing a Pucci geometric tunic and an antique lace head-dress. She is stitching a hem on a piece of tapestry. Hod is drinking from a silver goblet, hair slicked back, sideburns bristling. Etruscan lamps shed a diffused light over the whole shebang. We are living a quiet life, Eddie tells Dumayet. We are honest with each other. She is my woman, and he is my friend. They are married. We know each other well and we know each other's faults. We are honest.

And you are an antiques dealer, Dumayet asks. Yes, we are exporting antiques around the world to the tune of half a million sterling a year. (You can hear Dumayet's disbelief.) Eddie smirks some more. His latest win on the greyhounds netted him a hundred grand, he says. And yes, wasn't it strange that all the other dogs seemed so sluggish in comparison with the winner who streaked ahead?

The camera spends a long time studying Mariella's face. She had always thought she had a dull face, a thoroughly forgettable face with a look of docility that her near-blindness confirmed. But the docility set off eyes dark as lava and just as devouring.

And you, Madame? What is it you have left behind in England? 'Hypocrisy,' she says, her eyes glinting.

Here were three schemers and chancers deploring hypocrisy and avowing complete transparency. But the camera knows they are capable of anything. 'There are two things about Eddie that I adore,' Mariella wrote in *Club International*. 'One is that he has never lied about being a conman, a jailbird, an adulterer, blackmailer, traitor, thief or liar. The second is that Eddie is the only Englishman ever to have been decorated with the Iron Cross.' The next best joke was the pardon the British government gave Eddie for any outstanding charges from his days as a burglar.

For the benefit of M. Dumayet, Hod purred like a satiated Terry Thomas. Eddie hinted at scams involving greyhounds, forgeries, gold smuggling, and currency deals. Dumayet was lost for words.

Eddie was on a roll; Eddie, who had repeatedly risked his life for the British war effort, who had penetrated the German secret service and helped disrupt V1 attacks on London. Even until the late 1950s, German intelligence officers were poring over documents supplied by Agent Zigzag, his MI5 codename, which described non-existent anti-submarine gadgets. Eddie had extracted thousands of deutschmarks from Hitler's treasury, and saved the lives of thousands of his fellow Brits. Was he heroically courageous? Lieutenant-Colonel 'Tin Eye' Stephens wrote: 'Fiction has not, and probably never will, produce an espionage story to rival in fascination and improbability the true story of Eddie Chapman, whom only war could invest with virtue, and that only for its duration.'

It is quite likely that in moments of extreme danger Eddie was rendered nerveless. If so, this was the feature that drew him to the self-appointed Queen of London's Permissive Society. Mariella anticipated in a way no other woman had – and he'd known plenty – what made Eddie tick. Before he knew it, adrenalin was pumping through his wiry frame as fast as Mariella could command it.

'I look like an angel on the outside. That's how people see me,' she told him. 'But I am like a demon inside. I have known all the suffering of the world since I was a little girl.'

18

LA DOLCE VITA

At two in the morning on Via Veneto the heat was still heavy in the air. Mariella waved her fan with the monotonous regularity of a *punka wallah*. *La Strega* was the most fashionable café in Rome in which to be bored. A roar of engines announced the arrival of some fabulous motors. A greasy freeloader joined them at their pavement table. The cars kept speeding down the Veneto.

Being Mariella Novotny was a full-time job. She may not have considered herself a 'common prostitute' but she did see herself as belonging to the public. The poise, the etiquette, the tilt of the chin, the lorgnette on the bridge of her nose: this level of posturing takes fortitude and discipline. She would always be aware of physical weaknesses such as her poor eyesight, and she resented it bitterly. She did not want to look owlish, foolish, short-sighted, long-sighted or blighted. She did not want to look vulnerable. So her eyes, which were not large and violet-blue, but green and slanting, were made larger by make-up and mystification. Even so, she needed reinforcements.

'When we had set off for the eternal city I'd insisted on taking my bulldogs Slasher and Killer with me. Strolling up and down

Via Veneto in my skimpy gear with a pair of British bulldogs was a mindbender for the Latin lot.'[32]

She needed an audience. The *ragazzi* of Rome cleaved the sidewalks in an endless carousel, resounding with come-hithers. Every morning, Mariella drove into central Rome, so that she could stroll up and down Via Veneto in her brand-new, skimpy gear with two salivating bulldogs straining at the leash. Every evening, she returned for a digestif beneath the Hotel Savoy, off Via Veneto. Eddie took her to Dave's Dive – the 'in' bar for a certain kind of 'in crowd'. It was like being back in Soho. The former British boxing champion Dave Crowley owned the joint. He attracted the type with whom Eddie felt most at home – those who had been through the wars without any need for a world war, and had survived and prospered at any cost. Furthermore, these were the men and women who were just as likely to lose whatever they had gained as easily as they had acquired it. This life was a club; loss was its password.

Stars of the silver screen were the other draw at Dave's Dive. Anthony Quinn was a regular. He moved in fast on Mariella but she didn't dig his come-on. One night, a short, fat woman in late middle age wearing an exorbitant and unnecessary fur squeezed into the group clustered round Eddie.

'The coat was a disaster on her,' Mariella wrote.

A well-known scriptwriter pushed his way in.

'Rita, darling,' the bore gushed. 'I haven't seen you in years. You look marvellous!'

At night she drove past the city limits looking for sex. This time, Hod came with her. The Via Appia Antica stretched out before her, grey and ancient, an ethereal blue splintered by broken tombs and wasteland. She sauntered out, coatless, in the *gelsomino* air. She wanted to lose herself, to become so lost and tired that Mariella would exist no longer.

---

32. *Club International*, July 1973

One night in Soho, Mariella Novotny conceived a child with Eddie. This had never been her intention. One of the conditions for her marriage with Hod was 'no children'. He had readily concurred. She had avoided pregnancy thus far in her career, but far from home and her doctor, there was no way out. Pregnancy broke the spell. Eddie's back started playing up.

Whether he tired of her, or she of him is unclear. She maintained it was *she* who gave him the kiss-off. His wife claimed he had had enough and returned to her in England. With or without Eddie, Mariella gave birth to a baby girl. She called her Henrietta October Chapman. As soon as decently possible the child was packed off a private boarding school in Switzerland. There is no record of her birth and Mariella's references to her are obfuscating to say the least.

Henrietta does make a further appearance in Marella's story. Unfortunately, she serves to illustrate the consequences of the life Mariella chose for herself. As for Mariella, life depended solely on what she wrote about it. So she wrote and wrote and wrote. As for *la dolce vita*, it didn't last long.

PART TWO

'This book is an action, a political action where revolution is the goal. It has no other purpose. It is not cerebral wisdom, or academic horseshit, or ideas carved in granite or destined for immortality. It is part of a process and its context is change.'

19

GLAMOUR SHOTS

When Eddie refers to Mariella in the interview for French TV he dismisses her as 'a girl I met in a nightclub'. Their child, Henrietta October Chapman, was born in April 1964. Not only was Mariella the mother of his two-year-old daughter, she was, like him, an intelligent, enigmatic trickster. If she had been taken seriously, who knows if she would not have proven herself as morally dextrous in her manoeuvrings as Agent Zigzag?

One balmy evening in Rome in 1966, Mariella Novotny was sitting next to Mrs Eddie Chapman, her lover's wife, at the premiere of the movie based on his life. Mr Eddie Chapman's double-crossing escapades in the Second World War formed just one episode in a hectic life that would exclude Mariella from the authorised version.

The morning after the premiere of *Triple Cross*, Eddie Chapman's wife returned to England in a state of high dudgeon. She was prepared to indulge her husband's extramarital affairs, but she disliked and disapproved of Mariella. Her self-assured sexuality was anathema to a wife intent on keeping up a respectable appearance. Since the Profumo Affair the rumours that shrouded Mariella had taken on quasi-demonic proportions such as those that shaped the reputation of Wallis Simpson, Duchess of Windsor, who bewitched a king, or Mata Hari, who betrayed her countrymen. These women challenged the conventions that made people feel safe. They used sex to get what they wanted. Men loved them and took enormous risks to be with them. Society was titillated, then scandalised, and finally horrified.

In Czechoslovakia, Mariella's alleged uncle, President Novotny, was making an effort to revitalise his country's fortunes. He decreed that privately owned businesses should be allowed to set their own wage and price structures. The following year, he began the rehabilitation of victims of the Stalinist purge. But it was too little, too late. Dissent was fomenting and in 1968 Novotny was purged from government. This was a pivotal year, rocked by protests, disturbances and riots in Prague, Chicago, Paris, Tokyo, Belgrade, Rome, Mexico City and Santiago. Just as the crusades and epidemics of the Middle Ages respected neither frontiers nor hierarchies, these rebellions, mostly led by students, whether they were spontaneous or planned, swept away ideologies and classifications. By the time Antonin Novotny had been ousted by Dubcek, his niece's *ménage a trois* was crumbling into the dust of the Appian Way en route to Fiumicino Airport.

Where was Mariella's three-year-old daughter? I am guessing she was in London with Mariella's mother, Mrs Constance Capes. One day, in the downstairs cupboard of a rented terraced house, Mrs Capes found a trunk. Inside the trunk was a collection of whips, assorted S&M paraphernalia, and an

oho chicanery.
op for John N
well to run t
chmond. H
ostcards in
rapher's st

she asked Betty, aka Mrs Eddie Chapman,
ange friendship with the mother of her
ou ever saw it, was the answer. Soon
sent to the private boarding school
n, Eddie brought his ex-girlfriend,
their jointly owned health farm,
lla draped herself across the

But Eddie was fading into the background. Mariella was still married to Hod, whom she married, she claimed, in order to get away from her mother. Now she needed to get away from her child. It has proved impossible to verify whether she lived with her child for any significant amount of time. This child, now a woman in her fifties, refuses to comment. And although Mariella came back to London, she did not come home in any meaningful sense. So how could she provide a home for a child?

As a pit stop in her loneliness, Mariella made weekly trips to a den of iniquity in Soho. It was always the same collection of shady immigrants, a boxer or two, a minor TV personality plus some pretty, agreeable women. In this instance, it is one boxer in particular on whom we need to keep an eye. Between them, this boxer – Mariella called him Mr Fists – and a police officer at West End Central police station would lure her into a *danse macabre* that ended in the downfall of everyone who took part. But at this point her ambition is to hustle a living out of her wits, sex appeal and chutzpah – whilst retaining her air of haughtiness and elegance, of course. There was no use swanning back to the Hyde Park set. There was no money to be got there and she had blown her cover with them.

So she found herself frequenting all-night bars in Soho with strange, over-ripe characters. This was the place, above all other London hotspots, where fortunes could be made because you had the right look or the right sound. And those fortunes could be made overnight. Perhaps because of its foreignness, Soho had a quality of separateness to it, as though the rules were different from those that operate in the rest of the city. My sources for this book spent entire periods of their lives sustained by S█████████. In 1968 Tricky Dicky was fronting an adults-only █████████ Mason, a Soho purveyor of sex.

Before I introduce Mr Mason, it m█████████ hrough a roll call of his predecessors.

In the 1930s, Soho's sexpert wa█████████ is real name was Tom Fletcher, and he█████████ from Paris. These were photos take█████████ udio mimicking the dimly lit intimacy of a lady's boudoir, catching her unawares, *déshabillé*, in a state of reverie, dreaming perhaps of you, her voyeuristic admirer. Despite their name these postcards were never intended to be sent via the post; sending such a card could have led to a charge of obscenity, a hefty fine and maybe even some gaol time. Fletcher crossed the Channel to buy the only erotica available at this time. He brought the cards back to Soho and sold them through his bookshop. It is just as Joseph Conrad depicts things in *The Secret Agent*. The cards were sold under the counter and hidden in brown paper bags.

For characters such as Tricky Dicky, Mariella and Conrad's secret agent, Soho offered freedom from identity, background and origins. Mariella could invent herself as a Windmill Girl, as a refugee (from the Profumo Affair), as a gangster's moll (it's where she met Eddie) and as a sex worker. Tricky Dicky definitely invented himself in Soho. It's an unmappable confluence of murky, sinuous forces at work in the underbelly of London. History loses its linearity, events become a series of re-occurrences. Italians like my father, who was a waiter at the Condor, do not stay Italian or become English in Soho. Instead they act out their Italian-ness in restaurants, cafes and shops; they commodify themselves. Or they become both Italian and English, which is to say neither. Mariella sold herself and lost herself and found herself over and again in queer little bars above sex shops.

As Tricky saw it, experiencing the weirdest quarter of Londontown led to one outcome only: wanting more of it.

'I remember the drummer Ray Du Val,' he said. 'He was a session musician. Born on D'Arblay Street. He played on a hit song, "What Do You Want to Make Those Eyes at Me For?" He was heavily into bennies. Once he played non-stop on the drums at the Top Ten for two days. He broke the world record.'

It was not so much a record. He just could not bring himself to leave Soho.

Tom Fletcher, our purveyor of Parisian postcards, was called the Duke because of his resemblance to Errol Flynn, and his generosity to beggars and tramps. Like all good Soho-ites, he had shoulder-length hair and a Gauloise affixed to the left corner of his mouth.

Soho was sex and France. Soho and vice were synonymous. Londoners flocked to the un-square mile to stock up on French tarts. On the main artery, Old Compton Street, itself a kind of Petty France with its cafes and *boulangeries* side by side with taverns, French pimps brokered deals in the Admiral Duncan pub. Next to the Old Charlotte Laundry on Frith Street was a club called the Union. Its owner was the French-Algerian pimp Casimir Micheletti. He was known as the Assassin for his dexterity with a stiletto knife. A brisk ten-minute stroll away, approaching Shaftesbury Avenue on the narrow passage of Archer Street, was his rival based in a school of dance. Juan Antonio Castanar was a Spaniard, and a tango dancer who had appeared on stage with the ballerina Anna Pavlova. His school for dance was a front for 'white-birding', selling women overseas for £50 a pop. Both Castanar and Micheletti were extremely good-looking, suave, softly spoken, vicious and dark. They were rivals but their loathing for each other went deeper. It was as though in facing each other they saw themselves.

How does Mariella fit in to the machismo of the sex trade? A place where men growl and swagger and talk about their testicles and their mothers' virtue? She tried to match them, blow for blow. Each bedding was a sexual conquest. Not for her the question of ownership and possession of her body. She saw herself as being in command. How much of this belief in herself was delusion? Most of the bodies that piled up due to turf disputes between Castanar the Spaniard and Micheletti the Frenchman were women's. They were accompanied by excited newspaper reports.

In 1935, the well-known prostitute and not-so-well-known police informer 'French Fifi' was found strangled with her silk stockings. The murder had taken place in her flat above the Globe Club – on Archer Street, near the Spaniard's school of dance. Shortly afterwards her pimp was killed; Micheletti was suspected.

Shortly after French Fifi was found, another woman was strangled, this time with her scarf, on Lexington Street. Her tongue had been cut out. She had links with Micheletti. A brutal code was spelling out the dangers of indiscretion. Next to die was Dutch Leah, strangled with a copper wire in her second-floor lodgings on Old Compton Street. The last to die was French Paulette, who came from Croydon but faked a French accent.

Shadows were flitting across Soho and disappearing into the miasma of the city like spindle-limbed villains in a pantomime. The maiden in distress was big business, but livestock was clearly troublesome. So Tom Fletcher, Duke of Richmond, quietly continued to sell 'glamour' to England from his bookshop on Old Compton Street.

20

THE SEX TRADE

The key areas in Soho for buying sex were the courts west of Old Compton Street on the corner with Wardour Street. In a triangulation of doglegs comprising Green's Court, Walker's Court and St Anne's Court, this is where the past lingers more than anywhere else. The tottering buildings linked by a bridge conjure up early urban topography that is now being converted to paved pedestrian zones. Green's Court was the headquarters of Tricky's employer, John Mason. A bear of a man with a Soviet-style crew-cut, he paid off friendly cops at the De Hems Dutch pub in Chinatown. Over the next quarter of a century he amassed a personal fortune of several million pounds on which he never paid a single penny of income tax.

Tricky's job was to stand tall for Mason:

Mason had about six shops when I knew him – three next to each other on Old Compton Street. If he heard someone was going to buy a shop, he would buy it first. That stopped the competition. He also had a few on Walker's Court, and a couple on Windmill Street. I just had to stand around so that when the cops came in the staff could run out. I just stood there or I'd do a runner so they could chase me. Once I locked the police inside the shop. Another time I said I was a burglar. I got nicked 38 times over the next 20 years.

Once Mason had established that vast amounts of money were to be made simply from churning out photographs and suggestive text, the game was on to produce more. At this point, Ron 'The Dustman' Davey ambles into view. As his moniker would suggest, he was employed as a dustman by Hammersmith Borough Council. He also belonged to a Surrey nudist club. A Soho bookshop owner suggested he take photos of the female members of his nudist club.

Carefully folded thighs and blanched breasts were stapled by Ron on his Gestetner printing machine and dispatched to Soho. This soon developed into photos of women wrestling. His photos were so popular that by the end of the seventies he had raised three families, and owned a small estate in Hampshire. His books became known throughout the trade as MDs – the Millionaire Dustman.

Mariella was in at the beginning – a topless performer at the Windmill, and through her marriage to Hod an active participant in the orgy scene. She had another contact in the shape of her fifteen-year-old boyfriend of Swedish extraction who came from Bromley. 'Sven' was a model used by Stephen Ward in his promotional films for osteopathy and the early, amateur producers of pornography. The story of 'Britain's first porn star', as he terms himself, is the basis of Anthony Frewin's cult novel, *London Blues*. The images Sven helped create were photographed at country homes let out by impoverished aristocrats. In an email dated 3 July 2016, he told me: 'I first met Hod at Baron John Lubbock's house in Orpington, Kent. John's large gardens were used for "glam modelling" weekends (naked girls running around being photographed!). I was photographed, too.'

In the dying light of the twentieth century, along the entire length of Berwick Street, fruit and veg traders were setting up large, tattered wagons draped in green felt. A damp breeze washed over me carrying the scent of over-ripe fruit and last night's lager. I walked into the Green Man pub with a tape recorder and a notepad to meet Tricky Dicky. My uncle James had set us up. Against a backdrop of Britpop blaring from the neighbouring vinyl shop, and reverberations of market banter and clanging fruit machines, we chatted tentatively. Tricky had known my grandfather through my uncle James.

Charlie Taylor was a well-known fence for most of the stolen gear that was being circulated in South London. He was also notorious for his fits of petty vindictiveness: he could throw a friend to the wolves with no regard for the outcome. But, if you gave him a sob story, and you wanted a television, one would arrive on your doorstep the following day. Tricky and I discussed my grandfather's sudden fall from grace, his equally sudden death, and the characteristics of conmen, namely their evasiveness. It struck me as odd that Tricky, with such a handle, should not include himself in their ranks.

It is always dark in the Green Man, like some ancient grotto. It is shrouded in dampness and a mossy light refracted from mirrors and glass. The man sitting across the table from me was unobtrusive. He had thin, grey hair with a broken nose and small eyes. The only remarkable thing about his face was that he had no eyebrows. His whole appearance gave the impression of hyper-vigilance and injured innocence.

Under the table his feet were resting on an Adidas hold-all. I asked him if he had brought me the papers that my uncle told me he had stolen from Mariella's flat. He reached under the table and opened the bag. It was filled with loose papers and desk diaries. Like a Lucky Dip, he rummaged in the bag's contents, and picked a sheet at random. One triumphant gesture later, it was in my hands. I was looking at headed notepaper with a London address: 19 Nevern Square.

I could still hear a Mancunian vocalist and Cockney stallholders battling for supremacy, but I had taken a step back into the past. Once back from their Roman holiday, Mariella and Hod had leased a flat in a mansion block in Earl's Court.

'I was determined to be the best hostess of my age,' Mariella had written in histrionic green ink. The entry was dated 1967; she was retreading the Profumo Affair. The beer-stained table was now littered with diaries from the sixties to the early eighties and loose pages from a manuscript. Tricky grinned at my excitement.

'I suppose the smart set found it fun to start with,' she wrote, 'hanging out with all these call girls and scarfaces; sitting down with a shyster and an MP the other side. Then of course when the screw was turned they were bouncing all the way to kingdom come.'

Tricky nodded his head towards the bar, signalling that he was ready for a drink. I rushed to the bar, frightened that he (and more importantly his bag) would disappear if I turned my back on him. I didn't need a drink. I was already intoxicated. So I ordered a lime soda for myself, and a large whisky for him. When I came back to the table he was fussing over his reflection in a large mirror promoting tobacco. He asked me if I had seen the film *Scandal*, featuring John Hurt as Stephen Ward. The film had come out in 1989. The forty-six-year-old actress Britt Ekland had played Mariella in a scene depicting the orgy in the Hyde Park flat. But in real life Mariella had only been twenty years old when she was torturing the Man in the Mask.

'She never did say who he was,' said Tricky, stroking his chin and sighing. 'All the names are coded, or written as initials.'

This Adidas hold-all was beginning to acquire the magical proportions of Mary Poppins' carpet bag, and I was growing increasingly anxious to wrest it from Tricky's grasp.

In the melee of paperwork, I lit on a cutting from a magazine. The magazine was called *Espionage*. The date was February 1986, three years after Mariella's death.

'How did you get this?' I asked Tricky. 'I thought you burgled her flat *before* she died?'

'Someone sent me that,' he said, adopting his air of the *ingenu*. I skimmed the contents – there were details about the Man in the Mask party that only she could have given the author: a centuries-old refectory table staggering under the weight of roast peacock and badger ... avocado stuffed with caviar, suckling pig, quail on garlic toast, salmon soufflé. Mariella and her guests were greedy for sensations. Luxury fare was served on antique silverware laid on black Maltese lace napery. Above their heads, chandeliers tinkled with droplets of clear crystal. Heated salvers of sandalwood perfumed the air. The senses were reeling ... they were naked apart from socks and stockings and they had taken drugs.

Tricky sensed my impatience for more evidence. He zipped up the hold-all and looked at his watch, sighing. He had a grandson, he said. He was in hospital. 'He needs a kidney transplant,' Tricky said. 'We're trying to raise the money for private treatment.'

I nodded, hanging on to the last scraps of paper sticking to the beer-stained table. I scribbled down some *apercus* from Mariella's notepaper:

'Ivanov was known for being able to put information on Khruschev's desk twenty minutes after receiving it.'

'It was a dangerous time to dabble in the Occult.'

On the second page of *Espionage* magazine, the author was discussing the evidence Mariella had given to Lord Denning: '[She] blew the whistle on Keeler's simultaneous affairs with Ivanov and Profumo. She spoke of her American connections, the Kennedys and other powerful figures.'

Then something I had not heard before:

'Attempts were made on her life.'

The author posited the theory that Eddie Chapman was acting in part as her bodyguard. 'I practised shooting daily with a small pistol tucked into the top of one black stocking,' Mariella told him.

The journalist went on:

As the seventies came in she turned from international to internal espionage walking the dangerous tightrope as informer not only for the intelligence services and Scotland Yard but the underworld too. She became the mistress of gangsters to uncover multi-national swindles, and made herself available, as she put it, to pry bedroom secrets out of visiting foreign dignitaries for government intelligence sources. She was also briefed to spy on high-ranking police officials during corruption inquiries.

'I can rattle skeletons in many important cupboards,' Mariella told him.

He continued: 'And some of those skeletons were establishment moles recently unearthed beavering away underground for the Soviets betraying their mother country. Friends told her to be careful, she smiled and spied on. In her forties she was still a beautiful woman and tension had taken its toll. Someone, somehow, had got her hooked on drugs, something she had always despised in others.'

I handed Tricky a ten-pound note, wished him luck, and made my getaway.

I had always sensed that addiction was an important part of Mariella's story. Drugs and alcohol were more or less essential for the continued functioning of a post-war traumatised society. Mariella was not a woman who could bear to admit powerlessness and she never took a drink. But she took drugs and plenty of them. Like many others, she could not see this as a dependency. Neither does it take a psychoanalyst to figure out why she should be drawn to the role of dominatrix. She had seen too much of victimhood as a child.

Of equal significance was the author of this article in *Espionage* magazine. He was no prurient hack-of-all-trades. Richard Walton was a respected author and broadcaster on 'Voice of America', actively involved in politics, an early member of the American Green Party and a campaigner for social justice.

Finally, there was this quote from Walton: 'She was preparing a dossier on her life story.'

Walton's credentials shored up Mariella's allegations. As well as being a crazed sex and drug addict, this was an intelligent and articulate woman. In Walton, I had found another writer who was willing to take her seriously.

So there was this *femme serieuse* sitting in a bar in Soho investigating the sex trade and working out how she could capitalise from it. Mariella must have been aware of the market in pornography. For their orgies, she and Hod had made mileage out of the work of de Sade, *The Story of O* and Georges Bataille's *Story of the Eye*. The sex therapist Eustace Chesser had featured as one of her dinner guests. As a Soho regular, she would have seen the germination of a countercultural sexual revolution. As the decade marched on, the flowering of an anarcho-intelligentsia cross-pollinated porn with the gendered theories of feminists such as Andrea Dworkin and Germaine Greer. Commercial pornography – *Playboy* – was quick to present the bouquet. Under the tagline 'Entertainment for Men', *Playboy* fashioned an editorial assemblage that combined lustily submissive naked women with highbrow copy (by men). Vladimir Nabokov, Jack Kerouac, Roald Dahl and Norman Mailer were just a few of the luminaries. Reading *Playboy* 'for the articles' became the perfect alibi. In the seventies, the British version of Hugh Hefner, Paul Raymond, would fashion his own version. Mariella would be part of his vision.

But for now, how could she get a toehold in this burgeoning industry? How could she give voice to her intellectual aspirations when she was primarily known as a whip-wielding whore?

Tricky gave me my next lead. 'Every week, the managers, or bucks, met in a drinking club over the strip club on Walkers' Court. That's where Mariella met Jackie, a junkie on the game for Michael X.'

21

KANGAROO VALLEY

She was still giving interviews to the press, so she was still a public figure. On 22 September 1969 she was quoted by a reporter from the *Daily Mirror*: 'The swinging scene was a swinging shadow. I think there will be a much better quality about everything in the next ten years.' Mariella has the depressive's penchant for the macabre. She does not care for reasoned analysis of the past. But she was right. The Swinging Sixties had always been swinging on a gibbet. On a personal level, the decade had brought her infamy, insecure finances, a disreputable husband and an unwanted daughter.

'The one thing I will not do is write my memoirs,' she fibs. Instead she says she is writing novels. She was written four so far, all of which are in the hands of literary agents in London and New York.

'One is called *Mrs Bitch* and is a study of a certain type of British female. The other, *Mrs Fink*, is a study of her American counterpart. I'm glad to say I don't belong to their breed. They are obsessed with the battle of the sexes, but personally I have never found there was any battle.'

Mariella's words reveal an upper-middle-class disdain for 'female' issues and a female anxiety about being a 'nagging' woman. She had bigger fish to fry. She was casting her net for a new cause to champion and she needed money to pay for digs.

No. 19 Nevern Square was her new address. She and Hod had settled on the far side of Chelsea in a rundown mansion block in SW5. The preoccupations of her neighbours were scrawled in handwritten notices pasted in shopfronts – short lets, French lessons and intercontinental flights.

Nevern Square is a development in the Pont Street Dutch style dating back to the 1860s. It was designed for the second sons of prosperous families as a speculative investment. By the 1880s overbuilding had led to a glut of housing in London, and the great mansion blocks and villas began the gradual but relentless process of subdivision. The Second World War brought bomb damage, neglect and disrepair. The large Polish community in Earl's Court was joined by Australians and New Zealanders.

Mariella was living in 'Kangaroo Valley'. She is listed in the 1970 directory under the name of Stella Marie Dibben. Her telephone number is 01-373 5819. I could almost pick up my bakelite GPO corded phone. I could rotate the dial and hear the click of the numbers connecting to the other side of reality. She will answer in her splashy, sibilant voice. What will she tell me?

Mariella wants to be published. She wants to tell the true story of her time inside the Black House, her affair with the prophet of Notting Hill … except she hadn't been there and it was some other black dude she was digging. But this was fiction, so she was free to believe she was riding the rapids of London's underground. In reality, in order to do that you have to 'hang out', be part of a scene. You have to get close to people. This was a problem because there was very little intimacy between Mariella and anyone. Hod once remarked that Mariella was too fond of the gentlemen. But she was not in the least fond of them – she was only fond of their homage. Women? They did not pay her homage. At the beginning of her career, she had met a woman she liked: Suzy Chang. But Suzy was currently hiding her light in one of her Made-in-America marriages.

Mariella classified women as bitches or finks. If they were bitches, i.e., spiteful, critical or merely indifferent, perhaps she feared being judged or, worse still, ignored. If they were finks, on the other hand, they were blacklegs and informants. She couldn't trust them. They sneaked on her; they whispered behind her back. She feared their judgement, too.

But she had to get out from within to survive. So in her leap over the wall of solitude, she leapt over the notion of herself as a female. She was bigger than gender and she was smaller than adult. Perhaps she couldn't hang in there with other women because conversations about the politics and practicalities of womanhood and motherhood bored her. Those men and women who did befriend her liked her for her integrity and her kindness. But she couldn't stay around long enough. She wanted to fly.

She liked other high-fliers. If she had learnt anything from the Profumo scandal it was this: Ward had been a class rebel and a class traitor. He travelled up and down the social escalator. He wanted to know everyone and be everyone. Rigid social hierarchies had been broken down by the Beatles. But Ward moved too fast and you just can't do that. So she lost interest in courting the aristocracy.

The sixties showed Mariella that a media profile makes money. Martin Luther King and the fight for civil rights and a confrontation over Cuba were historically significant events. But Christine Keeler was the subject of a bidding war between national newspapers and she managed to steal the front page. If Keeler had not been seen to be involved with black men, readers of her story would not have been quite so excited at her involvement with a government minister, excited in a way they could not quite explain. Nor would that government minister have been quite so damaged by association. Mariella's new venture involved mixing high and low, and white with black.

It was the clipper and stripper Jackie, a friend of Tricky Dicky, who opened the door to the next phase of Mariella's development. Jackie was the kind of woman with whom Mariella could emphathise. She was aware of the hedonistic and hieratic nature of the prostitute's existence. There were no informants here. If there were, they got their tongues cut out. There were no bitches, either. They were a confederacy of outcasts. Jackie worked in the sex industry. She was matter-of-fact about it. She betrayed no signs of self-pity or intemperate suffering, apart from the cool front she exposed to society. When I met her, some forty years after Mariella's death, she was scarred and shrunken and sexless. It had all been sucked out of her. But in the late sixties, she was a foxy little teenager in a tight tee-shirt and spiked heels.

Jackie told Mariella about a scene taking place not so very far from Nevern Square. From the back of the block, Mariella's flat overlooked the A4 dual carriageway as it rolls past the Victoria and Albert Museum and onto Cromwell Road. From here, all Mariella had to do was to get into her Jag, cross Cromwell Road and she was on Kensington High Street. Continuing past Holland Park, she was on Ladbroke Grove. After her initial reccy, she probably left the car at home and caught the 52 bus. It was time for a new Mariella.

The object of her inquiries was a thug who looked like a cross between a pirate and a martyr. He was bearded, with a ring in one ear, and at least slightly charismatic. Like Mariella, he had many aliases; one name he used a lot was Michael Abdul Malik. But when he arrived in Britain aged 24 on a cargo boat that docked at Cardiff, he was half-Portuguese, half-Trinidadian and his name was Michael de Freitas.

Mariella and Hod Dibben on their wedding day, 29 January 1960.
(Courtesy of the Library of Congress)

Mariella at Sotheby's in 1964. (© Alamy)

Before Mariella there was Patsy Morgan-Dibben, who gained some fame as 'The Earring Girl'. (© Alamy)

Right: Harry Alan Towers.

Below: President John F. Kennedy.

Below right: J. Edgar Hoover, first Director of the FBI. (Courtesy of the Library of Congress)

Left: Christine Keeler.
(Courtesy of the Dutch
Nationaalarchief)

Below: Mandy Rice-Davies.
(Courtesy of the Dutch
Nationaalarchief)

Eddie Chapman, AKA Agent Zigzag. With Mariella he had a daughter, Henrietta.

The Pheasantry, headquarters of the Popocracy in Mariella's King's Road days.

Brown's Hotel, a place of some mystery in Mariella's career. (Courtesy of CVB)

Above: Soho in the early 1960s.

Right: Charlie Taylor, face about town and my grandfather. (Author's collection)

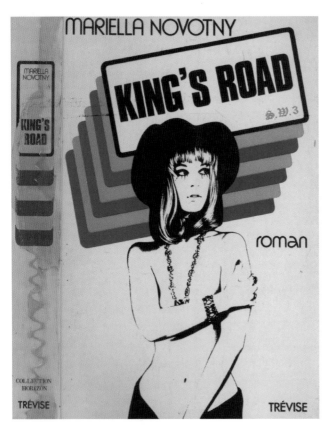

Left: One of the cover designs for Mariella's novel *King's Road*, prominently featuring her own portrait.

Below: The Soho Mariella knew lives on in some corners, such as Green's Court. (Courtesy of Paul the Archivist)

22

BLACK POWER AND ROTTING HILL

Michael came to London. He worked his way into the veins of criminal society. In Notting Hill, he managed prostitutes, ran gambling houses, sold drugs and collected rent for the property racketeer Peter Rachman, who had already had a go at bedding Mariella and blackmailing Hod.

Notting Hill was a radical departure from the *ancien regime* she had left in Hyde Park. A Black Panther movement had started in west London. In the wake of global uprisings and raised consciousness, England's black activists were finding their voice, inspired by their peers across the pond. But when they watched their black-and-white television sets, the Windrush generation saw that black liberation groups in America were brutally set upon by the police and mainstream media. So many were understandably unwilling to raise their heads above the parapet.

Like the labour movement, the Black Power movement became fragmented. In the case of Black Power the momentum was swallowed by the Universal Coloured People's Association, the Black Workers' League, and the Black Liberation Front – all splinter groups in which members failed to reach a consensus on strategy or aims. Only one man was prepared to take the heat.

Michael de Freitas changed his name to Michael X and dubbed himself the commander-in-chief of the Black Panthers.

'They've made me the archbishop of violence in this country.'

Michael X understood Rachman, an immigrant survivor, traumatised by experiences in the Second World War, renting to social rejects, poor black families and prostitutes – even if it wasn't out of charity. Michael had a heart. He was involved in a community school, a legal assistance programme, development of the Notting Hill Carnival and rent reduction. But he was a damaged man, and violence was his first resort. No one challenged the former enforcer for Rachman.

'White men have no soul,' was his *cri de guerre* – unless, like the Beatle John Lennon, they made a donation to his movement. March 1966 saw the founding of Michael X's London Free School, a kind of underground Citizen's Advice Bureau. Students, poets, musicians and hippies met in the basement of 26 Powis Terrace, in Notting Hill. If Mariella was aware of this burgeoning scene from her castle in Rome, she must have been itching to get back to it. And now she was.

One night Michael X appeared on television. He had Malcolm's look down to a tee, and he was working on his oratory. 'Today I can preach, for I have run the course and I know it. My record is behind me. I am a reformed man, I am a reformed heroin addict. I am a reformed ponce, so I can talk of reforming others.'

Mariella would have responded to his revivalist rhetoric and his kneejerk opportunism like an alcoholic lighting up at the popping of a champagne cork.

She enrolled Jackie in her efforts to infiltrate the action. One trip to Biba's later and she was decked out in a polo-necked white shirt, black suede hot pants, matching cap and shoulder bag. So into character did Mariella get that 'her family' thought she had become 'a drop out'.

'White birds were only tolerated by Michael if they were hooked on junk or brought in bread. At first I was uptight when I was present at various gatherings. But I knew I had to fool him somehow into believing I was a head.'

At the very least, Mariella was accurate in her observations. Women were only tolerated if they were mute and pliable and funded the men. Nevertheless, white women from across the class divide were to be found in the squats and night-clubs of Rotting Hill, where locals were plotting a Caribbean renaissance and a concerted response to the demolition of homes and schools to make room for a new flyover. Mariella took part in sit-ins and joined forces with Michael's devotees. First on their agenda was opposition to the proposed Westway, a two-and-a-half-mile elevated dual carriageway that joined Paddington to Ladbroke Grove. At the time Mariella was doing her researches, the artist Gustav Metzger was undertaking auto-destructive art performances on the Westway site along Acklam Road. In Mariella's hands the explosions in 'Viet Grove' become an incendiary threat to authority.

Tricesta, Mariella's fictional heroine, befriends (which means beds) a 'spade' called Apostrophe Brown. He blows sax in a rock-and-reggae band and is a community leader and ally of 'Edward X'.

'[You] never read anything about the flyover supports being blown up,' says Apos.

'What are you talking about?' Tricesta asked.

'A lot of things,' he replied, frowning, 'but specifically a certain flyover in the West London district; we made numerous applications to the council asking them to let us have a certain area beneath the flyover as a playground for the kids of the district, at first they refused us saying they wanted the space for a car park!' His indignation was genuine. 'Then one of the supporting pillars of the flyover was blown up. We re-applied to the council, urging them to change their "final decision".' They did, the kids got their play area.'

'Who blew the flyover?' she asked.

'That's not a cool question, baby,' he smiled, 'especially when you can guess the answer! The flyover in Edgware Road was also sabotaged, just a couple of pillars. That was hushed up too ...'

On application to local archives I found no trace of explosions in protest against the Westway flyover. But the passage indicates a familiarity with the subject-matter that is possibly gleaned from close scrutiny of local newspapers but also some interaction with the local community. I would guess that Mariella ventured into Ladbroke Grove and neighbouring areas with notebook in hand and simply, brazenly questioned people. As for the inside track, there were white women heavily involved with Michael X and his followers – middle-class white women – but I cannot be sure that Mariella was one of them. It may well be that Jackie was providing her with her source material. Or it may be that Mariella was in the Grove for the same reason as everyone else: drugs. Although she denied using street drugs and alcohol, she admitted to a dependency on prescription medication. And anyone who has been around narcotics knows that the best ones in terms of purity and efficacy are the ones that come out of a pharmacist's jar.

* * *

Drugs come up a lot in Mariella's novel. We know she knew her way around prescription drugs. Now, in the name of research, she became acquainted with street drugs. In the Grove and up the Hill is where her drug use got dirtier, to support her cover. This is the story she told herself. She was going to the places her peers feared to tread. While the Hyde Park Set were in their kaftans buying their return tickets to a revolution, Mariella's entree was not as a tourist, or a girlfriend, but as a reporter. Her sense of self, her very existence, depended on getting a story.

Mariella's story had to be political, had to be radical and had to shock an elderly square like Hod, who was rapidly taking on the role of her father. Echoes of Patsy's suppressed and distorted narrative emerge in Mariella's text. In it, her heroine repeatedly turns to 'delinquency' to escape the position society has established for her. Vulnerable, she craves 'power' above anything else.

Jackie was useful to a point. She took her to the brothels, the blues clubs and Powis Terrace, where the flats were overcrowded with newly arrived Caribbean families. The previous incumbents had been vast Irish families, some of them tinkers, some of them rag-and-bone men, most of them dealing in junk, often stored in hallways and corridors and gardens. Mariella documents the fascinating clash of cultures and trash that were making this part of London Britain's answer to the Projects. To get to the shebeen or the squat of the moment, our heroine had to claw her way over bicycle wheels, broken-down prams, battered bedsteads and the oppressed.

Our heroine – Mariella, that is – has a lot to say about enterprises like the HQ for the Malcolm X Montessori School in Notting Hill and the London Free School. She is sincere in her admiration for their aims and their commitment to the advance of equality. As a writer she is finding her vocation and her conscience. She is in favour of community activism, children's play groups and free schools.

At the same time, it is interesting to watch her distort the facts to suit her flair for drama. It would not be hard for a man as sharp as Michael X to see through Mariella's cover. She could not play a convincing doped-up dolly bird, or hippy hanger-on. All her play-acting went into playing herself. All this work concealed a frightened little girl who had seen too much – and gone blind. Michael X would have seen the cracks in her facade; he would have got shot of her very quickly. So she got in there, she met the major players, but there was no hanging out, let alone dropping out. This leaves the question: if much of Mariella's novel is thinly veiled fact, whose facts are they?

There are two contenders. Apart from Michael X, there was another Notting Hill messiah, who really did believe he was God, and who boasted two high-ranking women in his entourage. A girl like Jackie, born a nobody in a nowhere town, one of the many who are used, abused, or drably invisible, becomes, in Mariella's heroine, an avenging, deviant, veritable 'she-devil'. These women who really were supping at the table of Black Power become material for her shiniest manifestation, Tricesta St Regis.

The women who are the model for Tricesta were embedded in the upper echelons of Notting Hill. They were Gale Benson, the daughter of a Tory MP, and Diana Athill, a respected editor at the London publisher Andre Deutsch. Benson and Athill offer contrasting portraits of women who were dissatisfied with their role in society, who were trying to express their individuality, but who could not escape identification through their relations with men. Black men – wounded outsiders and passionate advocates for a just cause – were like honey to a bee for women with low self-esteem. They could surrender their own cause in the name of his. Their motivation for getting involved in black politics was a man called Hakim Abdullah Jamal.

Jamal was born Allen Donaldson in the ghetto of Roxbury in Boston, Massachusetts. Like Mariella, he was no stranger to misery. His mother left home when he was six, his father was a drunk, and by the age of fourteen he was an alcoholic and drug addict. Several times before coming to Europe, he had been accused of attempted murder. He had been in prison and mental hospitals and was destined to meet an early death.

Needless to say, he was a draw for ladies who had lost their way whilst looking for a lost cause. The 'well brought up' writer and publisher Diana Athill wrote a memoir about her flirtation with Black Power. At the same time as Mariella was strutting her hotpants round the Grove, Athill was coaxing the memoirs out of Jamal. Athill was a bourgeois bohemian in her fifties looking for hot new authors. The pinko press loved Michael X. Jamal had an even better story. He was distantly related to Malcolm X through his wife Dorothy, Malcolm's cousin. Malcolm X did not recognise the link. But Jamal used the distant kinship as a passport to fame. He converted to Islam and peddled racial oppression but mostly he peddled himself.

Fourteen years Athill's junior, Jamal wore a ring in his left ear and a heavy gold chain round his neck – jewellery that groans with memories of slavery and the price that is put on a man. A multi-coloured dashiki with Biblical overtones finished off the look. He had little going for him except his appearance and his knowledge of how to survive in impossible circumstances. This in itself was enough, but the myth that black men were sexually superior to timid whites was a persuasive weapon in his arsenal. Basically – and Mariella would have spotted this – he was a hustler. He used sex to gain power over the the enemy. In this instance, rich white women. It was the 'talk black, sleep white' strategy, and, in the closing years of this tumultuous decade, it worked.

Jamal came to England with impeccable references. He had met the French actress Jean Seberg while she was in America with her husband, the novelist Romain Gary. Gary was also researching a book – this one described activists like his actress wife and her friends who made themselves at home in black ghettoes. Romain Gary eventually published his story as *Chien Blanc* (*White Dog*). It tells the story of how a white liberal couple get friendly with black militants and are completely exploited. Still in the process of researching the book, Gary invited Jamal to Paris, where *he* started writing *his* book about his *ménage a trois* with Seberg and Gary. Everyone was writing a book, it seems. Soon, the English actress Vanessa Redgrave extricated Jamal from Seberg's embrace and bought his ticket to London.

She parked him with her brother Corin in Notting Hill. At a dinner party, Hakim Jamal met a friend of Corin, the disaffected daughter of a Tory MP. Gale Benson listened fascinated as Jamal talked of attending functions alongside Princess Margaret and her husband Lord Snowdon and the broadcaster David Frost. His brand of contempt mixed with greed was mesmerising. Since Corin was wanting to distance himself from his uninvited guest, Gale got there in time to offer him a new pad. She was a privileged if troubled young woman. She had married young, at twenty, to film director Jonathan Benson. Their wedding was reported in the papers under the headline, 'Silk, satin and lace', in reference to her bridal attire. Corin had been the best man and the newly-weds had moved into a big house in Chelsea. Soon after the honeymoon, Gale ran away to Argentina. When she came back, she went round to Corin's for dinner.

Soon, Gale Benson had changed her name to 'Hale Kimga', which was an anagram of her own first name and Hakim's. Her friends simply assumed that she had become swept along by the excitement of the time. It soon became clear she had not only lost her identity; she had lost her mind.

Seeing the cracks and fearing for his financial security, Jamal started touting his manuscript. Another of Corin's groovy friends took Jamal to the offices of Andre Deutsch to talk about getting it commissioned. Athill gave him an advance and a place on her sofa. From now on, Gale Benson and Diana Athill would take it in turns to look after the endlessly demanding and needy Jamal. Did Mariella see any of this? Was she inside the circle as she maintains? How else could she have known about these women and the exploitative situations in which they found themselves?

In 1970 Jamal moved into the Malcolm X Montessori School in Notting Hill. He telephoned Michael X and introduced himself as 'Malcolm X's cousin'. Michael X was living in the Black House in Islington and invited Jamal over. But he rarely went anywhere unless someone chauffeured him. He was paralysed by fear, anxiety and the growing conviction that he was God, a belief fuelled by the interpretation of Bible passages which speak of Jews and Gentiles living under sin. Since blacks were not mentioned, it followed they lived in grace. Jamal took this personally.

Together with Benson, Jamal hatched a plan. Their mission was to launch the mass migration of poor black people from America and Britain to Guyana. Most of the time they smoked pot in basement rooms in 'Viet Grove'. Perhaps this is where Mariella was watching them.

There is one conspiracy theory worth mentioning. In the film *The Bank Job*, which came out in 2008, Gale is depicted as working undercover for the secret services. According to the film there was an Establishment plot to infiltrate the Black Power movement.

Her brother, who survives her, discredits the notion. He simply believes that she was vulnerable to a man like Jamal. Frankly, it seems unlikely that she would be an undercover agent. But inferences can be drawn. Was there a woman working undercover in the circles surrounding Michael X and Hakim Jamal? Mariella would have us believe there was, and in her novel this woman's name is Tricesta St Regis.

In a crumbling terraced house, with paint peeling and faded curtains hung haphazardly at the grimy windows, Tricesta walks into a hall cluttered with broken furniture. The stale smell of cooking assaults her delicate nostrils. She dashes up the lino-covered stairs into a flat filled with the music of Jimmy Smith and finds white girls dancing with 'negroes'. Black Panther posters are stuck on the walls. Instead of freaking out she gets turned on and meets Brad, a 'great-looking spade'. Other kooky cats are to be found in the next room, supervising the hi-fi deck. In this inner sanctum, she meets Edward X, 'a real cookie, dressed in long black robes'. He is 'the most beautiful talker ... not tall but fabulous looking, in the face he resembles Cassius Clay'.

In the dens of Rotting Hill, Tricesta meets Janie Craig, a pretty, dreamy twenty-three-year-old English girl, the daughter of a High Court judge. Janie's profile chimes with Gale Benson's. Janie left home after a violent quarrel. She is raising her consciousness (smoking pot). She writes outspoken articles in *Our Times*, an underground newspaper of which she is features editor.

In *Make Believe: A True Story*, Athill tells a similar story to Mariella's. Both books are by women who claim to be sexually liberated. But both women betray a painful contempt for other women and collaboration with men in the domination of those women. Athill's tone is more matter-of-fact, more true to herself, confessional. But the confidence with which she writes belies the actions she describes. Her highly active sex life is an example of female masochism rather than Mariella's sadism, and yet female subordination is the result in both texts. The apparent frankness of both Novotny and Athill as writers is at odds with the suspicion they betray towards their own sex. In neither text can it truly be said that women are liberated. However, while Athill indulges her male subject at the expense of the women around him, Mariella shows him to be a fraud.

Mariella was no man-hater. Her novel's decent chap is Brad. Although he is the right-hand man of Edward X, he does not advocate violence. Although he runs 'girls' and pushes drugs, it's all for the cause of racial equality. He exploits women (who don't count for Mariella), but he respects her heroine and asks for her hand in marriage.

The need to appear cool about casual sex and mind-stripping hallucinogenics precluded any form of intimacy. Mariella's lack of curiosity about other people and inability to feel compassion or empathy make for an unmarriageable woman and a troubled narrative. Underneath Mariella's bid for sexual domination is Athill's thinly disguised female masochism.

On 2 January 1972, Michael X murdered Gale Benson in Trinidad. Athill remains, like Polonius, wringing her hands on the sidelines while the principals lurch into the murk of counter-cultural collapse and psychic disintegration. Like Polonius, her presence is self-justifying, unsympathetic to the female victim of this messy story and uneasy to contemplate. Mariella's response is equally unsatisfactory but more honest. She sees the victimhood and despises it. She sees the predator and deflates him.

23

LESLIE FREWIN

King's Road was published by Leslie Frewin on 22 November 1971. This small publishing firm was based at 5 Goodwin's Court off St Martin's Lane. Frewin is forgotten now, but his address, a cobbled alleyway with bow shopfronts and gabled windows, is redolent of the gaslit world of British publishing that once upon a time released gentlemanly anthologies of cricket lore and humour. Frewin was also the author of showbiz biographies. All his books, whether authored by himself or published by his firm, are brisk in tone, and pitched for a mass-market readership. In 1968, to the amusement of the *Spectator*'s John Wells, Frewin published an 'elegantly produced cocoa-table book, planned as a triumphant climax to the series which includes '*The Wit of Prince Philip* — and now *Three Faces of Wit: HRH Prince Philip, Sir Winston Churchill and President John F. Kennedy* [priced at 30s], *The Wit of the Church* [16s], and *The Wit of Harold Wilson* [15s]'.

Frewin's self-penned biographies include *The Late Mrs Dorothy Parker* (Macmillan, 1969), *Blond Venus: A Life of Marlene Dietrich* (1956) and *The Cafe Royal Story: A Living Legend* (Hutchinson, 1963). He was sufficiently well known to feature in a group photograph commissioned by Jocelyn Stevens, the publisher of *Queen* magazine, and taken by fashion photographer Patrick Lichfield in July 1967. The photo is called '*Out*' *Group* and features campaigners for social reform, some aristocrats, the boxer Billy Walker, and a clutch of literary luminaries. In the same month, Lichfield composed another group portrait called '*In*' *Group, young London* featuring up-and-coming theatrical stars Susannah York, Peter Cook, Tom Courtenay, the model Twiggy, and playwright Joe Orton.

As a member of the publishing Establishment, or at least its middlebrow stratum, Frewin did not just churn out stocking fillers. In 1969, his firm published *Edge of Violence* by John Summers, a Welsh journalist. A blend of fact and fiction, adventure and memoir, this was the story of the Aberfan disaster of 1966 in which a slag heap collapsed and buried a school in the Welsh village, killing 166 children. Apart from the tragedy of this case, there were political ramifications. Financial compensation was allegedly being held up by Westminster amidst suspicion that some of the families were connected to a Free Wales Army. The book concerns Summer's efforts to gain funds for these bereaved families. With the consent of his publisher, he played with literary convention in producing a work of creative non-fiction. In this way, the journalist's account of the political backdrop to the slaughter of innocents becomes a novel featuring members of the Free Wales Army who are threatening to blow up an abandoned factory tower if their demands for the funds are not met. In literary terms, *Edge of Violence* is most convincing when it details the story of Summers, a seaman turned journalist living on the edge of poverty, relating eyewitness accounts of his dealings with Welsh nationalists. In 1969 – a year that saw protests against war in Vietnam, British troops sent into Northern Ireland and revolutionary rhetoric – Frewin was chiming with public sympathies through Summers' ambition to revolt against an Establishment culture of complacency and consumerism.

In the end, the indictment fails to light up the page. It did, however, provoke proceedings for contempt of court over its proposed publication. Frewin consulted the libel lawyer Hilary

Rubinstein about whether he and his author would be sued, since the novel included charges of corruption and the plundering of the disaster fund. Rubinstein's response was that 'a million copies of this book should be printed and given away free to the public'.

The *London Evening Standard* quoted Frewin as saying: 'It is censorship without legal action. In the last few months the author has brought new facts to light, and these are incorporated in this edition. Now, for the first time, the story can be told.'

Edge of Violence did reach publication. Several journalists were prepared to review it. For reasons that are still difficult to determine, the majority of these reviews did not appear. However, the book was reissued in 1970 as *The Disaster* with a chapter taken out on legal advice. One can only assume it was the chapter in which Summers accused the Wilson government, and in particular the 'absurd' George Thomas, a minister at the Welsh Office and one of the first politicians at the scene, of trying to suppress his book. So by the time of publication of *King's Road*, Frewin had a reputation for producing provocative political novels.

He was also keen to infiltrate the best-selling territory of 'the man who invented sex' and godfather of the airport novel, Harold Robbins. Mariella must have seemed like a godsend when she walked into No. 5 Goodwin's Court. Her backstory was a marketing man's dream. Her credentials in the *demi-monde* were unimpeachable, and she looked good – blonde hair, pouting mouth, a willingness to strip off at any given moment. Her cover photo is revealing in every sense. If she is trying to create an image, the effect is that of a demented Julie Christie. Her hair is dressed in the same fashion as Christie's in the film *Shampoo*. It is a long, luxuriant golden bob. She is wearing a fedora hat and antique, ornate jewellery. She covers her naked breasts with one arm, while the other arm reaches down to her pelvis, pulling down the waistband of her Oxford bags. Her make-up is witchy, black spikes radiating outwards from hooded eyes. Her lips are moist and ready for action. So she had the goods; she had a story, but could she write? Leslie Frewin and Mariella Novotny are joint owners of the copyright to *King's Road*. This suggests that she couldn't. If this is the case, how much writing did Frewin have to do?

The prose of *King's Road* has the quality of a runaway train, much like the articles Mariella wrote for *Club International*. One can assume, perhaps, that the story is hers, and the momentum is hers. But maybe Frewin injected some colour, gave flesh to her characters and helped her shape the plot. He is certainly no Maxwell Perkins, the editor who licked Fitzgerald's *Great Gatsby* into shape. Nowadays Frewin would be making a living as a teacher of creative writing. Character, POV, plot, irony, tone and dialogue. Frewin knew how to make books. He was a businessman. But Mariella was an author who could not edit herself and who had no POV other than that of a traumatised child who thinks she is an adult. Besides this handicap, her shortsightedness comes to mind again, and there was her prolixity. I can imagine him asking her to cut 5,000 words and her writing another 10,000.

Frewin had previous experience of a celebrity author. This collaboration should have acted as a warning. In 1966 Chaplin v Leslie Frewin (Publishers) Limited was a case in which 'a minor entered into a contract with a publisher for the publication of a ghost-written biography of the minor'. The minor in question was the son of Charlie Chaplin, who employed Frewin to ghostwrite his memoir. On reading the results, entitled *I Couldn't Smoke the Grass on my Father's Lawn: Pot, Girls and Swingers in London's Ultra-Mod Set*, Chaplin Jr found that he did not like the contents. One of his complaints was the injudicious use of slang. To beef things up his ghostwriter had seasoned the text with the slang we find in Mariella's book: charge, bread, fuzz, cop, busted, heads, dames, pinched, gear, etc. But the contract was found to be binding as 'overall it was for his benefit in two ways: 1) In terms of money and 2) It gave him the chance to earn a living in the world of publication.' The judge's final verdict was 'the mud may cling but the profits will be secured'. This was language Mariella could understand.

When it came to the publication of *King's Road*, she pulled out all the stops. On the road itself, Mariella stepped through a giant-size replica of the book cover in a shop window. A photo shows a window cleaner getting a close-up view of topless Mariella with copies of her novel failing to preserve her modesty. Frewin touted this latest product of his stable as '*the* novel of Britain's Permissive Society' exposing 'in raw truth the whole of the high life and low life of London's "turned-on, beautiful people".' He told the reporter from the *Kensington Post* that the demand for rights to her novel was so great she had been dubbed Britain's first Common Market authoress and 'the natural successor to Harold Robbins'. His quote was placed above an advert for the London Masseuses Agency.

24

CHELSEA GIRL

In a piece of advance publicity on 29 September, the *Daily Mirror* plugged Mariella's forthcoming book as a 'scorcher'. In a section of the tabloid devoted to finding jobs for 'clever girls', the article on Mariella claimed that the authoress was working for

> ... another publishing firm selling encyclopaedias. And because of her novel they have suspended her. Mariella, 29 (who was hostess at the masked man party in those days of Stephen Ward) was doing well. She thinks they are annoyed that she is being published by another firm. She says she did offer them the book. They returned it, unread.

I do not know if Mariella was working as a door-to-door saleswoman. But bankruptcy was a regular occurrence in her life with Hod. Going back to the 1940s Hod was in and out of Queer Street, and played fast and loose with his creditors. Sometimes he got caught out. In October 1964 he had obtained credit from Harrods without informing them that he was an undischarged bankrupt. At their Auction Rooms in Sloane Avenue he had placed bids for three lots of furniture which were knocked down to him for a total of

£169 and that payment was made with a cheque signed 'Mariella Dibben'. The cheque was returned marked RD. No payment was made, though three letters were sent to Hod, who was well known at the auction rooms. In 1965, under the name of Marie Stella Dibben, Mariella was declared bankrupt. In 1966 Hod was declared bankrupt. The couple were struggling to stay afloat.

Not so Tricesta St Regis. We have already seen that Tricesta is a fantasy version of her creator. Tricesta never had to resort to door-to-door selling of encyclopaedias. Tricesta had the film-star looks, the aristocratic background, the disingenuous disregard for her family's wealth and prestige. Tricesta is 'the leading light of the King's Road'. Mariella wanted to make that claim for herself. She had been on friendly terms with senators in Washington, MPs in Westminster, Mayfair debs and guardsmen, and the boss of Britain's underworld. Now she wanted to infiltrate the Chelsea set that included Mick and Marianne, who had a flat near the Flour Mills on Chelsea Wharf.

She never got there. So she wrote about it instead – from 8 a.m. to 6 p.m. every day ('until I am knocked out', she told Frewin). His cover blurb describes her as

... a disarmingly frank and open person, with no pretensions or fears. She wants to go to university (where, unquestionably, she would prove a bewitching distraction!). She lives in Mayfair, London [by 1971 when the novel was published she had moved out of Earl's Court], writes to the accompaniment of strident hi-fi jazz – preferably Buddy Rich – aided by countless mugs of tea. Very 'mod', she is always ahead of fashion. Yet for all her sophistication, she remains an incredibly 'quiet' person, preferring work to the social scene. She is now writing not one – but three novels at once. Mariella Novotny belies the saying that 'beauty cannot boast brains'. In her case, it can – and does.

She does not drink alcohol of any sort ('May I have a Coke?'), does not smoke and believes in God but spurns 'organised religion'.

So here we have another description of her frank and open nature (and lack of self-awareness). The emphasis is on teetotalism – in almost every interview she makes the pledge. Why? Who is she trying to impress? Did her mother drink? Or her mystery father? Or some father figure in her childhood? Hod definitely drank. He was a just-about functioning alcoholic. At any rate, she had lost her appetite for inviting people to dinner. That most feminine arena – food, cooking and the kitchen – is now absent from her writing. Mariella mentions toast and eating soul food at the Mangrove. The rest of the time it's coffee, diamorphine and Tuinal. She listens to Buddy Rich. He was the jazz drummer she met in LA, with whom she had the best sex of her life, she told her readers in *Club International*.

The connection between intensity, turmoil and writing is strong in Mariella. As well as depicting her heroine listening to Rich's frenetic drumming, Tricesta listens to The Who, Black Sabbath and Jimi Hendrix. By the fourth chapter she has avoided a vice charge in New York, had sex with her brother, seduced her grandfather, roared down the King's Road in a bronze E-type, 'swallowed two sleeping pills, reflected on this barbiturate-soaked society, told herself not to feel sad', and on awakening taken an unnamed upper that 'doesn't give you the shakes'. This writer is possessed by sounds, stories, surfaces and voices. Her writing is haunted. Henrietta, the name Mariella gave to her daughter, becomes in her novel the name of Tricesta's grandmother who went down with the *Titanic*. Tricesta's brother looks like a cross between the actor David Hemmings and the Rolling Stone Mick Jagger – so he's vulnerable *and* upfront. He, in turn, is obsessed with Tricesta and constantly pressing her for sex. She, meanwhile, is blackmailing their uncle Eric who raped her when she was fourteen. Uncle Eric duly gives her £100,000 to open a boutique on King's Road. She has one foot in the antiques trade and the country house set (shades of Hod) and another in the trend for period clothes and interior design (the Chelsea set). She gets the curse. It's a drag. She's sold on jazz, she fights with or fucks the men in her story and the same goes for the women.

That's not all. Tricesta bags the US senator who 'gets so would up and tense … he's got to have it every other day'. Just to clarify his dilemma, 'a ten-minute bang is enough'. The conservatives don't like him and he makes a bid for the black vote. Tricesta finds his politics patronising, dishonest and harmful. She contends that the black community will find their real leader from within. Eventually he becomes a man who is so cynical she cannot make love to him.

Back on the King's Road, a lovely blonde girl schemes to supplant her; a clutch of rejected girlfriends retreat and plot; the help she does receive from female friends is so casual they could equally well be hindering. And she's very busy. She plants a bug that 'looked like a leather covered cigarette lighter' in the office of Edward X. She cracks the Ingersoll lock of the safe in his office. She retrieves his blackmail tapes. In the background, riots are covering most of Europe and the States. In the foreground, Edward X persuades her to fly to New York and gives her the blueprint for a series of Black Power riots to be triggered by a signal from the movement's HQ in Harlem. The transatlantic 'collective act' is only prevented when Tricesta is arrested with the blueprint in her possession. (The randy senator gets her off.)

On her return to London, Edward X presents her with recorded evidence of her relations with her brother. He forces her into a relationship with Michael Flaxman, an MP. This should be easy, she figures, as with Flaxman's wife being over fifty, 'I don't suppose he's had his monthly rights in years.' It is Tricesta's job to force Flaxman to present a private member's bill in Parliament in favour of Edward's cause. Before she has to apply pressure (evidence of their affair) she fucks a friendly burglar who steals the *kompromat* on her and her brother from Edward X. She then watches the assassination of Edward X at a Teach-In at the Roundhouse in Camden. While all this is going on, she is 'the sexiest bird in Belgravia', she forces another woman to undergo a vaginal piercing, and visits her parents who are of course wish-fulfilment status symbols. Father is a surgeon.

Mother is the only child of the Earl of Prestigne, Lord Lieutenant of Westingshire. Father has just been knighted for his services to medicine. Mother is a successful 'movement' painter. Tricesta and her brother went to Dartington Hall 'because of our artistic talent'. With Eric's money, they open 'one of the finest antique showrooms in the King's Road ... ultra-modern interiors with period furniture ... After nine months in business people have taken to our ideas and it's swinging.' But Dr St Regis is too busy saving lives to notice. Mrs St Regis is ethereal and intellectual, has no substance and offers no support or protection. Both parents are mere mouthpieces for an absence, leaving Tricesta to battle her way to survival.

By the end of the novel, Tricesta's 'friend's' piercing has become infected. She has enjoyed long chats with Edward X about black history and with Michael Flaxman about pressing social issues. She decides to write a book, listens to Cream's newly released LP and talks to the tired-looking mother of three small, half-naked black children down the Grove. The place is derelict. The conditions are appalling. Brad convinces her, 'People like you can help, just by being aware, by not denying its existence.'

In a final flourish, she goes to the Carnival, the land of Grenfell Tower, and actually witnesses a column of fire, 'flames funnelling upwards ... roaring towards the roofs. The draught encouraged by the open windows caused the fire to travel in a spiral, all the time moving upwards.' Her 'friend' has her piercing removed. The MP, Michael Flaxman, dies and leaves her his entire estate. Brad proposes marriage. She goes home to listen to Ben Webster and think about it. Brad takes over as leader of a 'non-violent Black Power movement'. Tricesta decides to open a shop in Paris. Her 'friend' has released herself from the vaginal piercing, but she has become 'a hopeless junkie, destroyed in body and soul'. She is Mariella Novotny's shadow self.

The other characters get their egos massaged and their happy endings. *King's Road*, Frewin concludes, 'is a novel of *now*'.

In Mariella's hands, the re-writing of women's subordination to love and romance becomes a gathering-up of an insurgent force of energies which patriarchy has sought to contain and finds horrifying. Mariella winds this female monstrosity into a warped articulation of excess – both sexual and political – Tricesta, dressed to kill in the shortest mini you've ever seen, nipples pushing against fine fabric, fingers bedecked with antique rings, embodies a transgressive and fuck-you strategy. Mariella was writing this novel in the vanguard of the women's liberation movement, although the publication of *The Second Sex* in 1949 or *The Female Eunuch* in 1970 had had no visible effect on her. This is, on the one hand, an example of her lack of interest in self-awareness, but also her lack of interest in women's place in society. Her real motivation was to beat into submission the Hyde Park Set who had rejected her, to nail prevailing trends to her masthead, to smash the fake power of the false prophet and expose any dreams of a new order as being the performance of a bully who belonged in the gutter.

'When you're a child and you are told something long enough and loud enough you eventually believe it and it stays with you,' Tricesta says. What message did Stella Marie receive as a child that grew into a voice she could not stop hearing?

Despite the fact that Mariella Novotny is described by her publisher as possessing 'a sex appeal that is like a sledgehammer in its effect', women are ultimately powerless in her worldview. There is no sisterhood for the preposterously named Tricesta St Regis. They are competitors, victims, bitches and finks.

In real life, there was no money to offset her insecurities. In real life, Mariella was living in Earl's Court with an ageing bankrupt. The *Sunday Times* Insight team had done a big piece on auction rigging. The game was up. Hod had a go at the scaffolding business, which he ran out of a shed in the Boltons, a garden square in Chelsea (now fantastically expensive and eerily quiet).

Over in Goodwin's Court, Leslie Frewin sifted through advance reviews for his latest wannabe bestseller. He needed to promote the controversy, the salaciousness, the hard-earned insight into a world closed off from his average reader. These were the quotes he selected for the back cover of the book:

'... hailed by her publishers as the natural successor to Harold Robbins ... she is certainly extraordinary...'
Evening News

'The girl who once shocked the nation ... Mariella Novotny takes the lid off upper-class layabouts...'
News of the World

The ellipses say it all.

25

A LITERARY HIT-LIST

Frewin claims in his cover notes that he has signed 'Europe's most provocative authoress' to a six-book contract. His *protégée* shows no interest in the craft of writing or no sign of having read any books whatsoever. Apart from her perfectly reasonable desire to earn some money, she is possessed with the desire to knock other people's tomes off the bestseller lists.

But in order to gain a wide readership a writer has to broaden his or her appeal and be appealing in the first place. There was something in Mariella that was inherently uncomfortable. Photographs from this period show a woman who flaunts her nudity in a series of misjudged poses. It is as though deep down and unbeknownst to herself she actually wants to repel her audience.

The only thing she admits to liking is sex and because it is the Age of Aquarius she gets further into the esoteric. *TIME* magazine ran a cover story in 1972 that declared 'Satan Returns'. Horror mainstay Hammer Film Productions was in its heyday. Mainstream cinema saw the underground rise in the form of *The Wicker Man* and *Blood on Satan's Claw* – witchcraft was a cinema ticket or trip to the newsagents away. So Mariella was not alone in exploring her interest in the supernatural.

This is where David Litvinoff comes in. The boutiques along the King's Road, the antique galleries, the Pheasantry pub, where Litvinoff held court, were located in Chelsea and Knightsbridge. The Pheasantry was a Georgian building built in 1769. In 1865 it was occupied by a game dealer named Samuel Baker who raised pheasants for the royal household, hence the name. In the early twentieth century studios were let to artists and models like Eleanor Thornton, the inspiration for the Rolls-Royce mascot, 'Spirit of Ecstasy'. After the Second World War the ground floor became a nightclub that survived into the seventies and the upper building was let as apartments. Rock guitarist Eric Clapton and journalist Martin Sharp (editor of *Oz*) were two of the counter-cultural heroes who lived here. Germaine Greer wrote *The Female Eunuch* here. It was a place in which to be seen, juxtaposing the charm of dereliction with the happening of now.

To get here from Earl's Court was a dogged trot through bedsit-land, fast-food joints and Hod's scaffolding yard in the Boltons before finally broaching Chelsea via King's Road. The bird from bohemia wanted to make her nest here. Through her association with David Litvinoff, she caught the attention of London's most famous antiques dealer, Christopher Gibbs. When I spoke to Mr Gibbs via the internet in 2013, he was wintering in Morocco. He told me that he first saw Mariella at Sotheby's in the early sixties when she was being squired by the notorious one-armed philanderer and MP for Thanet Billy Rees-Davies.

'My long dead friend David Litvinov [*sic*] knew [Hod and Mariella] well,' wrote Mr Gibbs. 'We all used to see Mariella at the auction houses. David [Litvinoff] knew Hod from around the fifties onwards, and spent time with them both until he died.'

'David Litvinoff was a character to whom you always referred by his full name,' said another contact, Patricia Goldstein. In befriending Litvinoff, Mariella had hit a cultural nerve, because Litvinoff was at the epicentre of the Chelsea Popocracy – a confluence of pop stars, aristocrats and drug-dealers. His favourite haunt was the King's Road. The road belonged to the King when

Charles II built it to link St James's Palace to Fulham. Four hundred years later King's Road had a decadent feel to it. It was here in Mary Quant's shop Bazaar that the mini skirt was invented. As well as the Royal Court Theatre there were risqué shows at the Chelsea Palace theatre down the road from Bazaar. In the fifties, Paul Raymond, Mariella's future employer, put on a show called *Burlesque*, which featured twenty separate acts such as Miss Blandish and Her Famous Moving Nudes and the Sex-Appeal Girls.

Boutiques abounded, just as described by Mariella in her novel: Girl, Just Looking, Kleptomania, Take Six, I Was Lord Kitchener's Valet and the famous Chelsea Antiques Market. Smiling like a Cheshire cat, a cravat loosely tied round his scarred neck, in the saloon bar of the Pheasantry, or in Christopher Gibb's Sloane Avenue gallery, Litvinoff was there even if he wasn't.

In 1954 the Soho artist Lucian Freud had painted David Litvinoff's portrait. He called it *The Procurer*. Like Mariella, David Litvinoff emanated from post-war Soho. From 1972 until 1975, he lived in Davington Priory, a former Benedictine nunnery in Kent owned by Gibbs. Characters who joined him here included the antiquarian bookdealer Patricia Goldstein and her husband Gerry. When I met Patricia in 2015, like Jackie the stripper, she was a recovering addict.

Even at the height of Soho's rush hour – 6.15 p.m. – Meard Street retains its quiet. With all these hints of mystery whispering in my ears, I walked along, taking my time to think. I was heading for a house converted into tarts' parlours, a film company and Gabi's trattoria. Fitted out like a ski lodge that had been abandoned at some point in the seventies, Gabi's offered a Peroni and spag bol to Soho's working girls. I had arranged to meet Patricia there. She told me that she and her husband Gerry had been freebasing cocaine and injecting heroin since the seventies. They had always lived amidst the roadworks, gridlock and cracked cement on the exhaust pipe of West London, Goldhawk Road. From their modest flat above a Bangladeshi minimart, she and her husband sallied forth to meet with other esoteric treasure and pleasure seekers. These are characters who have passed into London's lore and literary hinterland, placed there by the Bards of London, Iain Sinclair and Chris Petit.

Patricia met Mariella through David Litvinoff. Some background first: her main drug of choice was buying and selling, receiving and stealing rare books and collectibles that explained and revivified the past. Patricia had a nose for finding Sexton Blake mysteries in East End markets. Her flat – anonymous and tired from the outside – was an Aladdin's Cave within. Floor-to-ceiling bookcases were lined with trophies she and Gerry hadn't offloaded and literary curios they couldn't let go. They were the big game hunters – and the rat catchers – of the book trade.

They collected people, too. 'There was a whole crowd of people in Chelsea in the seventies – rebellious aristocrats like Lord Lambton's daughter. Litvinoff was the fixer for them. He was a great raconteur. One morning he told us he woke up, and half his head had been shaved. He was hanging by his feet from a window overlooking Ken High Street. He owed money to the Krays. Some weird throat scars were down to them, too.'

Litvinoff's real achievement was as 'Dialogue Coach and Technical Adviser' to Nicholas Roeg on the set of *Performance*. Author of lines such as 'what a freak show' and 'shut your bloody 'ole', he gained a toehold on the silver screen and some kind of immortality.

Patricia was a lively and intelligent woman; her husband was a sensitive book-hound. 'By the eighties it got a bit out of hand. We were boosting books out of Mayfair...'

Their drug use had got out of hand. But what kept Patricia going was the prospect of finding a lost treasure, a manuscript by Alistair Crowley liberated from a basement in Fitzrovia, a sketch book belonging to Camille Pisarro sourced in a conservatory in Streatham. There is something of Mariella in this. Always looking for the jackpot whilst rummaging in the dust of old closets.

As a digression, Patricia alerted me to a literary descendant of Mariella's: the character of Karen, Catherine Ballard's secretary in J. G. Ballard's novel *Crash*. Karen is part of a lesbian sub-plot Ballard devised for his novel. In the final draft, Karen has no surname. Patricia had found a previous draft of *Crash* in a house clearance of a publisher in Hampstead. In this previous draft that Patricia told me was called *The Atrocity Exhibition*, Ballard gave Karen the surname Novotny.

Like me, Patricia had been looking to substantiate the rumours that surrounded Mariella since she first met her. She suggested I look at Iain Sinclair's BFI book on *Crash*. I did, and I found the trace of Mariella's existence and the impression she made upon Ballard. Sinclair reckons that the choice of surname for Karen summons up cartoonish spy stories and mock glamour. He sums up *King's Road* and its ghostly author thus: 'A trashy docu-novel ... written by the Czech "model" and amateur spook, Mariella Novotny ... The book features all the usual elements of sex/dope craziness, including lesbian couplings and voyeurism.'

Mariella becomes an abandoned notation in a forgotten manuscript. But Patricia had not finished.

'The other book you should look at is *Thus Bad Begins* by Javier Marías,' she said. 'It was published in England in 2016. Gerry was reading it when he had his heart attack. I picked it up and read it to him in the hospital when he was in a coma. I only mention it because there's a photo of Mariella in it.'

Javier Marías, a Spanish author, chooses two images to illustrate a four-hundred-page novel that takes all those pages to reveal the answer to the initial mystery. The final revelation as to why the hero's friend 'behaved in an indecent manner' is shockingly anticlimactic. There is an answer for me here. More than this, lying just beneath the surface of his novel of a marriage and its secrets is the guilty conscience of post-Franco Spain.

The first image Marías reproduces is an eighteenth-century painting owned by the hero that depicts a cavalier on horseback. The cavalier looks back over his shoulder in the direction of the viewer, 'as if wishing to retain, before he rode off, the image of the deaths he had caused'.

The image to which Patricia alerted me is a press photograph of Mariella, who appears as a minor figure in the novel. The photograph shows her 'wearing a ridiculous and yet very modest hat' at the moment she is arrested by an FBI agent from the era of J. Edgar Hoover. What does this image mean for the author? I looked again closely at her silly hat and thought about what Bobbie McKew had said – that Mariella always wore a hat. He never saw her without one, even in bed. I looked at other photos of a hatless Mariella and saw that her hair had the quality of a glossy, mannequin's wig.

I thought of fashions, and what Mariella said about the nasty incident she saw behind the woodshed in the disputed displaced person's camp. How her hair fell out. Did it ever grow back, I wondered? Is that why she always wore hats and wigs? I thought of her ability to transform herself with each passing decade – adopting the latest fashions and sometimes surpassing them. The image Marías chose of Mariella, perhaps more than any other, demonstrates the way she relates to her life, turning everything into fiction. Now that she is long gone, any photograph of her suffers the same fate. She, too, looks like an invented person who never existed.

26

PERFORMANCE AND PUBLICITY

The weekend Patricia spent with Litvinoff and Mariella left the usually articulate Patricia shuddering in recollection. Patricia was no *ingenue* when it came to apocalyptic couplings. In 1978, after the collapse of the Sex Pistols, she and Gerry hosted the guitarist Sid Vicious. They sourced him his drugs in an alleyway at the back of the minimart below their flat. He slept on their sofa for several days. Nancy Spungeon collected him before she and Sid caught the Piccadilly line from Hammersmith. From here, they made their way to Heathrow Airport en route to the Chelsea Hotel in New York.

Sid and Nancy were puppy dogs compared to Hod and Mariella. A weekend at Litvinoff's frightened Patricia. It was not just the drug use, it was the atmosphere Hod and Mariella brought with them. It was the kind of emptiness around which you can only imagine the worst because there is no one there.

I thought we were the only visitors that weekend. The village was deep into Harvest Festival and walking down the high street all you could hear was the clinking of sherry glasses. We got some disapproving looks – we weren't Home Counties material. Litvinoff had all his hippy friends lodging at the Priory so he was used to disapproving looks. Behind the house there were green fields and a winding path through trees. I went off by myself down a dirt track through the oaks, stopping to climb over gates. Finally I came over a rise, and walked down toward a cluster of sheds by a pond. Standing there was Mariella in some kind of riding outfit – all in tweed. She had a bundle of twigs in her hand. Hod was standing with his face pressed against the trunk of an old oak. I thought he was tree-hugging. When he heard me approach, he jerked his head round. Mariella just gazed at me. The three of us stood there for a few minutes without saying anything. I was paralysed and I couldn't tell if it was fear or fascination. They were looking at me like a lamb chop had just arrived on their plate.

Back in the Boltons, the greenhouse of Chelsea, in 1972 Mariella made a brief attempt to get into the interior design business. Hod was renting a shed from which he ran his scaffolding business. Mariella was reinventing herself as an interior designer. It was a short-lived career. Her main client, she claimed, was Prince Faisal M. Al-Saud. She writes in *Club International* that he took her to dinner and discotheques. Annabel's was his favourite night spot. He asked her to decorate his flat with pictures and furniture. She dragged him round Sotheby's and Christie's but possibly not Harrods, where her cheque had bounced. She wrote that Faisal resembled an Arab as played by Spike Milligan. She boasted that lavish presents arrived at her flat. If her claims are true, the prince she was fleecing was Prince Faisal bin Musaid Abdulaziz Al Saud, the nephew and assassin of King Faisal of Saudi Arabia. Prince Faisal was fond of blondes. His regular girlfriend was a West German fellow student at Berkeley, California. I can't back up Mariella's claims. It is possible he spent some time in London and he had a documented taste for drugs. (In 1969 he picked up a charge of conspiracy to supply LSD.)

It is possible he fell for Mariella. He also had a taste for outsiders. His girlfriend told reporters that Faisal had become radicalised during his time at Berkeley. He spent a lot of time with Arab Marxists and supporters of the Palestinian Liberation Organization. He was anti-Zionist and embarrassed at being part of a socially conservative royal family whose main interest was in cooperating with American oil interests. Reports from the time show a young man who was struggling to find his place in a highly politicised society. So it is conceivable that he could have spent time with a woman like Mariella. Especially if she could hook him up with some drugs.

She also managed to bag the Secretary General of the Arts Council. She kept names out of it but dropped a few clues. He was a Knight and CBE, he wrote articles in the *Sunday Times* and Mariella made love to him across a fabulous Chippendale pedestal desk. This one transposition of furniture – from bed to desk – turned an ordinary lover into an extraordinary one, she said.

At the very end of the twentieth century, in 1999, Freud's portrait of Litvinoff sold at Christie's for £1,156,500. The catalogue described its 'medieval quality', the 'weather-beaten head ... wrapped in a coarse scarf'. Straight out of Breughel's Flemish Renaissance. Straight out of Soho more like.

One summer's day in 2016 I was sitting in the bar of a hotel in Earl's Court surrounded by Portuguese estate agents. They were attending a conference on promoting resorts and health spas in the UK. Over two Americanos, Tricky Dicky told me of a reading he had attended in Bloomsbury. The talk had been given by Kieron Pym, the author of *Jumpin' Jack Flash*, a biography of David Litvinoff. Tricky was amused to hear members of Pym's 'middle class' audience tut-tutting at the Kray twins' behaviour. When I asked him if he had enjoyed the event, he shrugged and said, 'It was something to do.' He thought about it a bit. 'It was something for them to do as well.'

(I had a sense that he was enjoying keeping me hanging on: now that he had agreed to tell me the story, he would do so at his own pace and in his own way. That is the prerogative of the one doing the telling, and the person listening has none at all, or only that of giving up and leaving.)

A long time ago, he continued, when he had been on the run, Tricky had stayed in Litvinoff's mews house in Kensington. The twist in this particular tale (and there is always a twist in Tricky's tales) is that he was the guest, not of Litvinoff, but of the Krays. Litvinoff owed them money. So the twins had taken the lease to Litvinoff's flat and a spare set of keys as security for the debt. When Tricky did some favours for them and needed a place to stay, they gave him Litvinoff's keys.

'He came home, found me sitting on the sofa and offered me a drink,' Tricky said. 'Didn't know who I was. Didn't turn a hair. Just offered me a drink.' This was the key to Litvinoff's character. He comes home to find a shifty-looking stranger sitting on his sofa, making himself at home, and he shows no alarm, no indignation, not even curiosity. He just offers him a drink and sits down for a friendly chat. Litvinoff adapted to a constantly changing set of circumstances in order to survive, even if it was only for the next five minutes. There was no end to him. There was no end to his performance.

Litvinoff could chat to anyone, as could Mariella. This was the cautionary tale. He could be whoever you wanted him to be, so don't go looking for who he was because he wasn't. If Mariella knew this, she didn't care. If she recoiled at his clingy charm, she did not show it. Litvinoff capitalised on knowing stuff about people. He avoided intimate relationships, not even indulging in casual sex. He was the sexless yin to her sexually aggressive yang.

In Chelsea, Mariella slid silently and inexorably, like a shadow, to the edge of the crowd. She watched the potheads and ate some soul food. She denied using drugs or alcohol but her conflicting attitudes spoke of someone who glamorised her own use and belittled that of others. Heroin made a deep impact on the counterculture, on the student left, and the New Left at large. Mariella saw herself as part of the radical set, and the ritual of heroin consumption was a sort of everyday radical praxis. So she hung out with Michael X, the leader of the Viet Grove Set, and with

David Litvinoff, the Court Jester to the Chelsea Popocracy, and shut behind her the door to self-destruction.

* * *

On 6 May 1972 she was interviewed by Ray Connolly for the *Evening Standard*. Connolly covers the conflicting versions of her origins, citing Blackpool, Prague, the FBI and the Czech Embassy. Mariella insists that her name is Novotny, and that Mariella 'is too silly and stagey – so I just stick to Novotny – not Mrs or Miss – just Novotny'. She was trying to reinvent herself.

Next Connolly tackles the question of her age. She could be anything from twenty-seven (to which she admits) to thirty-three. She will in fact be thirty-two in three days. He states that in a couple of weeks she is off to America for the publication of *King's Road* and that she is putting the finishing touches to her next novel, *The Big Sell*.

Next he describes her apartment. It's in Mayfair. It is tiny and smells of joss sticks. It is sparsely furnished. She does not need very much other than her records – and her multi-postered walls are testimony to her interest in rock music. Jim Morrison stares down at us. She tells us again of her childhood displacement and a return to England at the age of ten. In an undisclosed location she met her mother, whom she did not know.

Then there is a new development. 'After that I was sent to stay with friends in France, and then with friends in the Russian sector of Austria. I always seemed to be in places where I was isolated and afraid of something big and bad outside.'

I have no corroboration for this but she was clearly getting a handle on her early misfortune. When she finally came back to England her mother moved them to Hampstead. Mariella claims she sent her to a finishing school to learn all the right things, and then 'because I considered myself very beautiful I became a model. And for a while I did quite well.'

'But I didn't know anything about men – nothing at all. Not even how babies were born, and although there were all these fellows trying to date me and score with me, I always used to go home. Then I met a man who was much older than me called Hod Dibben who restored historical buildings and after a week he asked me to marry him. I met him at a party with my mother.'

Connolly had done his research and read the cuttings. He interpolated on behalf of his readers that they actually met at the Black Sheep Club where she worked as a hostess. Her reinvented self was not convincing him.

Well, I didn't know what to do but I agreed to marry him on condition that I didn't have to do any housework, any cooking or have any children. And he agreed. We were married at Caxton Hall when I was 18, and I had an 18-tiered cake – one for every year of my life. Then on the wedding night I went to bed in my pyjamas and with a book by Somerset Maugham – and Hod eventually had to tell me all the clinical details. When I heard I said 'that's not for me' and so three weeks later I was still a virgin. He was very patient. And then it happened. And I began to think 'this has possibilities!'. I mean my curiosity was definitely aroused. That's probably why I am like I am now – making up for lost time.

Some of the details differ from her written account – she was reading Bertrand Russell not Maugham. She had sex with a stranger, not with Hod three weeks later, but the gist of it is there. Rehashing the Man in the Mask story, she produced the very mask from the drawer of a sideboard, asking Connolly to observe the delicacy of the workmanship that had gone into it. Then, 'after all that bother', if she didn't go and get pregnant.

'At first she couldn't believe it. But there it was and she had a daughter in February 1964. She called her October.'

Where is the child now, Connolly asks.

'She went to a boarding school when she was six. Hod and I are getting a divorce this year, and we live apart now.'

This was news to me: the first mention of a split between her and Hod. Connolly is more concerned with little Henrietta/October. He asks if she misses her mother.

'No, I give her a lot of attention. And I send her letters and go to see her. What about children in homes – do they get any parental love? Did I get any parental love?'

Oh dear.

How much did she see of October? Connolly persists.

'Oh – like any other child - half terms, full terms. She comes here, or goes to stay with my mother or relations. She gets so many invitations. I'd like to have another child some day – a boy.'

Very quickly we move back to the subject of her books. All six books have been written and sent to her agent in New York. Two completed manuscripts are lying neatly typed on her desk.

'I usually write four days a week. And work very hard. I'm also working on a documentary for the BBC and I want to write a play next.'

She revels in her nickname of Naughty Novotny 'and there's no one naughtier than me. It's fun and I like it. I don't drink or take drugs [once again], and I think the most exciting thing I can do is to make love. Nobody ever dies from making love, do they?'

And what of the future?

She replies in that airy manner that disguises everything and hides nothing – Oh, so many people keep asking her to get married when her present marriage is dissolved. But for the future all she wants to do is to keep on working and writing and being naughty...

'For a girl with her background (whatever it may be) she remains totally, incomprehensibly naive.'

The accompanying photo shows Mariella bottomless. A black tunic with a low-slung belt, the same spiky eyes and Julie Christie bob, draped over a desk, pen in hand, looking over her shoulder at the reader, caught in the act of thinking naughty thoughts.

She kept writing but no one wanted to read her. *King's Road* is a cold text. It isn't autobiographical and it is autobiographical. Reconstructed from Novotny's misadventures in the world of sexpionage and sexploitation, the account does not adhere too closely to actual events. Real characters come and go, their names changed. Mariella does not appear in palpable form. She does not tell everything that happened, nor did everything happen that she tells. It is as though the truth is too incredible, so she has to make up something incredulous.

All I could really see was that she was very productive. During the gestation of her novel Mariella had also been involved in writing a memoir with the aid of Michael Eddowes. 'This is the age of conspiracy,' says a character in Don DeLillo's *Running Dog* (1978), 'the age of connections, links, secret relationships.' The possible nightmare of being totally controlled by unseen agencies was never far away in either of their minds. Eddowes wanted Mariella's input on the assassination of John F. Kennedy. He was determined to uncover the real identity and motivation of the killer. To Eddowes, Novotny was the link to a Soviet plot to discredit Western leaders. As mentioned earlier, he claimed to have discovered a group in London 'who had destroyed Profumo and sent a young woman, Maria Novotny, to destroy the character of President Kennedy. She was the cousin of President Novotny of Czechoslovakia.'

Eddowes' book, *November 22nd: How They Killed Kennedy*, suggested that Lee Harvey Oswald had been replaced by a lookalike KGB agent when he went to the Soviet Union. He spent over $10,000 in October 1981 on legal fees and exhumation costs involved in reopening Oswald's grave. He arranged for a new autopsy with the consent of Marina Porter (Oswald) to see if the grave contained Oswald or a double. Accusations of conspiracy theorist of course hang around him, but it is worth recalling that Eddowes was a respected solicitor; he had obtained a Royal Pardon for Timothy Evans and had written a best-selling book on the case, *A Man on Your Conscience*. In Stephen Dorrill's analysis of Eddowes's conclusions, he finds it strange that although central to his theory on the assassination, Mariella is only briefly mentioned in the introduction to the book.

This could be because he was three-quarters of the way though Mariella's Jackanory when two men broke into his flat and beat him badly, leaving him bleeding on his bed. They warned him to stay away from her. The day before, one of Mariella's boyfriends reported to his other girlfriend that Mariella had narrowly escaped a serious accident in her car. The steering had failed. Bolts had been cut. Hod passed on this information to Eddowes. He burned the manuscript. He would pursue the matter no further.

The idea of conspiracy offers an odd sort of comfort in an uncertain age: it makes sense of the inexplicable, accounting for complex events in a clear, if frightening, way. To put it another way, 'writers' like Eddowes and Mariella offer an alternative, shifting vision of reality, creating a master narrative, a grand scheme capable of explaining all the complex events assailing the readers of news media. Their writings have the added bonus of being virtually impossible to confirm. Yet this built-in impediment to certainty is precisely why their theories and postulations continue to flourish (at least online) in an age supposedly marked by the disappearance of grand explanatory schemes and master narratives.

For Mariella, already an adept in the Occult, her theories came with a quasi-religious conviction, a sense that the conspiracy in question was an entity with almost supernatural powers.

27

WOMEN'S LIBBER –
AND GROWING UP

The surge of conspiracy narratives that swept through Mariella's life stems not from a specific historical development – such as Watergate, the Kennedy assassination, or even the Cold War – but from the larger sense of diminished human agency, a feeling that individuals cannot effect meaningful social action. 'At this moment in history,' wrote R. D. Laing in 1967, 'we are The Culture *of* Paranoia all caught in the hell of frenetic passivity.' In other words, our minds were disturbingly lively, and our bodies were frightening inert. In 1972 Mariella met a woman she liked. Serena Wadham was a photojournalist specialising in social issues, a committee member on various do-good agencies, a woman with an agenda. Wadham was a doer. This is what she had to say about Mariella.

Mariella Novotny, 27, is the first hardback novelist to be photographed without the cover of her clothes. Her first book, *King's Road*, was published in Britain last November, and it will appear in Germany later this year. Its publisher, Leslie Frewin, is negotiating sales to other Continental countries and to the USA where it will be in paperback. Mariella was married at 18 to a man much older than herself and she has one daughter, who is now at the preparatory school for Benenden, where Princess Anne was educated.

Fact check: Mariella was thirty-one in 1972. She was quite possibly the first novelist to be photographed by Wadham nude. In the background, Frewin had negotiated a French translation and a US edition which were duly published. The German edition has not come to light. There is not and never has been a prep school for Benenden.

Later this year, Mariella hopes to get a divorce. Her husband is Hod Dibben, and he is interested in restoring historical buildings and in night-clubs. They do not live together. Mariella has a flat in Dover St. near the Ritz.

So Mariella was plotting her escape from Hod. She was living alone in Mayfair. This could be the same flat in which Mariella was photographed for Ray Connolly's article. Dover Street is the nexus of London's Club Land. The Albemarle, the Arts Club, Drone's and the Empress Club are the most illustrious. This last was a ladies-only club set up by one of Queen Victoria's ladies-in-waiting. Mayfair was where 'fashionable bachelors lurk disconsolately on their evenings at home', according to Evelyn Waugh. It was where you went if you had to attend a ball at the Grosvenor House Hotel. Green Park to one side, Hyde Park to the other, and the brothels of the notorious Shepherd's Market in the middle, Mayfair catered for indoor activities as well as outdoor. Long the retreat of London's wealthy and famous, where fortunes were won and lost at exclusive gambling clubs, Mayfair must have been heaven for Mariella.

Soon after her marriage, Mariella left for the USA to work as a model. When she was lunching with Peter Lawford, John F

Kennedy's brother-in-law, in New York, they saw JFK across the room and Mariella was introduced to him. It was the beginning of a friendship.

True.

After J. F. Kennedy's assassination, Mariella was asked by a lawyer with access to secret information in the CIA's files to write a book about it. There was a meeting with a publisher, but the project was abandoned after Mariella had been threatened by four unknown men.

The specificity is convincing. Why four? Why not one or two? This could also be a clue to Mariella's introduction to the British Secret Services and her subsequent work for them.

Revolution, rape, murder, Black Power (and now Women's Lib) are all ingredients of Mariella's world of romance and violence. As a cousin of President Novotny of Czechoslovakia, she has been used to them since her childhood.

As has been seen, accounts of her childhood vary. But rape in some form or another is almost certainly an ingredient of her world of romance and violence. And yes, she was used to it since childhood.

Her plans for the future include more books and more fun. She loves five people, she says, including her daughter.

So who are the others? Before we can summon up these ghosts, Wadham quotes Mariella. 'I'm only good at two things. One pays the rent and my bills and the other is for kicks.' I'm guessing sex paid the rent and her bills, and writing was for kicks.

Wadham offers a perspective on Mariella that is worth recording. She photographed countless squats, sit-ins, demonstrations and peace marches in and around London. Between the mid-sixties and the mid-seventies she assembled a long series of studies of women at work, from the sculptor Barbara Hepworth and the composer Elisabeth Lutyens to scientists, writers, gardeners, a coach driver, and a London cabby. Her aim to publish them in book form never materialised. But her notes for this book as quoted above show that Mariella was taking herself seriously as an author and women's libber and that she was separating herself from her *roué* husband.

It was time to move on. Women like Wadham were making names for themselves and they were inviting Mariella to play her part in the liberation movement. Wadham called Mariella a sixties mini-icon and a British Barbarella.

With a write-up like that, who needs a bankrupt like Hod?

***

Leading trauma theorists hold that the mark of a traumatic experience is that it escapes language. This reinforces my belief that Mariella kept writing because she was trying to put into words what had happened that left such a deep imprint on her psyche. But she was living in a society that had not fully learned yet to respect women's voices. Where these voices were beginning to be heard caused a new set of problems for Mariella. She was a woman who stood outside feminist hierarchies and theories of liberation.

So Editions de Trévise published in France and New England Library published in the States. Although she did not publish again, she did not stop reporting on her activities. The seventies saw Mariella adapting to survive. Her decision to write was not a confirmation of a creative, life-affirming vocation. It was a form of incoherence, of mumbling, an early indication of what was her curse. Without getting her heart or soul involved, she continued to broach a heavy subject – the relationship between sex and power.

She had found a new reading public, and it was very private. Between 1975 and 1978 Mariella was working undercover for the Pain Inquiry, an investigation headed by the Chief Constable of Kent into police corruption in the Flying Squad. Her chief target was my grandfather, Charlie Taylor, a London conman who had high-ranking officers in his deep pockets. Mariella brought them all down.

The claims she made are incendiary. British secret services set her up with Persons of Interest. They sent her to Brussels in the capacity of a 'party hostess'. She met technocrats and MEPs and Black Power activists. She kept notes of everything, but the evidence gets sketchy and frustratingly vague. The burglar and his portable archive disappear in a puff of smoke. The men who write about her – historians and journalists – dismiss her in pejorative terms, focussing on her strident sexuality.

Still in the glare of publicity from her novel's publication, on 11 January 1973 she was interviewed by Paul Callan for the *Daily Mail*. She was writing her second book, she told him. 'Tentatively entitled *The Hot Years*, it promises – judging from the synopsis – to be a most provocative *oeuvre*.'

Callan reports that the book's most 'revealing' section is her meeting with Stephen Ward and 'the subsequent invitation to the Soviet Embassy where she met the Russian diplomat Eugen Ivanov'. The reasoning behind her decision to ditch the second novel in favour of a memoir was unclear, he said. Especially since 'at the time of her publication of her novel … the blurb writers really went to town. "The natural successor to Harold Robbins" was the wail.'

So what made Mariella change her mind?

Callan tells us that the previous October Mariella had attended the Labour Party conference in Blackpool. She discussed prison reform with the social reformer Lord Longford. Her way into the conference was possibly through one of the extra-curricular debates that year. Dubbed a 'Press Gang' by the *Observer* newspaper, this was a public meeting held on 2 October 1970 organised jointly by the Labour Newspaper Group and the Free Communications Group. The exercise was an effort to get the Labour Party to realise that anxiety about press bias was real and that the future of the industry was under threat.

In her flat I picture Mariella surrounded by piles of paper and bric-a-brac that Hod could not shift. Newspapers were still in black and white and blissfully thin. Only the Sundays carried more than one section. I imagine her trawling through the editorials and features grasping at the zeitgeist. A weekend in Blackpool might clear the air.

The Free Communications Group was thought to be a revolutionary body. But it was actually made up of left-wing newsmen and television professionals whose concern was that media outlets would get into fewer and fewer hands through takeovers and mergers. The Labour Newspaper Group included MPs who were practising journalists, such as Michael Foot. The group contended that within ten years there would likely be just two daily newspapers in Britain.

The head of the Labour Group designed a poster for the Blackpool meeting that looked like a playbill and listed the speakers like music-hall acts. Lord Longford topped the bill. Malcolm Muggeridge, 'straight from the pulpit', was making an appearance. Stuart Hood, former controller of BBC1, was speaking. Act number five was Dick Brigginshaw, the powerful General Secretary of the newspaper union NATSOPA. He was billed as 'a worthy representative of the working classes'.

Longford would have been a fascinating figure to Mariella. He had befriended the notorious Moors murderers, Ian Brady and Myra Hindley. When critics asked why he did not do more for the victims of crimes, Longford responded with the motto of St Augustine: 'hate the sin and love the sinner.' He was a campaigner and author; he waded into the moral quagmire surrounding the crimes of child sex abuse, rape and murder. The wings of hair that framed his balding pate and trademark pebble glasses would have singled him out for Mariella as her kind of target. But she kept her interest legit. She was into politics now and Lord Longford walked the walk. She must have made a favourable impression on him because he turned up to the preview of a film made by her next collaborator.

Mariella was being taken seriously as a thinking woman rather than as a pretty woman. She was discussing prison reform with a Law Lord in a febrile party-political setting. How seriously Mariella was able to enter into this conversation, what insights she might have had, remain intangibles. Judging from her television interviews she was able to retain her poise and focus under pressure. She was used to dinner-party conversation with the likes of Dr Eustace Chesser, Lord Astor and an assortment of aristocrats. She enjoyed controversy. She needed to shock and to educate.

This new venture was a film intended for sex education classes in schools, and it was called *Growing Up*. In recent years there have been investigations into the circle of protection that enveloped disgraced clerics, do-gooders, DJs and politicians. It is now acknowledged that in all cases where sexual abuse has been proved, the victim or victims should be the primary concern. In the seventies there was still a taint of guilt, or at least shame, associated with the victims of sex crimes. It is safe to say that in the minds of judges and the general populace, sex workers and young girls in mini-skirts were fair game. Some would claim that the age of consent (sixteen in Britain) was a bit of a movable feast, and that some teenagers of fifteen or so were no longer children, so 'paedophile' was not the exact application. Well into the eighties boundaries were blurred around the notion of paedophilia, with the notorious Paedophile Information Exchange even receiving government funding in the spirit of permissiveness and open-mindedness. Mariella herself had cloudy notions of what constitutes abuse, so she was not alone in perpetuating its horror.

The director of *Growing Up* was British sexologist and campaigner for abortion reform, Martin Cole, dubbed 'Sex King Cole' by the *Sun*. Mariella would have applauded his credentials because at this point they looked impressive. He was Chairman of the Birmingham Group of the Abortion Law Reform Association and involved in setting up clinics for advice on sexual matters, contraception and abortion. Following the Abortion Act 1967 he was a founder of the Birmingham Pregnancy Advisory Service (which later became the British Pregnancy Advisory Service). This laudable organisation assisted women to get legal abortions, initially using the front room of Dr Cole's home for consultations in 1968. His standing is at least partly undermined when we learn that Dr Cole was a Doctor in Plant Genetics and that in 1971 he married one of his students from Aston University, where he lectured in Botany. I would hazard a guess that extra-curricular interest was in human reproduction.

In 1966, he established an Institute of Sex Education and Research; whether this was also in his front room I cannot say. Dr Cole was especially notorious for pioneering 'surrogate partner therapy' for shy virgins. This took place in a clinic that used 'sexologically trained women' to have sex with men who were experiencing erectile dysfunction.

'I am obviously in a position to advise him on several sex matters,' Mariella told the *Daily Mirror*'s gossip columnist. Hers was a voice to be reckoned with in the radical new field of 'sex therapy'. Via the Labour Party she had entered an arena where concerns surrounding a nascent neoliberal marketplace were being aired. Pro-prostitution discourse had begun to present the sex worker as an empowered and rational businesswoman peddling her wares just like any other worker. Mariella wanted to advertise herself as educated, sophisticated, appreciating fine wines and gentlemen, and coming from a good family. She presented herself as having entered into prostitution in order to satisfy her ravenous sexual appetites.

It was the 'middle-classing' of prostitution and it happened organically as a result of the increasing practice of focusing on individual experiences rather than on the collective or in terms of broader trends; on what things look like, rather than what they actually are. Mariella would have argued that sex work is a job that, while not exactly like any other, still contains the sorts of tensions, vexations, financial pressures and freedoms that define the lives of other workers under capitalism.

Like so many issues involving women, debates about sex work are bogged down in the question of whether sex work itself is 'degrading' or 'empowering'. She would have enjoyed the attention, the cut and thrust of debate. Ultimately, however, whether it is good or bad, whether sex workers are deluded or voiceless victims, sex workers are associated with sex, and to be associated with sex is to have a short shelf life.

In 1975 I find Mariella at the wrong end of Fulham. She is back with Hod. She is suffering. She is suffering because Leslie Frewin, who had published her novel, had not followed through on his contractual obligation to publish her sequel. Also, she thought it was the noise from the street that was bothering her. But it was not. It was the silence – except for Hod, who had the impertinence to want to talk to her.

He was bankrupt again. This latest insolvency followed a series of articles by the *Sunday Times* Insight team on price-fixing in auction houses. With this latest setback in mind, she sat at the Louis XV *escritoire*. It was a reproduction. So much of what Hod is reported to have said and done dissolves into fakery like a salesman's patter. But while it lasted he created the illusion that prospects were good.

Unlike Hod, Mariella was busy addressing herself mentally. I see her making herself ready to embark on another chapter in her strange and turbulent history. I see her mind clouding and notorious figures from her past emerging from the mist. Mariella's involvement with Dr Cole was a tip-off from Jackie. By the time I met the former stripper and long-time waif, she had found her way to the meeting rooms of 12-Step recovery.

The great thing about recovering addicts is that they have a great need to talk. So alongside the rapid speech patterns of a detox-ing junkie I was assimilating trends in Japanese game avatars, genomics, bio-informatics, and online platforms. I was stuck in the doorway of Number One Frith Street, the Soho Centre for Health and Care. It is a large, welcoming doorway, which was just as well as it was raining. Jackie had popped out of a meeting of Narcotics Anonymous for a cigarette. She was an incongruous sight: a tiny sixty-year-old woman in baggy sweat pants and a hooded top. Next to us was a very excited man having a heated conversation with his mobile. 'Neuroscience,' he said, 'is just a concept enjoying its moment in the sun.'

I was finding it hard to concentrate on the sad, shattered story Jackie was delivering between drags on her fag. I was stuck in a doorway but it wasn't just any doorway because it was a hub for the transfer of diverging strands of information. The media type, with his messenger bag tucked between his legs and his phone nestled between ear and shoulder was superficially more compelling, energised by blossoming systems of thought and new ways to commodify. I felt guilty as I eavesdropped on his conversation while Jackie's monologue rehearsed the cause of her present situation. Finally I brought her back to Mariella.

'After the Michael X scene I met her at a strip club in Moor Street. I was working the curtains and the record-player. She wanted me to pass round cards to men in the audience. She had been in discussions with Cole to set up a London branch of his sex clinic. The address she gave me was a room in Mayfair. It all seemed a bit iffy to me. I told her she should try stripping. Strippers didn't get paid much but they did a lot of gigs. You used to see them running round Soho with shopping bags full of outfits. I told her I knew one girl who was putting her boy through private school. She asked for her number.'

The film *Growing Up* was released in 1971 and Lord Longford joined Mariella for the London showing. He then went on to debate in the House of Commons with Mrs Thatcher, Secretary of State for Education and Science, whether the film was pornography. It *is* 'a kind of pornography', said one reviewer, 'that makes sex a cold, loveless place and the stealer of dreams'.

Dr Cole – advocate of 'wife-swapping' – was finally discredited when on 6 December 1972, Jill Knight, MP for Birmingham Edgbaston, brought a motion to the House of Commons. She told the house that Cole offered sex therapy in a clinical setting. But when Knight's constituent applied for a position with him, Cole said that she should use her own flat. There was no question of a clinic. Among the reasons he gave was that some clients might want to stay for a weekend. Knight's constituent, Miss X, was paid £1.50 per session by Cole. When she asked about contraception he said, 'We must not have any of our therapists getting pregnant, although you need not worry – we can always get you an abortion.' As Dr Cole helped establish the first abortion clinic in Birmingham, he had the right contacts for this.

Knight went on to tell the House that Miss X was warned she might have to deal with some very weird types, and that some might be on drugs. But Cole said that he thought he could recognise any potentially dangerous client and she was not to worry.

In the final analysis, it was decided that Dr Cole was not a sex therapist and that he was in fact running a brothel. The film, like Mariella, was a strange sign of the times, and thankfully disappeared as quickly as it surfaced.

Mariella held on to the phone number Jackie B had given her. She still had her room in Dover Street and in 1973 New England Library published the paperback of *King's Road*. There was still a chance for her to join a new movement of feminism. The pursuit of sexual freedom without exploitation was one of the core themes espoused by Germaine Greer in her numerous contributions to a magazine called *Suck*. While *Suck* was never intended as a specifically feminist 'sex paper', Greer's contributions prefigure what became known as 'sex-positive' feminism. This was a minority position that emerged in response to the 'sex wars' of the seventies and the calls for censorship by such groups as Women Against Pornography. Greer's self-help-inflected, body-positive essays bore such titles as 'Lady Love Your Cunt', 'Bounce Titty Bounce' and 'Ladies Get on Top for Better Orgasms'. The tenor of female empowerment was echoed by other *Suck* headlines such as 'Women Need Whore Houses' and 'Can a Woman Fuck a Man?' Mariella would have had the answer to that one.

28

CLUB INTERNATIONAL

Revisionist historians might be tempted to view feminist porn as a radical feminist triumph. Mariella would have. But the catalyst for this woman-focused copy was still male desire. In writing about sex Mariella was distorting her fears and desires through the lens of a male readership.

At some point in 1972, Tricky Dicky came across a semi-clad, bewigged woman in her early thirties in a room above a film club in Soho. The sex shops and strip clubs had spread so thickly that between the restaurants, pubs, coffee bars and delis there was an intermittent frieze of leering, bulging women. The signs contested in shrill superlatives: 'SEXIEST', 'SAUCIEST', 'NAUGHTIEST', 'MOST EXCITING', 'MOST GLAMOROUS', 'MOST INTIMATE'.

We were a long way from Second Empire Paris. Open from 11.30 a.m. until 2.30 the following morning, the Princess Club offered a 'lunchtime scene' with four strips every Thursday, Friday and Saturday. There was an admission fee of just 10 pence plus pub-price drinks and cheap pub grub. The Princess was billed as the 'ideal businessmen's meeting place', offering 'fabulous strips' by the 'International Sex Queen, Mariella Novotny'. If that didn't promise enough, you could always dive back into the network of alleys, around the doorways and the Aladdin's lobbies where the neon flickered and the lamps flared in haloes highlighting curves and contortions, and meet up with porn queen Fiona Richmond (in the flesh) at Raymond's Revue on Walker's Court.

Jackie taught Mariella to strip. They tried out the *nom de strip-teaseuse* Lady Henrietta Bath for a while. But her need to cash in on her notoriety won out over her desire for anonymity. Maybe she had school fees to pay, but she was entering the underbelly of whoredom.

Naughty Novotny, a burglar called Tricky and Jackie converged on a node of sexual frustration and suppressed violence. Men watched while Mariella peeled off her boa and satin gloves and strutted on a stage in tail feathers and stiletto heels. She is followed by a brunette (Jackie) lying on a spot-lit divan. She wears a black gossamer bra, tiny black pants, fishnet stockings, the thread of a suspender belt. She unfolds a *billet doux* that leads to the biting of her lower lip. Her eyes start to gyrate. Her underwear re-jigs itself. Ranged in front of her is a board meeting of company directors. In the makeshift theatre's amber glow, the tiered rows of lounge chairs are coiled with cigar smoke. Through the strains of 'Blues in the Night' comes the clink of ice in G&Ts, and the grunt of expert pundits.

Over on Walker's Court a well-dressed man is making a killing out of naked women. In 1971 his fortune was estimated at around £3.5 million. Meet Mariella's next employer.

On 21 April 1958 in the former Doric Ballroom on Brewer's Street, a thirty-two-year-old Glossop-born dealer in nylons was reborn as the owner of Raymond's Revue Bar. A neon sign over the entrance in Walker's Court proclaimed Raymond's Revue to be the 'World Centre of Erotic Entertainment'.

Paul Raymond's business interests had major consequences for the locals. The writer Daniel Farson attacked the negative impact of the sex trade on the 'authentic artisans' of Soho. However, there is an argument that the authentic article that kept Soho going was sex. In the first fortnight of takings for the Revue, Raymond accepted over eight thousand membership applications. This netted receipts over £4,000.

'Very good going for a club which has been opened for 11 days,' a police spokesman said. The Revue Bar was described by Raymond's press agent as 'the Athenaeum of the strip clubs'. This was no joke. The names of the members were confidential. But a reporter from the *Spectator* noted that among those listed were 'ten MPs, eight millionaires, more than sixty knights, thirty-five peers and enough businessmen and captains of industry to drain dry the Stock Exchange and the Savoy Grill when a new whipping act is being staged'.

In 1964 Raymond branched into literature. He started the first imitation of *Playboy* magazine in the UK, called *King*. His lasting contributions to the top shelf were *Men Only* and *Club International*. The first of these lasted longest because it showed no reverence whatsoever for the written word.

Club International was launched in 1972. Editor Tony Power – a wannabe wideboy and hipster – and art director Steve Ridgeway – a superannuated Georgian popinjay – assembled a diverse pool of contributors, including art critic and cultural commentator George Melly, and, in a rare lapse of taste, the Stately Homosexual Quentin Crisp. The artwork was where the real action was. It relied heavily on soft-focus nostalgia: Victorian brocade petticoats, ostrich fans, and velvet pantaloons curled around breast- and crotch-shots. Men's fashions were of the peacock variety, usually accessorised by a naked woman, as were the adverts for cars, whisky, cigars and other assorted male paraphernalia.

Mariella's debut appearance was in the May 1973 issue. 'Exactly ten years ago,' the introductory blurb reads, 'a major scandal rocked the entire British Parliamentary system ... after much soul-searching, [Mariella Novotny] has finally agreed to *Club International* serialising her life during those and later, scandalous times. This first instalment implicates many famous personalities, one of them the most famous American politician of this century.'

29

FROM THE CARPATHIANS
TO NEW YORK

So, another chapter. Her portrait is engraved on the Czech nation's banknotes. She suffers an isolated childhood that is forgotten the moment she tastes power via sex with JFK. Brought back to Southampton, she finds her ageing husband and fretting mother waiting for her. She has memories that cannot lie down, particularly her recollection of that 'Russian military gang-bang':

> I was put to bed with a sedative. I awoke the next day to find that my vision had dropped to a nine-inch radius. No one could explain the whys and wherefores of this sudden optical loss ... I had to settle for spectacles. This, in a way, is a blessing, as now I do not have to see who or what I don't want to see.

This first instalment keeps tripping over Mariella's mother and her desire to rise above her.

'Over the years I gathered a sack full of tricks to outwit her. I once pretended to have lost my memory and power of speech when she showered her wrath upon me for not devoting myself to becoming a brilliant ballet dancer.'

An education is obtained. She is working on her story at breakneck speed. Always in the same dishevelled room, bedecked with trophies. With the hi-fi blasting out the voices in her head, she puts pen to paper.

The day the Reds deposed the government, I heard my Father say that the *putsch* was coming. He refused to leave the resistance. Mother refused to leave him. So I was to return to England with the family agent. We bumped along the rough track for miles on a cart pulled by mules. It took us through the plains into the river valley. We watched as trains thundered by with their carriages and sleeping compartments. Somewhere on the border with Austria we found an inn. The landlord led us into the cellar. We lay side by side on the stone floor surrounded by barrels. 'If only he had listened to us,' Rutter, my father's agent, was lamenting. I tried to follow him back and forth, as he tried to figure a way back to private property and the rule of the elite.

I woke as dawn came through the wide slats of the latched window. The rising sun did its best to chase away the images that were floating across my mind: the city's boulevards, the palaces, and spirals. I turned to look for Rutter. He had gone, but he had pinned a note to my coat with some currency. I would have to try and get on without him.

Mariella pauses. She picks up the sheet of paper she has just completed. Both sides are filled with the overwrought calligraphy I glimpsed in the pub on Berwick Street. She cannot stay still. Instead of pursuing her adventures across the Carpathians she has moved the scene to New York and her debacle with J. Edgar Hoover's FBI.

'Months after Suzy Chang and I played nurse with "the Senator", I was in another room with another man. He was a cop. I was a minor.'

She is so real to me I can see her putting the pen down. She frowns. Somewhere in her file she has a cutting from the *New York Post*.

It is dated October 1961. She must find it. It confirms what she has always known. Someone, somewhere, is listening to her.

'Mariella Novotny, the beauty involved in vice charges here with British TV producer Harry Alan Towers, is the object of frenzied bidding by English book publishers who want to put her first-person story between the covers. She's received several movie offers, too.'

So she continues. 'FBI agents smuggled me on board the *Queen Mary*. By the time I got to Southampton, I was ready to sell my story of teen vice, the President-Elect and Agent Towers to the *News of the World*.'

Pretence was endemic in a world where survivors reinvented themselves and in the process shook off guilt. By the seventies the Second World War had dwindled in importance, but it was like one of those family feuds that last for generations. It was best not to talk about it or where you were or what you were doing while it was going on.

Some kind of study facilitated Mariella's entry into high society. Possibly between them it was the ministrations of Stephen Ward, the Svengali to dozens of provincial teenagers, and Hod, the creator of Patsy Morgan Dibben. The result was a woman who professed herself an adept at the hunting, shooting, fishing lifestyle:

'My gun looks like a donkey's hind leg because I shoot from my left shoulder but use my right eye, hence a two and quarter inch cast-off. My shooting parties became particularly popular especially in the autumn. Tall bracken can make an excellent hide for a quick poke.'

Shooting parties took on a new meaning:

'I can claim a record for having every male member of the party without any one of them guessing I'd had all the rest.'

Then her artistic credentials are enumerated.

Peggy Guggenheim, who I had known in New York, Venice and London, had turned me on to the Modern Art scene with the help of Prince Ashwin Lipple, curator of Chinese Art at the Metropolitan Museum in New York.

Over the years I've made friends with characters such as Feliks Topolski, Count Manfred Czernin, Count Paolo Barrozzi, Count Luciano Bortolotto, Katy Howard of Castle Howard, Viscountess and Viscount Monck, Lord Asquith, Dr Eustace Chesser, Lord Longford, Jack Profumo, Steve McQueen, Jimi Hendrix, Sammy Davis Jnr., Jayne Mansfield, Walter Flack, Charles Clore, Huntington Hartford, Peter Lawford, Rita Hayworth, Richard Johnson, Anthony Quinn, Sean Connery, and so on.

I like to specialise in Presidents.

But the truth is she mixed with men like Ward, who 'held forth on Red politics and pink personalities as the temperature around him rose to feverish climaxes'. She discusses his fetish for high-heeled shoes and her kindly ministrations in facilitating one of his own feverish climaxes.

From Vegas to British parliamentary scandal to 'the horror of the Russian rape' – this is a scattergun approach to memoir. It is as though the monologue she has been rehearsing all her life is spilling out of her unchecked onto several pages of a men's magazine. It would perhaps be more suited to an analyst's couch because in essence she sexualises everything, even abuse. Perhaps the most telling line is this:

'I had once seen my father naked and erect but had no idea what it signified.'

This brings us back to Mariella's parentage. Christine Keeler and our old friend Swedish Sven are at one on this. Mariella's mother was a 'tart'. This is probably the most credible version of events. If this was the case, Stella Marie could have witnessed many scenes of sexual exploitation and even been exploited herself.

Mariella's inaugural article signs off with the farcical episode of her bridal night. 'The actual wedding was chaotic. I was given away by a surgeon-gynaecologist. This was because my father, at that moment, was having a life-and-death hassle in Prague with my uncle.'

The same photographer who snapped the pair on the day at Caxton Hall is the photographer who provides portraits of her for *Club International*: David Bailey.

30

FROM BRIXTON TO BRUSSELS

On 7 June 1973, Sex Pistols manager Malcolm McLaren and the record label Virgin arranged to charter a private boat and have the Sex Pistols perform while sailing down the River Thames. In July, Mariella informs her readers that she has attended the Silver Jubilee celebrations of a girls' preparatory school in 'Snobton'. In London, celebrations were hijacked by the news that police launches had forced a boat to dock, and constabulary surrounded the gangplanks at the pier. For once Mariella is playing it safe. She is marking the Queen's jubilee at a boarding-school jamboree because she has 'a goddaughter aged seven, or is it eight, being brainwashed there'.

In order to preserve her privacy and that of her daughter, Mariella invents a goddaughter. But she cannot disguise her lack of interest in this or any other child.

'Henrietta is a doll ... She holds me in awe (quite right) and specially requested that I show up.' The day passes with a Fortnum and Mason's picnic on the lawn, and a speech from the headmaster of Roedean, John Maitland Hunt. 'Henrietta said nothing, thank God, she sucked her thumb instead.' Prizes were presented, and 'I concealed my annoyance at the fact that Henrietta wasn't getting one or more'.

Riding events, dress parades, tea, gymnastic displays and a swimming gala do nothing to relieve the tedium. 'At 6pm I departed, exhausted but cheered at the thought that it would be a whole year before I would be called upon to attend another "open day".'

So bored and disillusioned is she that there is only one solution. She asks a 'spade' she knows, 'a super-stud' called Len, if he can fix up an all-black gangbang for her. She has already reminded us that Michael de Freitas AKA Michael X is locked up in Trinidad awaiting his appeal against the death sentence. She tells us of time spent in his circle: 'What I saw was shattering, but unfortunately he eventually broke my cover and tried to have me murdered.'

She goes on to say, 'The Black Power Party will never get me to sign the petition for clemency they are organising on Michael X's behalf. Rachman is dead, his henchman should join him. Much of my novel *King's Road* was thinly veiled fact and there is a lot more left for me to write about that period, sexy and sinister. I will tell you the story in full – or anyway in part – in my monthly column.'

Next for the enlightenment and elucidation of her readers Mariella embarks on a horrific foray 'on the south side of Battersea Bridge'. She arrives at a brightly painted terraced house in a district she does not know. This is Brixton.

Imagine a district in South London in a state of siege, its residents, mainly black, confronted by repeated police raids, with or without warrants, the trashing of their houses, searches, and assaults. Black people were told that if they didn't want to get arrested they should stay indoors. The widespread use of Section 24 of the 1824 Vagrancy Act led to its infamous nickname – the 'Sus' law.

> ... every suspected person or reputed thief, frequenting any river, canal, or navigable stream, dock, or basin, or any quay, wharf, or warehouse near or adjoining thereto, or any street, highway, or avenue leading thereto, or any place of public resort, or any avenue leading thereto, or any street, or any

highway or any place adjacent to a street or highway, with intent to commit an arrestable offence ... shall be deemed a rogue and vagabond and would be guilty of an offence, and be liable to be imprisoned for up to three months.

I lived close by in Brixton Hill. Mariella had yet to enter my family circle. Even as a seven-year-old I knew that Brixton was a no-go zone. As I came into my teens I grew even more wary. The Sus charge was one that affected young people most. 'Loitering with intent to commit a crime' was the justification for at least a stop-and-search. The Lambeth I knew consistently ranked highest in London for Sus arrests. So much so that most young people really did stay indoors.

Mariella found a room in the back streets of Brixton. Len led her up a dimly lit stairway into a bedroom. It was sparsely furnished and reeked of cannabis. The rest of the house was 'jam-packed already' according to Len. 'They're reading, listening to soul sounds and gambling ... shall we start?'

Mariella proceeds to have sex with around twenty-five black men. The next day she goes back for more. By the end of the month she has had hundreds. It is as though Mariella had to outdo the worst that men could offer. Her articles were being published in pages devoted to the type of pornography in which the basic components of sex crime are laid out amidst the iconography of glamour photography. The female body – and Mariella wanted it to be hers – was fetishised, displayed, adored, only so that, in the final analysis, she could be resented, possessed, profaned and finally sacrificed. All this in the same issue in which she holds cheap a child's need for a caring presence.

August 1973: Novotny has now dropped her first name and added an acute accent to the 'y' in Novotny. She tells her readers that she is working as an escort for captains of industry.

This was quite the fashion statement suitable for a magazine concerned with style and fetish. Again we can find precedents in history. Among the more fashionably progressive 'sexcorts' were the *grandes horizontales* of the nineteenth century, courtesans like Cora Pearl, a client of Charles Worth, the era's first celebrity designer; and Catherine Walters ('Skittles' to her public), riveting on horseback as she paraded through Hyde Park sewn into her riding ensemble.

Escorts offered 'the girlfriend experience'. The idea was to look conservative enough so that a client could take the escort to dinner, but to insert a throwaway, *risqué* detail, like thigh-high stockings. So Mariella adopted the A-line skirts with heels and a skimpy top. A scout called Thelma booked twenty or so escorts to entertain male execs after their works do. Mariella turned up at a Mayfair hotel suite and picked up a freight broker. They discussed the wheat, barley and maize markets. He told her he had lost a packet a couple of years back when the cold currents coming up from Antarctica took a wrong turn and swept the coast of Chile. He was heavily into the Chilean pilchard harvest but it bottomed out.

'What do you do?' he asked her.

'I write books,' she said. They had sex.

In September 1973 Mariella sits alongside an interview with the 'girls who edit that extremely radical women's magazine *Spare Rib*'. The journalists Rosie Boycott and Sandra Rowe 'do not approve of publications like *Club International* and *Men Only*, but nonetheless, the conversation proved a most entertaining experience'. Mariella meanwhile has 'captured the imagination of the country, and her mail to these offices is reaching astronomical proportions'. She is building up her readership with lengthy descriptions of penises and vaginas and their intercourse. This month she attends a reception in the The Hague, along with assorted VIPs and politicians. She is taken to tea at the House of Commons and spends an evening in the company of a famous boxer.

I can only infer that Mariella has taken a new direction. She tried stripping; that didn't pay well enough, and Mr Raymond over at the Revue Bar liked them in their early twenties. Her next bid for gainful employment was working as an escort. From here she moved into a position for which she was well qualified: hosting parties for businessmen, technocrats and those aforementioned captains of industry. The party that she describes in September 1973 was organised by an outfit called Parkland Research Europe S.A. She was hired to arrange the guest list.

Parkland was the company responsible for producing the riveting page-turner *A Guide to national practices in Western Europe: a guide to commercial, business and legal practices and attitudes in the continental EEC countries and Switzerland*. It was written primarily for the benefit of English businessmen contemplating sales or direct investments in Europe following the enlargement of the EEC. For some of them, it probably *was* porn.

'It's rare for the Chamber of Commerce to sponsor a presentation of this kind,' Mariella comments. But they did, and the British Embassy in The Hague assisted in promoting it. It could well be at this point that security services approached Mariella with an offer of extramural employment: industrial espionage, or honeytrapping. MEPs are not beyond the pale. For now, all we know is that Mariella came into contact with the editor of the guide, Victor Selwyn. A graduate of the London School of Economics, Selwyn went into journalism and wrote articles for Fleet Street papers on subjects ranging from economics to scientific and medical matters. He was best known for editing anthologies of war poets, for which he gained an MBE. Selwyn gave Mariella *carte blanche* as to whom she should invite to the historic Kasteel de Wittenburg.

She invited, among others, 'Peter R', a Conservative pro-EEC MP; 'Michael E', MP for Nottingham West, Socialist and anti-EEC; 'Sylvia P', granddaughter of Korea's last king; and Serena Wadham, photojournalist.

(In 1973, outside Korea and Japan, any Asian girl could have said she was granddaughter of the last king of Korea and no one would have questioned her. The family tree of the Gojong dynasty was complicated; its twiglets scattered across the globe.) In Kasteel de Wittenburg Mariella could flaunt her fake credentials. The drawing room was illuminated by candles set in crystal chandeliers.

Titbits were arrayed on silver salvers. The French windows opened onto a terrace overlooking a formal garden and lake. Mariella was wearing seventeenth-century black lace. Sylvia was in full escort mode in a long dress with deep cleavage. Serena was taking photographs. Talk was of the newly splashed Lambton Affair.

A prodigiously unfaithful husband to his wife Belinda, Lord Lambton had a number of mistresses and was a user of both prostitutes and drugs. Nemesis duly arrived in the shape of Norma Levy, a member of a call-girl ring servicing upper-class clients. Levy told police that her husband Colin, a conman who connived in her liaison with Lambton, was threatening to expose it. As well as compromising shots of the Lord, Levy had photos of other prominent people. The story broke in 1973, evoking memories of the Profumo Affair. Secret files released in 2004 contained the names of three *eminences grises* but they were redacted.

Mariella shows no interest in joining in the debate, maybe because she is not at the centre of it. Michael E divulges a *faux pas* involving cabinet minister Barbara Castle that lost him his government post. So the evening goes on with more gossip and shop talk. On returning to London, Michael E invites Mariella and Sylvia to tea at the House.

'The sun shone on the Thames as we sat facing the G.L.C. building and watched the water traffic pass by. Sylvia dug the privilege of tea there but was speechless after tackling the so-called beef and tongue sandwiches.'

Even here, in the House of Commons, Mariella can find no one to flagellate or fellate, so she takes her weekly trip to Soho.

Some of us have an inexorable inner logic that pushes us towards places that can only be described as the end of the road. This place was a depository of lost souls on Gerrard Street called the New Cabinet Club. Down you went to the cellar, and there was a square, dark room. The avant-garde, wolves and drunks like caves. The New Cabinet Club was a cave run by the gangster Billy Hill's ex-wife Aggie. She liked clubs that hosted men like her ex-husband. This one hosted refugees from more salubrious clubs where showbiz types mixed with scarfaces. The basic premise was if you weren't good enough for the more titillating venues, you came here. It was a place of nostalgia and regret, of afternoon drinkers, homeless chancers and *Club International*'s racy columnist.

At last Mariella met the boxer I mentioned a while back, 'Mr Fists'. A party at his luxurious flat resulted in 'the usual fun and games' and the end of Mariella's stint as a columnist. In 1974 Tony Power left his position in Raymond's publishing empire. The magazine was sinking under the weight of hardcore rivals. It was time to move on, and it was at Mr Fists' *soiree* that Mariella's career took a new direction.

She does not name Mr Fists, so I am assuming he needed to keep a low profile. But one particular reference to Billy Ambrose emerged later in the decade. If Billy Ambrose is Mr Fists, this explains Mariella's burgeoning career as a police informant. Ambrose was a one-time contender for the middleweight championship of Great Britain. So he was famous, as she said. But he occupied a hinterland where secrecy is vital to survival. In other words, he occasionally grassed up his mates to the cops. In particular his CV boasts a connection to an elite network of international fraudsters and forgers that helps join the dots of what happened next for Mariella.

Her version of events is that she made herself available to the British intelligence services, and they in turn invited her to compromise 'persons of interest' to the state. What is certain is that Mariella initiated a maze of deception and entrapment from which only Ariadne could emerge unscathed. And it all started in Mr Fists' luxury flat.

31

LORELEI

When we last saw John Mason, it was 1968. The bear-sized crew-cut porn king was standing rounds at the De Hem public house off Shaftesbury Avenue. Around him were gathered his friends from the Dirty Squad. When we find him again in 1976, he is giving evidence at their trial at the Old Bailey. In court, Mason testified that he had been bribing officers of the OPS for over twenty years. To put a figure on it, he was paying a licence-to-operate fee of £1,000 per month plus expenses.

Where was Mariella? From street level, she was a bit-part, an extra, a flash of flesh in a peep show. From her own viewpoint, she brought down the whole Soho shebang.

After the trial, the Pils-swilling Mason fled to his villa in the Costa Del Crime. Soho's power vacuum was filled by Bernie Silver, a former runner for Maltese criminals. Back in the fifties, the *Sunday People*'s crusading journalist Duncan Webb called him one of 'the two most evil men in London'. By the seventies, Silver was known as the Godfather of Soho, making profits from prostitution and nineteen of the twenty-four strip clubs in Soho. Silver's sidekick was 'Big Frank' Mifsud. The one-time traffic policeman had left Malta in the fifties to make a name for himself in London, where his 18-stone frame would ultimately earn him the obvious handle. 'Big Frank' recruited Maltese compatriots to the Soho gang that would become known as 'The Syndicate', a vast call-girl empire built up over twenty years.

Any criminal about to make a bid for property in Soho had to go through the Syndicate. Silver had spotted some loopholes in recent legislation that led to his dominion over Soho. After the Rent Act of 1957, landlords could charge what they wished. Silver duly let out leases with six-month break-clauses. This was ideal for low-overhead operations. Maintenance was not an issue. Sex tourists like the patina of dinginess. Peeling plaster walls, hand-written signs, a red light bulb, net curtains, an iron-frame bed and a wash-stand. Silver was renting out flats for prostitutes, as well as gambling and illegal drinking clubs. Working from an office on Romilly Street, Silver went further even than Mason. He bribed a whole generation of police officers.

In 1973, on the back of *King's Road*, Mariella was serialising her memoirs in Paul Raymond's *Club International*, describing her relations with anonymous VIPs in Westminster, Rome, New York, LA and Washington and with unemployed black men in Brixton. Mary Whitehouse and Lord Longford had been called upon to investigate a film made by her friend, the 'group-sex therapist' Martin Cole, who was charged with living off immoral earnings. Mariella was transitioning from working at the coalface to writing about it with some hustle on the side as a stripper or an escort.

In 2013 I was teaching a course in Creative Writing at the City Literary Institute where I met an elderly woman who knew Mariella. Caroline had been sub-editor at *Club International*. She had invited Mariella to a meeting of Women in Media, a serious organisation initiated by serious women like Mary Stott, editor of the *Guardian*'s women's page from 1957 to 1972. Women in Media functioned as a feminist pressure group campaigning on issues such as equal opportunities, tax inequalities, abortion and the representation of women in Parliament. The group held seminars on issues of discrimination and stereotyping. On the back of their researches, Stott and her colleagues lobbied Parliament and the Equal Opportunities Commission, which had been established by the Sex Discrimination Act 1975.

Caroline liked Mariella's matter-of-fact presentation. She liked her friendly, open manner and her frank admissions of sexual largesse. She liked the fact that Mariella took herself seriously as a writer. Sadly, Mariella was not the committee type. The meeting was brought to a halt when Mariella passed out in the toilet after smoking a joint.

Pressures were piling on the showgirl turned writer. She was paying school fees for a child whose father showed no interest in her. Hod could no longer support her. Her youth was in question as she got deeper into her thirties. This was the greatest pressure of all. Mariella was driven by a need to be noticed, admired, and set apart from other women. The sad fact was she had become one of those people no one thought about with passion or concern. Hence the drive to succeed was even more pronounced, and her particular skill set was about to be put into motion.

Another place Jackie and Mariella hooked up was in a membership club, a cramped, damp cellar – a 'flea-pit'. Here Mariella took off her clothes just for kicks, Jackie said. But all the while she was wondering where the money went. It goes like this: at minimum outlay, a basement room opens, whisks in a crop of members for an annual fee of £1 a head, closes a month later, and reopens elsewhere under another name to continue the shake-down.

'Well, Mariella had a friend at the West End Central police station,' said Jackie. 'She knew him from the Profumo days. Through him, she started reporting to the Chief Constable of Kent. He was investigating bent coppers.'

It was 2015 and I was talking to Jackie on my uncle James's mobile. We were standing outside the health centre in Frith Street. I kept finding myself here, picking up scraps of stories, waiting for the payload. On this occasion, at my uncle's invitation, I was waiting for Jackie to turn up to a Narcotics Anonymous meeting in order to pick up her ninety-day sobriety chip. But over the telephone, she explained she was otherwise engaged in a business meeting in a hotel room in King's Cross. 'That's how she started investigating your grandfather.'

Uncle James took his phone back and smiled. He had the face of a naughty schoolboy and the confiding smile to match. He spoke to Jackie briefly, got her location and headed off to meet her.

My uncle had first met Jackie at my grandfather's hotel, where she turned up for a party in Mariella's tow. James had suggested I meet her just as he suggested I meet Tricky, the man who recovered the evidence that would link Mariella to the British government. Since the frenzied blur of the seventies the three had kept in touch through the long years of the eighties and nineties, weaving from recovery to relapse.

It was through linking their recollections that I realised how Mariella found her next job. On her return from the King's Cross interlude, I met Jackie again. She was now collecting her one-day chip of sobriety at Frith Street. We repaired to the Lorelei on Bateman Street.

I entered a classic Soho lair where the customer trips over bags of flour in the doorway to enter the restaurant's one room. Thirty covers; plastic condiments on each Formica-topped table; a waitress with other things on her mind. The room was dominated by an old coffee machine and a life-size mural of the siren after whom the place was named. I pointed to a picture of a prawn cocktail on the laminated menu, and waited for Jackie to begin. She was still jaundiced and her hands were shaking. As happens with chronic addicts and alcoholics, her cheeks had caved in and yet she was blasé to the point of being cheerful.

'His death was stage-managed.' Jackie was referring to my grandfather. Despite the strangeness of what she was saying, it was her manner that struck me more deeply. It was as though I was watching Mariella in the video clip I have of her from 1978. In it she is presenting herself as a Resistance heroine chipping away at a rotten male Establishment.

'The coroner's report said "myocardial infarction." Jackie paused. 'A heart attack is easy enough to fake.'

She took a moment to suck hard on the Marlboro Lite I had given her. I swallowed a slice of avocado so unripe it had to go down whole.

'A hypodermic filled with hydrogen cyanide is all you need to fool a coroner. With a sharp needle, even the victim wouldn't know what had happened to him.'

Before I had a chance to respond, she added, 'Mariella knew she was next. "They'll disappear me, or I'll be found dead of an overdose. No note."'

In the bristling silence, I got the distinct impression Jackie was taking me up and down flights of stairs in an apparently vast government building before stopping at a door that turned out to hold official secrets that pertained to me personally. Who were *they*?

'This officer she knew from her party days.'

'The officer at West End Central?'

'Yes, him. She started telling him about Silver and Humphreys and the Dirty Squad but he didn't want to know. He rubbished her. "He doesn't believe me, Jackie," she kept saying. But she persisted. She niggled and nagged at him. Finally, she got him the evidence that he couldn't ignore.'

She 'niggled and nagged at him' – the mode of discourse allotted to women, the language that crushed my proud mother and nearly got me. The language of women that is endless in its import because it never scores a point, it never 'ends'. Just as I was pondering the significance of what she had said, Jackie left, leaving a chill in the air and a dog-end in the ashtray. Not just that, however. Sensing something was missing, I looked about me and realised she'd taken my pack of Marlboro Lites.

32

LET ME ENTERTAIN YOU

I gathered my notebook and pen and made my way to Greek Street. I entered a cocoa-coloured café that is informally known as the Recovery Café because it's cheap and the owners don't mind people sitting there all day and into the night. 'Espresso,' I said to the juggling *barrista* behind the bar. The satellite TV was jangling. The door opened behind me. I got a glimpse of neon flickering in the twilight. Two trans girls tottered in, and my uncle James followed behind them.

'Looks like it's going to be another quiet evening,' he said, peering at the notice board feathered with self-help adverts. My uncle's face was immediately companionable, welcoming confidences.

'Tell me more about Mariella,' I said.

'Well, she liked the cover of darkness, didn't she?' He was putting in the fancy brushwork but I kept with him. 'She didn't like to feel people were looking too closely at her.'

'So she didn't like being held to account?'

I was beginning to wonder if he saw something of himself in her. I wanted to know more about her covert activities but he was more interested in the show she put on.

'She liked to make an effect, make a splash. Then,' he made a flourish, 'she'd run and hide. That's why she liked Soho. Round here, everyone keeps schtum. It's the perfect cover.'

I was gathering impressions not so much of Mariella but of a circus performer who lights up the ring then fades into the darkness that surrounds the Big Tent. Outside, on a muddy common, under a moonlit sky she and others like her occupy smaller tents and the next day, before sunrise, they hitch their wagons and are gone.

The next figure to hitch his wagon to the story is a minor villain called Jimmy Humphreys. Jimmy wanted to get into Soho's sex-shop business. A Bermondsey-born graduate of Rochester YOI, HMP Wormwood Scrubs and HMP Dartmoor, Jimmy was the kind of alert, adrenalin-fuelled young man who was always going to make a name for himself. This drive would lead him to a starring role in the *Sunday People*'s scoop of the seventies.

The path to glory was paved with his wife's ambition. She was a stripper called Rusty who had started her career at the Casino de Paris on Wardour Street. As a wedding present, she wanted him to buy a strip joint at 5 Walkers Court. Rusty's theme song was 'Let Me Entertain You' from the musical *Gypsy*. She wanted to put her experience to good use. On sketching the sex-tourist's map of London, Jimmy saw a hoarding opposite the address his wife had found. It advertised Raymond's Revue Bar,. Next door to No. 5 was the showcase for Bernie Silver's bookshop empire. So the Humphreys' new club would be a centre point in Soho's Sexlandia. Jimmy thought it a splendid idea. So he went ahead and made inquiries about the property.

What he didn't do was to ask permission of Bernie 'The Godfather' Silver. Since no one could get into Soho without Silver's permission, Bill 'The Architect' Moody, aka head of the Dirty Squad, refused Jimmy a 'licence'. This was a setback for the putative baron and baroness. But Jimmy was unstoppable. Ever the obliging go-between, he had recently done the police a favour. The inmates at HMP Gartree had been planning to attack the governor because of his treatment of fellow inmate

'Mad' Frankie Fraser. When a Flying Squad officer asked Jimmy to intervene, he obliged. On the back of this, Jimmy wangled an introduction to Wally Virgo, 'the man upstairs'. Very soon, Jimmy found himself sitting next to Commander Virgo from Scotland Yard. Together they were enjoying a Freemasons' dinner at the Criterion Restaurant in Piccadilly.

During the various trials that revolved around the Obscene Publications Squad, it emerged that membership of the Freemasons was a prerequisite for any detective who wanted to join the squad. Everyone had to be 'on the square'. After the dinner, Virgo 'came across', and arranged a meeting for Jimmy with Bernie Silver. This was how business was done in the early 1970s in Soho. But it is worth reiterating, nevertheless: a high-ranking police officer requested permission from a gang leader for a minor villain to open a strip club in central London.

Jimmy's club on Walker's Court was a success. When Rusty wanted to open a bigger club on the corner of Berwick and D'Arblay Streets, she called it Queen's. As an invitation to the opening night, Jimmy sent out forged pound notes with Rusty's bust replacing the Queen's. The Bank of England threatened prosecution. No matter. By now, Jimmy had his moneyman who handled the cash and met with Silver's moneyman for coffee at Valerie's to divide the spoils. He had Ronnie King, the fastest knife man in London, Coloured Pat and Maltese Charlie, his second-in-command. He also had Kenneth Drury in his pocket. Drury was Commander of the Flying Squad and a regular at parties held at my grandfather's hotel. This hotel in suburban Streatham also served as a discreet bolt hole for lodging prosecution witnesses.

'What happened next?' I asked Uncle James.

'Rusty [Humphreys] asked your grandad Charlie to look after "Pooky" Garfarth. He was a two-bit hotel thief, and he was hiding from her and Jimmy. She was anxious to find him.'

Why?

'It turned out,' Uncle James continued, 'that Rusty had been having an affair with Pooky for as long as she had been married to Jimmy. Now Jimmy was not a man to be messed with. He suspected something was up when Rusty was doing a spell in Holloway. One Sunday he turned up and saw Pooky's name in the visitor's book. He'd visited her four Sundays in a row.'

'And?'

'Well, it was more than Jimmy had, and he was her husband. So, anyway, Pooky was warned to stay away from Rusty. This was after he was slashed with a razor and beaten up by six masked men. That was in the toilets of the Dauphin Club in Marylebone. After that, the cops persuaded Pooky to turn supergrass. They were under pressure to clean up their links to the porn trade.'

I wondered if Mariella's information was finally filtering through. Uncle James continued to warm to his subject.

'Through your Grandad Charlie's connections with Commander Ken Drury, Charlie put Pooky under police protection in our hotel in Streatham.'

He paused to allow me time to catch up. Just as I was framing a question, he picked up the thread again.

'As you know, our hotel was a meeting-place for Flying Squad officers and villains. It was there of all places that Mariella popped up again.'

His face screwed up with disgust. His pride was wounded. Why?

'Mariella was in business with Rusty,' he continued. 'She was arranging for Rusty's strippers to come to the hotel for parties. That was how I met Jackie. We got talking one night in the greenhouse in the garden – we were shooting up speedballs with some junkies I'd met in the 'Dilly. It turned out we knew a lot of people in common, and we both felt there was something more going on with Mariella than met the eye. It turned out we was right.' He sighed. 'It was all a long time ago,' he said, and then with a flash of ceramic teeth, he dug into his pocket.

'Let's have another coffee. You're going to need it by the looks of things.'

33

THE FLEA-PIT

In October 1973, the 'Old Grey Fox' Bert Wickstead, one of the Big Five at Scotland Yard, was leading the Serious Crime Squad, a crack detective unit stationed in Limehouse, east London. The squad had been set up as a specialised CID unit in 1971 to deal with organised crime. Wickstead was given a free hand to form his own team, one of the first of the specialist units set up within the Metropolitan Police. When Wickstead set his sights on Soho, he found that an amorphous organisation known as the Syndicate had taken over most of the vice. Said to be earning as much as £100,000 a week, the organisation was run by a Maltese Jew called Bernie Silver, and 'Big Frank' Mifsud. Wickstead scratched his head in his Limehouse police station, wondering how he could unpick the tapestry Silver had stitched so tightly that it was part of the fabric of the city.

Wickstead had his desk removed from Soho to keep his officers incorruptible. Mariella did her investigations *in situ*. Mine were conducted in a state of suspended animation in front of a microfiche in Colindale, at the far end of the Northern line. In the dark cubicle of the reference library, I was building a file. In the murk of London in the seventies there was a lot of confusion as to who were the goodies and who were the baddies. Officers from the West End police squads were so entwined with the owners of Soho's porn shops it was hard to tell them apart. No wonder Mariella could not get officers of the law to listen.

George Fenwick was the operational head of the Obscene Publications Squad and very good friends with the lager-drinking Mason. For £100 per issue he 'sub-edited' Mason's spanking magazine *Janus*. He even offered to write for it. Amazingly, Detective Chief Inspector George Fenwick was also the senior officer responsible for the 1971 prosecution of *Oz* magazine. Not surprisingly, Fenwick's arrogance was drawing the attention of Bert Wickstead over in Limehouse.

Another person of interest was 'the Architect', Detective Chief Superintendent Bill Moody. But Moody was well connected, and despite Wickstead's protests he managed to install himself on Wickstead's team. At that time the OPS squad was a unit within the CID's central office, known as C1. Selection was largely in the gift of the C1 commander or the superintendent heading the squad. From 1964 until 1972 the OPS was under the umbrella of Moody. While heading one of the biggest investigations into police corruption, 'the Architect' was simultaneously collecting lavish bribes from Mason, Silver and Humphreys. So was his superior, Commander Wally Virgo.

Based at New Scotland Yard, Virgo had overall control of nine squads including the Flying, Drugs and the Dirty Squad. Three senior officers: Moody, Virgo and Fenwick. For most of the seventies they were raking it in, having the time of their lives; they were untouchable.

This is what irked Mariella. She didn't like men who were untouchable. While these men were taking kickbacks secreted in the pockets of their Cecil Gee suits, she was on display in a flea-pit in Soho. But she was picking up information all the while.

While it worked, it worked like a dream. Moody, Virgo, Silver and Mason had a well-established system that ran far, far better than British industry. They thought of everything. The passwords for police raids were 'Ryman's' or 'W. H. Smith's'. This translated as, 'Clear up the display and remove compromising material.' On the other side of the coin, if one of the porn merchants' rivals annoyed them, they could get a copper to pay the unfortunate interloper a surprise visit. This helped keep up the requisite number of arrests. As far as career progression went, officers would serve a spell on the OPS, and, when transferred, pass on vice contacts to the next man to keep the ball in play.

As a matter of interest, there was also a ready supply of indigent Soho authors who were only too happy to supply copy for the pornographer's press. At the French pub on Dean Street one boozy lunchtime in the 1990s I heard a man brag he had made 'one fuck last for 42 pages'. Pornography is one of the oldest patrons of the poor scribbler. The junkie existentialist Alexander Trocchi boasted that he could knock out a lewd novel in two weeks. Joining him was the poet Christopher Logue (writing as Count Palmiro Vicarion) and, later in the millennium, spin doctor Alastair Campbell. In the early 2000s I joined their ranks, serving up smut for the *Erotic Review* in Carnaby Street. For decades, the indigent hacks who crowded the pubs of Soho prided themselves on the potency of their craft.

Watching everything, the Old Grey Fox Bert Wickstead was biding his time in the Limehouse police station, still trying to find a way into the Syndicate. He was up against Silver's intelligence and wealth allied to his superb police contacts. Silver's contacts weren't limited to just Fenwick, Virgo and Moody. They went all the way to Commander level at Scotland Yard.

Twilight was slowly descending over Soho. On the corner of Old Compton Street and Wardour Street, girls and boys with newborn faces and bruised eyes lurched towards pedestrians holding polystyrene cups. 'Any change, please?'

Behind the counter of the sex shop where Tricky Dicky stood tall for Mason was a cool, black-painted cave. The walls were lined with racks filled with video cassettes in white cardboard cases. Each spine had a four-digit number written by hand in a black marker pen. They all had a logo that read 'Original Climax'. Big Jeff Phillips of Original Climax Ltd was the biggest movie maker in Soho. The numbers referred to a title listed in the catalogue behind the till.

It was Big Jeff who inadvertently gave Bert Wickstead a hand in his pursuit of Bernie Silver. A crack was opening in the facade. Reporters from the ever-vigilant *Sunday People* were observing Big Jeff – and then who should pry open the crack a little bit more but everyone's friend and associate, Jimmy Humphreys?

Big Jeff's movie house was on Denman Street and the *Sunday People*'s intrepid reporters were on to him. After meeting with Jeff in the guise of porn dealers, they went to visit Jimmy at Queen's Club. They struck up a camaraderie with him that, to someone like Jimmy, was suspicious from the off. Maybe they were trying to win his confidence but in telling him about their dealings with Big Jeff, they let slip they had observed his friendship with officers from the Dirty Squad.

Jimmy called Wally Virgo at Scotland Yard to alert him to potential danger. Half an hour later Jimmy and Wally met at the art-deco masterpiece that is the Regent Palace Hotel, just off Piccadilly. Wally and Jimmy weren't there to admire the chandeliers and gilding. Wally agreed to check the credentials of the putative buyers. When he got back to D'Arblay Street, Jimmy dialled the hotline to the Dirty Squad. He told Moody to put the word out to all the Soho bucks that an investigation was in progress. Tricky Dicky was just one of the managers who toned down their displays, while Jimmy called the undercover reporters and filibustered them with titbits of information about his rivals.

Once off the phone, Virgo got back to him and confirmed that the mystery buyers were working for the *Sunday People*. Jimmy then arranged a meeting for the journalists at the Hilton Hotel. He sent Big Jeff's frontman along, together with his solicitor and a photographer. The snaps taken at the Hilton were immediately circulated to all the bucks so that the reporters would be recognised.

The undercover reporters only had half a scoop but they ran with it anyway, and Jimmy was about to get deeper into the conspiracy. He had got friendly with another Commander from the Yard. This was Ken Drury of the Flying Squad; the same Ken Drury who frequented my grandfather's hotel. Jimmy decided he needed a holiday. He invited Commander Drury to join him in Cyprus. Both the wives were there, Rusty and Mrs Drury. It was all very relaxed. Drury couldn't help mentioning that he had heard from Moody about Wickstead's operational base in Limehouse. Jimmy somewhat nervously asked for the bill. Drury spilled some more beans. He told Jimmy about Wickstead's impending raid of Soho's dens of vice. What Jimmy didn't realize was that the *Sunday People* had forgotten about Big Jeff and were onto him. They had flown another of their undercover reporters out to Cyprus. This one obtained a copy of the hotel receipts including use of the mini-bar. This was the evidence the *People* needed.

The story was a showstopper – Commander Kenneth Drury, head of the Flying Squad, holidaying in Cyprus with a notorious Soho porn baron called Jimmy Humphreys. The story just got better when Commander Drury explained to the *Sunday People* that he had taken Jimmy to Cyprus in the hope of finding the Great Train Robber Ronnie Biggs.

Over in Limehouse, the Old Grey Fox was visited by no less than Commander Wally Virgo. Wally was understandably hot under the collar. He wanted to request that Wickstead leave the cleaning up of Soho to the Flying Squad. Wickstead refused to see him.

Tradition demands that the plot thickens and at this point it does. One of Wickstead's officers reported that his 'action book' detailing which OPS officers were next to be interviewed was stolen from his office. He also surmised that his phone calls were being tapped. Lo and behold, Bill Moody, head of the Dirty Squad and Grand Master Freemason, rocked up to the station in an Alfa Romeo. The officer who had requested assistance in locating his action book was taken aback. His own car was an Austin 1800. Moody took one look at it, and said, 'Is that the best you can do?' When the officer checked on Moody's car, he found it belonged to a pornographer.

Despite the good offices of the *Sunday People*, Wickstead's investigation was stuttering. Because of the publicity, Drury's warning had got through to the Godfather and his enforcer, Big Frank. In February 1972, just as Wickstead's men were poised to pounce, Silver and Mifsud left the country. In response, Wickstead leaked a story to the press that he had given up the case. The papers complied with the story of 'The Raid That Never Was'. The ruse worked and members of the Syndicate started to return to London. Then came a stroke of luck for Wickstead that saw the eventual downfall not only of the Syndicate but my family as well.

34

EVERYONE SANG SONGS

On 23 October 1972, Rusty Humphreys' lover, Peter 'Pooky' Garfarth, was savagely attacked by four men in the lavatory of the Dauphin Club in Marylebone. Rusty had been released three days previously from Holloway following a six-month sentence for possession of a firearm. The attack gave Wickstead's team the perfect excuse to involve themselves in the Dirty Squad's manor.

By mid-December of 1972 Jimmy had obtained a false passport in the name of Leigh Back and was nervously waiting for something to happen. According to Jackie, who was working for Rusty at the time, Mariella climbed up the narrow stairway to his first-floor office on D'Arblay Street.

She pulled a face at the stale aroma of fear, sweat and tobacco. Mariella was fastidious. 'I could see her from the kitchen,' said Jackie. She made some vague pretext for her visit about needing the phone numbers of some girls to take to a party in a hotel in Streatham. Jackie continued to shoot the breeze with Jimmy's minders. They were all in a state of high alert having just returned from exile in Amsterdam. 'We all heard Jimmy say: "The phone hasn't rung. I don't like it."'

He opened the door to his office, which he had locked from the inside, with some force, nearly knocking Mariella backwards down the stairs.

'Jimmy,' Mariella drawled after the retreating figure, 'Rusty said I could get some numbers.'

Jimmy rushed out of the door. All he knew about a hotel in Streatham was that Pooky Garfarth was in hiding there, waiting to give evidence against him. The minders took up the pursuit of their boss. Jackie sat in the kitchen and watched as Mariella walked into his office, rifled through his drawers and stashed the contents in her shoulder bag.

What happens next is pure hearsay. But if she handed over her findings to her contact at West End Central and he passed it on to Bert Wickstead, it could have been the key he was seeking.

Official accounts state that one Saturday morning at the beginning of 1973 Wickstead and his team hit the West End shops, smashing down doors and seizing some forty tons of porn. The raids netted several important dealers, including Big Jeff. Shortly afterwards, Rusty was arrested and charged with keeping a brothel at an address in Greek Street owned by Jimmy. At this point, back in Amsterdam, Jimmy started singing. He wrote a personal letter to Wickstead's boss, Deputy Police Commissioner Starritt, who was technically in charge of the Soho inquiry. The letter was a twelve-page statement which was to have been the basis for Jimmy's autobiography. What it lacked in literary quality it made up for in detail.

Cases of corruption often hinge on the apocryphal writings of dubious characters. During a raid on Jimmy's home, Wickstead made the discovery of a detailed ledger of the Syndicate's police payoffs. It listed payments to seventeen different policemen including Ken Drury, the head of the Flying Squad.

This document along with the diary would ultimately lead to the dismissal or forced retirement of hundreds of Met officers. The ensuing corruption trials in 1976–77 resulted in thirteen detectives – including two ex-Commanders, the highest-ranking British police officers ever to be convicted of corruption – being sentenced to a total of ninety years in prison.

The Godfather of Soho, Bernie Silver, was arrested while he was having dinner with his girlfriend at the Park Tower Hotel on

30 December 1973. Other members of the gang were seized at the Scheherazade Club in Soho. By now, Wickstead had entered into the spirit of things and made the raid a theatrical event. In the early hours of the morning, this burly, square-jawed man in the mould of Spencer Tracey stepped onto the stage in his raincoat, suit and tie. He made the spectacular announcement that everyone was arrested.

A member of the audience shouted out, 'What do you think of the cabaret?' Another responded, 'Not much!'

The guests, staff and even the band, were taken to Limehouse police station where the band continued playing and everyone sang songs. The main point, for Wickstead, was to get them as far away as possible from Soho.

Where does Mariella come into all this, I asked my uncle again.

'It was Mariella who nicked Jimmy's diary and the tape of Moody speaking to a buck.'

The transcript of this tape goes as follows:

Don't forget always to let me know straight away if you need anything because I know people everywhere. Because I'm in a little firm in a firm. Don't matter where, anywhere in London, I can get on the phone to someone I know I can trust, that talks the same as me. And if he's not the right person that can do it, he'll know the person that can. All right? ... That's the thing, and it can work – well, it's worked for years, hasn't it?

35

A COMMONWEALTH CONNECTION

'She was working the peep shows. They were like sex shows with cucumbers and stuff. Guys went into booths and girls danced for them.'

We were on the phone again. I found Jackie was more communicative over the phone than face to face. The Security Services had asked Mariella to help them compromise 'people of interest', Jackie reminded me.

'Do you remember anyone specifically?' I asked.

'She spent the night with a Commonwealth leader. He was black, from the Caribbean, and they wanted independence. That was in Brown's Hotel. She told me there were two-way mirrors and hidden mics in the room.'

Was this a wild goose chase? Or was it another lead? Eventually I narrowed down the Commonwealth leader to Patrick John and the island to Dominica. In 1976, at the village of Salisbury in Dominica, Patrick John announced his intention to take the country to independence. The statement was issued as the Salisbury Declaration. In March through to May 1977, constitutional talks on independence took place in London.

This time, I told myself, I would pin Jackie down. The address she gave me was on the other side of Old Compton Street in a nightclub. She said she would meet me there in an hour.

The interior was as dark as a cave, except for the soft lights behind the bar. Two hung-over women were smoking cigarettes. I walked over to their table. I tried to make eye contact and asked if they had seen Jackie. One tutted and removed a shred of tobacco from her lip. The other looked at nothing; she blew smoke up in the air and flipped her ash. Together they were as lifeless as cardboard cut-outs, and about as forthcoming.

'I understand she works here,' I said.

The woman whose skin was whitest turned to me and looked me full in the face. 'Listen, love. I'm supposed to talk to people who buy me a drink,' she said. 'Then I put my hand in their lap, and we talk about what happens next.'

I got the message and left. At least I knew Jackie had told the truth about the Commonwealth leader. Mariella had mentioned Patrick John, the Prime Minister of Dominica, in one of her diaries. Now Jackie was saying Mariella had met him at Brown's Hotel. I guessed she had met him for sex and it was another honey trap. As luck would have it, I knew Lennox Honeychurch, a local historian from Dominica. I knew him because I had gone to the island in 2005 to research a biography of the novelist Jean Rhys. I emailed Lennox and asked if he knew of any plot by British secret services to compromise the movement for independence in Dominica. He replied:

This is the first time that I am hearing about this supposed episode in Dominica's quest for independence. I was a member of the delegation that went to London to discuss independence in March and May 1977. At the time I was a member of the House of Assembly on the opposition side led by Mary Eugenia Charles. Together we had meetings with as many members of the British Parliament that we could, to have the issues thoroughly debated when the time came for the motion to come before both houses of Parliament. The distinct impression that we got of the British, on both sides, at the time, was that Britain was keen to clean out its colonial filing cabinets and get rid of as many former colonies as possible.

Another dead end. I was disheartened.

Now my laptop started ringing; someone was Skyping me. MarieAntoinette, the caller-ident box read. I recognised the handle: it belonged to another friend of my uncle's. This was a woman who in the eighties had become engaged to a conman called Leonard Knowles – who in the seventies had been 'engaged' to Mariella.

'Can you hear me?' the voice asked. I said I could. 'Don't activate your camera,' the voice instructed. I didn't.

'Lennie was terrified of Mariella,' the voice told me. Despite the fact that she must have been in her seventies, she had the gushing tones of someone who would be attracted to a conman.

'Lenny said she was working for the dirty tricks department of MI5. When he left her the brakes on his cars gave out.'

I made a wild guess. 'Did he ever talk about his work with her?'

A pause. 'I think he was trying to engineer a *coup d'etat* in the Caribbean,' she said. Somewhat taken aback, I asked for more detail.

'The idea was that Lennie and his friends would open a Mayfair embassy for this island in the Caribbean and sell shares in five-square mile plots. They thought there was oil underground.'

This sounded like a fairly standard scam but it got complicated when Lennie hooked up with an old friend, an international property lawyer, and claimed for himself sovereignty of the island and the surrounding seas (and fishing rights). In an endeavour to gain control of the island he anointed himself head of state. I thanked her for her time and emailed Lennox again. I asked him if he had heard of a rather erratic character called Leonard Knowles.

He hadn't. But talking of erratic characters ...

'Patrick John was an erratic character,' he admitted. 'I did hear Miss Charles saying that the chauffeurs provided by the

Foreign Office were taken aback at the activities of John's team of delegates, in relation to visits by women. If I recall correctly she had an account of John demanding a chauffeur to drive all the way to Bristol for some encounter.'

Mr Honeychurch continued: 'We three delegates had made our own arrangements for accommodation in London. Miss Charles and I stayed at the Royal Commonwealth Society. Patrick John and his team stayed together at some hotel in West London, I cannot recall the name.'

This was getting warmer. Then suddenly everything made sense:

'Do not confuse all of this with the time Patrick John tried to strike some deal with South Africa and various dodgy individuals, a Major Banks, and a Lenny Knowles among others.'

So the smoke and mirrors contained some truth. In 1974 Patrick John unsuccessfully attempted to overthrow Eugenia Charles as Prime Minister of Dominica with the backing of white supremacist groups. Mariella's encounter with Patrick John may well have been because British intelligence forces were observing his movements.

36

THE HUNGARIAN CIRCLE

It is 1976 and Mariella is mooching along the King's Road, enjoying the heatwave and the attention her legs are getting from male passers-by. She stops outside a shop called Sex at number 430. Her eye has been caught by a scruffy, pencilled announcement. Someone calling himself Sid Vicious is looking for people to form a band with him.

'No flares,' reads the stern message.

Styles were colliding violently that season. The mainstream look was Chelsea Girl and Lord John. But Mariella's strip act had incorporated a new aesthetic.

'She used to wear wigs when she stripped. By the mid-Seventies it was a spiky punk wig, like Hazel O'Connor. High heels, skimpy clothes, and a swastika arm-band,' said Jackie.

Lady Henrietta Bath, aka the International Sex Queen, was undergoing a metamorphosis. Just as the King's Road was trading on its fading reputation as swinging London's trendiest thoroughfare, Mariella had taken on board a new, edgier trend. She had gained some ground from the Soho money men and their counterparts in the OPS. She was in the market for a new look, a new vibe. Sure, there were still the loon pants and star tops, tulip lapels and stack heels, and there were plenty of tourists to support the cowboy-boot-and-cheesecloth shops. But this was a more seditious vibe, and Mariella was fully into it.

All around her, she could see the *ancien regime* was in tatters. The gay charade of the swinging sixties, like the roaring twenties before it, had dissolved into the wreckage of a dying economy, bitter strikes, terrorist bombs and moral confusion. Sex sold cut-up shirts with portraits of Karl Marx. The walls of Chelsea were plastered with posters promoting David Bowie's *The Man Who Fell to Earth*. Schoolkids had a fad for felt-tipping swastikas on Bowie's cheekbone. Siouxsie, the lead singer of the Banshees, wore a Nazi armband. The new attitude, in short, was to be un-liberal, in a reaction against the progressiveness of the sixties. Mariella was reinventing herself.

As far as indigent authors and conmen were concerned, hitting the proverbial and much-longed-for jackpot was nigh impossible and there was a lot of competition for it. The *Daily Mirror* reported that a team of investigators had shown that of all the men who wore regimental ties, six in ten were impostors. Still, Mariella kept trying.

Parallel to the King's Road and snaking away from fashionable Chelsea and South Ken, the police were watching a second-floor flat on the Fulham Road. A relatively drab but very busy thoroughfare, Fulham Road was home to a mysterious blonde calling herself Miss Henrietta Chapman. The police were watching her second-floor flat because men from the 'Hungarian Circle' of international criminals were frequenting the address. This surveillance forms an intriguing part of one of the biggest police operations ever mounted in London and possibly the world, boasted the commander of Scotland Yard's Serious Crimes Squad.

'It was the biggest fraud plot of all time,' and had it not been prevented, 'it would have been very serious indeed for the Western economy.' Bearing in mind gloating coppers and prosecution lawyers have a flair for the self-aggrandising and apocryphal, the sums involved totalled at least £240 million, and the potential for more was limitless.

Mariella cannot be blamed for thinking she was getting close to hitting the jackpot. In the guise of Miss Henrietta Chapman, she was mixing with criminal masterminds who belonged to an organisation that, amongst other things, laundered money for the mafia. Their speciality was international draft transfers. These were ordered from one bank and cashed in another. Not one of the banks targeted revealed how much they had lost. The police were unable to trace most of the transfers. But they calculated that the full amount drawn was likely to have been hundreds of millions of dollars. The mastermind of the operation was the elusive Henry Oberlander.

Like Mariella, Oberlander was possibly of Czech descent. When she met him, he was a striking figure with a vast stomach, an overflowing beard and a confessional manner. He often told the story that he had been incarcerated in Auschwitz and watched his family die there. He said he had been ordered to dig mass graves – including his own – at the camp before being wounded in the leg and falling into the pit with the bodies. He told of staying in the mass of corpses until dark and then crawling away to his escape. He managed to get to Hungary and then Vienna. He claimed to have helped agents track Nazi Adolf Eichmann through South America and that he found the Angel of Death Joseph Mengele on a ranch in Brazil. He said he was hunted by the ex-SS agents of ODESSA. But then he said lots of things. His most revealing testament was Henry's Rule: 'Everyone is willing to give something for whatever it is they desire the most.'

Oberlander held twenty-five passports in as many different names and from as many different countries. He used these passports in the passing of forged bank drafts that were so convincing 'bank officials could not believe their eyes'. If we remember that bankers' drafts were issued in one bank and cashed in another and were guaranteed for immediate payment, then we see what an effective scam this was.

To his credit, it is true that Oberlander was known as the Scarlet Pimpernel for his work in the Jewish underground, and it is true that international barriers were as nothing to him. How did

Mariella meet him? Through her old friend, the boxer from Soho, 'Mr Fists', AKA Billy Ambrose. The police had been watching Ambrose, because he often met with Oberlander, and had become suddenly and inexplicably very rich. Ambrose was working as a bookmaker in a gambling establishment in Soho. Not many Soho bookmakers can afford a large house in Sandown Road, Surrey, opposite the Sandown racetrack. And he was driving a Rolls-Royce Corniche. One day the police followed Oberlander from Ambrose's Surrey mansion to the gang's forge in Bayswater.

This was where Francisco Fiocca, the world's most accomplished forger, was hard at work. Silver-haired and bespectacled, with an air of quiet distinction, Fiocca was born in Argentina. It was his forgeries that caused bank officials' eyes to pop. They were so good that even those officials whose signatures had been copied found it hard to accept that they were not genuine. When the police raided the workshop in Vere Court, they found it packed with forged bank notes, bank drafts and 'everything needed to beat the system'.

The gang's quartermaster had an equally colourful pedigree. Andre Biro was responsible for obtaining the specialist equipment used by Fiocca, who was his *protégé*. A Romanian with a Brazilian passport, Biro came from Bucharest, where he had moved in the best circles. But for reasons that remained obscure, he had been obliged to leave his native country. He had worked in Hungary until 1956 when he fled from the Russians during the uprising. So I'm sure he, too, had lots to talk about with Miss Henrietta Chapman.

The confederates arrested at Mariella's flat included Emile Fleischmann, a stateless Hungarian who joined the French Foreign Legion at the beginning of World War Two, subsequently escaping to Britain and joining the Free French Forces in Soho. Fleischman was the confidence trickster who met with bankers to negotiate the bonds that were used for copying. He used his talent for disguise and assimilation to pass forged bank drafts around the world. His companion that day was Jorge Grunfeld, born in Romania, emigrant to Argentina. He posed as a property dealer with an import-export company doing business between the Argentine and Eastern Europe. He was one of the couriers who travelled the world collecting genuine bank drafts for copying.

Although Billy Ambrose was part of the Hungarian Conspiracy he managed to avoid sentencing. It is possible that Mariella and Ambrose were complicit in informing on the rest of the Circle. But how did Mariella fool these consummate professionals? Their covers offer a clue. They were a mixed lot of refugees mostly from Eastern Europe, although their numbers also included an All-England squash player and an ex-Nazi tank commander. Around 1974, they set up a hand-operated press at the back of a junk shop in Notting Hill. Mariella had all the camouflage necessary to smuggle herself into their midst. Neither was their game so far from her own dear husband's: he was passing off fake antiques; they were churning out passports, bankers' drafts and travellers' cheques as well as dealing in fake gems. Biro's Jewels on Portobello Road was the address that fronted for the Circle. As well as producing phoney bankers' drafts, Biro organised the runners. They would cash Fiocca's cheques. So there were various men with dubious backgrounds coming in and out of various addresses in west London, looking for some downtime maybe, to kick back and forget who they were pretending to be for the moment; and here was a woman who, *like, totally got that.*

The more I read about the Hungarian Circle the more appropriate it felt that three members of the gang should be arrested whilst in her flat. One of these men must have been Billy Ambrose. They were charged, tried and sentenced. But not Billy Ambrose. Did he turn informant? Did he ask Mariella to use her contacts at West End Central to get him off the hook? They would have jumped at bait like this. When the case eventually came to court, the Yard was still celebrating the demolition of the Kray gang in East London, and the the Richardson gang in the south. The breaking of the Hungarian Circle was seen as another significant victory against organised crime.

It is also worth pointing out that Billy Ambrose was super-slippery. Remember the Great Train Robbery of 1963? Well, there were twenty-one men who were part of the train robbery – sixteen of whom were trackside. And six of these twenty-one were never identified and got clean away. Billy Ambrose was one of them. In the years that followed the Great Train Robbery accusations were made that some of these suspects paid off the police to have their fingerprints wiped from the scene. Other accusations were made that most of the money taken was still missing.

As for Mariella, she had reinvented herself to such an extent that she had convinced a gang of international men of mystery that her daughter was her sister and that her husband was her father. This deception was so necessary to her *amour propre* she probably believed it herself. According to my Skype contact, MarieAntoinette, Mariella was affianced to Mr Leonard Knowles for an entire year. During this time, Lennie thought she was a twenty-one-year-old unmarried Girton graduate.

The flat in which members of the Hungarian Circle were arrested was rented by Lennie and his new girlfriend whom he met in Wedgie's night club in Chelsea. Dai Llewellyn, variously known as the 'Conquistador of the Canapé Circuit', 'the seducer of the Valleys', or simply 'Dirty Dai', owned the club. Mariella and Lennie got their flat at Wedgie's because their landlord, twenty-six-year-old Lord Anthony Burghersh, heir to the 15th Earl of Westmoreland, was its manager. Burghersh's role seemed to involve a bit of PR work, organising the odd VIP party, and schmoozing rich toffs. This was in a city that still wove a web of reciprocal favours and backhanders. So it came to pass that Lord Burghersh leased the lovely Miss Chapman and Lennie Knowles his flat on Fulham Road while he pursued business interests in the Middle East and America.

The deeper I get into Mariella's story, the further I get from any sense of knowing her. She is vanishing before my eyes. But what I am left with is a keen desire for some kind of truth – her kind of truth – to be told.

So what about Hod? In the same year as Miss Chapman was cohabiting with Lennie, Hod, who was now seventy-three, was living in quiet seclusion at No. 3 High Street, Weybridge. As a bankrupt, the property was not leased in his name but that of Stella Marie Dibben. So she hadn't exactly left him behind, although her daughter's whereabouts remain a mystery. The only facts are that Mariella's new fiancé was a fraudster and conman, and that within a year of her moving into a flat in Fulham, three criminal masterminds were arrested in it.

However hard you look for the Hungarian Circle, I defy you to find them. The gang originated in West Germany. Its fifty or so members engaged in multi-million-pound frauds involving fake Nazi gold, fake jewels, forged bank documents and fake paintings. The subsequent trial was one of the biggest to come before the Central Criminal Court in its history. But neither Oberlander nor his co-defendants would ever be heard of again.

37

AT BROWN'S HOTEL

So Mariella met persons of interest at Brown's Hotel. This was work for a different sort of escort agency. It was more discreet than Thelma's, and Dr Cole's, but far cloudier in its intended outcomes for clients. An unnamed representative of this anonymous organisation sent Mariella to Brown's Hotel, on Albemarle Street in Mayfair. Brown's Hotel was a byword for discretion and luxury, or the luxury of discretion. It was opened in 1837 by Lord Byron's valet, and if anyone should know about discretion it would be him. For Mariella, she was back in her favourite postcode, basking in the perfect backdrop for her brand of escorting. She was on an actual mission; she was being taken seriously. For a woman who had been disbelieved and scorned this must have felt like vindication.

Mariella's new mission and the identity that went with it was triggered by Commander Bert Wickstead's zeal to stamp out corruption in the Met. As we have seen, Wickstead was not a man to take a bribe. And when the opportunity arose, he pursued his quarry with relish. As well as jailing thirteen corrupt members of the Obscene Publications Squad, he had also investigated the case of the prostitute Norma Levy, which was to lead to the downfall of the Conservative minister Lord Lambton. Unimpressed by the trappings of wealth that dazzled some of his colleagues, Wickstead lived in a council flat in Plaistow, east London, with his wife and three sons. The members of his squad, whom he liked to call the Incorruptibles, were devoted to him.

He was not without his detractors. Wickstead's most controversial case was the torso murders investigation of 1976–77. Dudley and Maynard were retired north London 'hard men' who had once run a gang called the Legal & General. The two men claimed in court that Wickstead had fabricated their confessions. He had been gunning for them for years, Dudley said. Dudley ('The Laughing Burglar') explained the statements read out to the court were 'classic verbals', which used terms no self-respecting criminal would utter. As he was taken from the dock, he shouted at Wickstead: 'You got the Tibbs, the Dixons, Silver, and now us. You fitted us all up. But don't worry, you'll be fitted up in the end, by your own kind.'

A decades-long campaign to free the men followed, and in 2002 three Court of Appeal judges quashed the convictions. So the Old Grey Fox had his own grey areas. Digging deeper, we could say that he saw his bosses get public commendations for work he had done; if money did not motivate him, maybe the need for recognition did.

The top job at Scotland Yard was being held by Sir Robert Mark, assisted by his Deputy Commissioner, Sir James Starritt. Both men had been knighted for rooting out police corruption. Sir Mark represented uniformed officers. These men and women, the bobbies on the beat, were the moral core of the police. As such, Sir Mark sought to channel press attention and plaudits towards them. In this he was facilitated by a number of high-level incidents, such as the Balcombe Street and Spaghetti House sieges in 1975. These enabled him to demonstrate the quasi-military efficiency of the uniformed branches.

Sir Mark and Sir Starritt were at the zenith of their respective careers. But with extra funds going to the constabulary, a rivalry was opening up in the Metropolitan Police.

The uniformed police were there to bear the brunt of society's violence. Whether it was political, industrial, criminal or hooligan, they were up close and personal to it. On the other hand, the CID, the plainclothes officers, regarded themselves as an elite body, higher paid by way of allowances and factually, fictionally and journalistically more glamorous than 'plod'. No one wants to be called 'plod', and uniform had long resented the airs and graces of CID, generally known as 'the department'.

The Old Grey Fox, CID, had a lead on a pair of detective chief inspectors close to Sir Robert Mark and his Assistant Commissioner 'C' (Crime), Sir Jock Wilson. The two men in question were DCI John Bland and DCI Reginald Davis, members of the elite Flying Squad. In order to bring them down, Wickstead earmarked a thirty-seven-year-old 'company executive' from Lincoln called Leonard Knowles.

Before Lennie met Mariella he met my grandfather Charlie. This was in 1975. Lennie was a slight, fair-haired man with, by all accounts, an engaging personality and a *retroussé* nose. Charlie met him through a 'creative' accountant of their mutual acquaintance. Charlie was in the market for new business interests and Lennie was on the run from a fraud that had gone wrong in his home town of Lincoln.

'I liked him straight away,' Charlie told Steve Haywood, a reporter from *Time Out*.[33] 'I thought he was an honest man and before long I'd have trusted him with my life. I misjudged the man, I see that now.'

Lennie told his new friend that he was hearing rumours that the police were interested in his Lincoln-based activities. He asked Charlie to use his contacts at the Yard to find out more. Charlie duly contacted his friends at the Yard, and discovered that Lennie's company was under suspicion for fraud. Then in February 1976 Lennie was charged with fraud, arrested, and released on bail. Charlie stood him bail of £30,000. Lennie's trial was scheduled

---

33. *Time Out*

for Lincoln Crown Court. Charlie apologised but his contacts in the Met could not stretch that far. This was a blow for Lennie. The charges against him were very serious, and Charlie could withdraw bail at any time. With this leverage, Charlie was putting pressure on Lennie to get more involved in his business interests.

If Commander Wickstead had some grey areas, Charlie was gunmetal grey all over. My grandfather had a lucrative trade in charging criminal associates for standing them bail. As a fixer it was standard practice that he take a cut. But he took it too far. He started tipping off the police *before* crimes were committed and then when they started to investigate, he offered to use his influence to help his friends wriggle out from under the net.

At the same time as Mariella and Lennie were attempting to get a read on each other in a booth in Wedgie's, Charlie was taking a sight-seeing tour of Ireland in his chauffeur-driven Rolls-Royce. Accompanying him were DCI Reginald Davis of the Flying Squad and his wife. On their return, Charlie was invited to lunch at New Scotland Yard. Through Reginald and DCI Bland, Charlie met other high-ranking officers. Thursday night parties at the Leigham Court hotel in Streatham were attended by Crystal Palace footballers and officers from the Flying Squad. Crooks like the Krays' older brother Charles, and Teddy Machin from the East End Tibbs gang, gathered for after-hours drinking alongside local police officers. When Rusty Humphreys ran out of strippers, my uncle James bussed in student nurses from local hostels.

The apogee of Charlie's social calendar was an invitation in 1975 to the Dorchester Hotel for a dinner to celebrate DCI Davis's promotion. Charlie was photographed sharing a table with Davis and Sir Jock Wilson. Remember Jock's position in the Scotland Yard hierarchy. He was Assistant Commissioner 'C' (Crime), the third-highest-ranked officer in London's Metropolitan Police. Sitting next to him was Sir Robert Mark.

Mariella approached Lennie under the revolving disco ball at Wedgie's. They smooched. They got friendly. They met the following day at Brown's. She intimated that she knew all about his 'problem at Lincoln'. He said nothing, wondering who this intriguing young woman with the plummy accent was. She told him that Charlie had been giving the police detailed information about his activities. Alarm bells started to ring in Lennie's head. Mariella explained that her 'family' had been interested in Charlie for a long time. She insinuated she would 'appreciate' any information he could provide. This could be a way out, thought Lennie. Afterwards he claimed to be sceptical until, he told Haywood, 'she produced statements purporting to be from Taylor to the police, the contents of which assured me that what she was saying was authentic'.

Oblivious to this new reality, Charlie, ensconced in his hotel in Streatham, had just that day been schooling Lenny in a complicated scam very popular in the seventies. It was called the Dollar Premium Fraud.

38

MISS HENRIETTA CHAPMAN

Forward to 21 September 1977, our location the West London County Court. A trial is taking place that sheds more murk on the murk that already surrounds Mariella and her fiancé Leonard Knowles. Lord Anthony Burghersh, the young aristocrat playboy who once boasted 'every night is party night', has fallen on hard times. The Lord, an Old Etonian whose parents are close friends of the Queen, is deep in debt and has nowhere to live.

In court, his counsel, Derek Wood, said his client's only asset, a £22,000 London flat with a £15,000 mortgage, was rented out – and he wanted it back.

The plight of the twenty-six-year-old entrepreneur, nightclub worker and heir to the 15th Earl of Westmorland emerged on the first day of his application for a possession order on the flat. It caught the attention of national tabloids, especially the *Daily Mail*, which delighted in stories of raffish aristocrats, especially those down on their luck. But it was not just sympathy for the rakish lord. It was curiosity about his lovely young tenant, Miss Chapman, and her fiancé Leonard Knowles. Readers discovered that the three were introduced at Wedgie's nightclub in Chelsea through a business partner. Mr Knowles signed the rent agreement to his lordship's flat as a witness and moved into it with Miss Chapman.

Counsel Derek Wood said, 'Mr Knowles is a man with quite a long criminal record, with apparently a record for forgery and fraud. Did you know that?'

Lord Burghersh said, 'I found out about it but I didn't know it at the time the tenancy started.'

Mr Wood continued to tell the court that Lord Burghersh had been naive and rented out the flat in an 'amateurish' way. He let it because he thought he could get a job in the Middle East or America, but the deal fell through. Now he was facing eviction from his present home.

Lord Burghersh told the court he had been forced to 'scrounge for a living'. He was well known to London's jet set but despite his trendy image he was feeling the financial pinch badly. He said that Miss Chapman was an ideal tenant at first, but then she stopped paying the rent, refused to speak to him or to open the door to him, and opened his mail.

Miss Chapman told the court that since she had moved into the flat she had been researching a book, which was entitled *Power, Politics and Pleasure*. She had not offered it to publishers. She also told the court she had not previously written any books. In other words, even the prospect of some free publicity could not persuade her to break cover.

She explained to the court that her research involved interviews and discussions at Lord Burghersh's flat with representatives of heads of state and international companies. During the last three months of 1976, she had been meeting six people a week there and 'others at other places'. Her research did not just mean 'interviewing people, but it is very delicate. When it comes to foreign representatives of heads of state, and industry and their representatives, and so on, I want to see documents and they are very reluctant. It takes me a long time to assure them that they can go to a flat and not be disturbed.'

When Mr Wood asked her whether they paid her any money, she replied, 'Definitely not.'

On 11 October, the same day that the child-killer Mary Bell was sentenced, and Princess Margaret told the gossip columnist Nigel Dempster she was unlikely to marry again because 'it would probably be too much of a bore', a sensational allegation was made in West London County Court. The girl in the case of Lord Burghersh's flat was not twenty-two-year-old Henrietta Chapman after all. She was in fact thirty-five-year-old Mariella Novotny. And the man she called her father, seventy-three-year-old Horace, was not her father. He was, in fact, her husband. The allegations were made on the fourth day of the case in which Lord Burghersh sought repossession of his flat in Fulham Road.

Hod, calling himself Horace Ronald Chapman-Dibben, took the stand for the defendant. He claimed to be based in the eighteenth-century Netherton manor house in Weymouth. (There is no Netherton manor house in Weymouth, although there is one in Hampshire.) He also told the court that the woman in the dock was his daughter. Earlier in the trial Mariella had denied marrying him in 1960 under the name of Stella Marie Capes. Now Hod agreed that he *had* married a former dancer called Stella Marie Capes in 1960 and that they had lived together for three years. But that was as far as he would go. Mr J. J. Davis, for Miss Chapman, said, 'It has been suggested that the woman with whom you went through that marriage ceremony is the defendant?'

'No, she is my daughter,' insisted Hod. He said that the woman in the dock was born in 1955, which made her twenty-two. He said he gave his daughter £200 a month as an allowance but often had to pay other bills. When pressed on the source of his income, he said he got his money from selling his antique collection as he had no earned income. Hod was clearly enjoying his day in court because he elaborated on the subject of daughters, stating for the record that he had *two* daughters named Henrietta. The one in court he called Henry I. The other, whose mother was Mariella Novotny, was known as Henry II. The younger Henrietta was now aged twelve. He claimed that Henry II's mother was living in California.

Mr Derek Wood for Lord Burghersh asked, 'Is California a convenient place for losing people's identity?'

Mr Chapman-Dibben sidestepped the question and said that Henry II was in an institution in Chelmsford. Whether this was a boarding school or a state-run care home is unclear but it does indicate the state of relations between Mariella and her daughter.

Of more immediate concern to Mariella was the preservation of her alias. Mr Derek Wood made the claim that Mariella had named the Man in the Mask in an interview with Lord Denning. The headline writers were in raptures over the Riddle of the Blonde Lodger and the Jet Set Lord. Miss Chapman's counsel, Mr J. J. Davis, was forced to ask Prosecution to withdraw the allegation that Henrietta was the witness's wife. He said her character was being besmirched. He dismissed as 'pure James Thurber' the allegation 'this isn't your daughter, this is your wife'.

Deputy Judge Simon Goldstein said Prosecution's claim was a sensational one and he thought there had been a 'serious error of judgement'. He said he was not called upon to make a decision 'but looking at Miss Chapman I find it very hard to accept that she is the thirty-five-year-old Mariella Novotny'.

So at least she had him fooled. But the *Daily Mail*'s team was not about to give up. They contacted a stripper called Tui Alba who said she had taught Mariella some moves at a strip club in Soho. So if anyone should know her to be Mariella, she would. The *Mail* also contacted a former neighbour from Hyde Park Square who was similarly puzzled at the similarity between Mariella and the woman in the dock. Mrs Margaret Foggarty said, 'When I saw the papers I could have sworn the pictures of father and daughter were really Mr Dibben and his wife. Mrs Dibben used to call herself Mariella. She always wore sunglasses, even in winter, and huge hats tied with a scarf.'

Mrs Foggarty confirmed that the couple had left Hyde Park Square around 1971. (This would have been when they moved to Nevern Square.) She paused to recall the late-night parties the couple used to give. 'The parties weren't noisy but the biggest cars would draw up. I remember reading in the Sunday papers about "Naughty Novotny" and her parties, and thinking that's them that lived next door.'

The following day the who's who mystery took a new twist when society doctor, Teddy Sugden, who gave Mariella away on her wedding day, told the *Daily Mail* that everything pointed to Mariella and Henrietta being the same person. So while Mariella and her husband stood in court continuing to assert she was his daughter, Dr Sugden accompanied the *Daily Mail* from court to the disputed flat in Fulham Road. Sugden went into some detail about his knowledge of the couple. For six months after the marriage, he told the *Mail* that he had shared a flat with the newly-weds in Eaton Place. The wedding was 'an extremely giggly affair. I took her to the ceremony from the flat.'

The accompanying photograph shows Hod sporting sideburns, ponytail and deer-stalker. Next to him Mariella exudes the glamour of a bygone era in a fur cap and blue-lensed metal-rimmed glasses. She is looking over her shoulder, apprehensive and defensive. Perhaps she has spotted Teddy in the crowd because he stood less than ten feet from her as she walked with Hod to the flat's entrance.

Afterwards he said, 'I could have sworn that they were Hod Dibben and Mariella. I'm sure I recognised them both. It was not just her face but her mannerisms and even the way she walked which were distinctive.'

He went on to say that he had received a phone call the previous night. 'Hod rang me up at midnight and said, "You've put me and Mariella in a very dangerous position."'

The trial ended on 12 October, and Miss Chapman was ordered to leave the flat within twenty-eight days. Deputy Judge Goldstein ordered her to pay costs, understood to run into several thousands of pounds, plus six months' rent, which came to a total of £950.

Behind the grimy blinds and broken door bell of the Fulham flat, no doubt mulling over the financial disaster, Mariella refused to emerge for waiting photographers. When Hod slipped out to a nearby pub he was pounced upon and asked where Mariella Novotny might be. He replied, 'I'm not answering.' When he returned he was accompanied by a dark-suited representative of a Sunday newspaper who was believed to be in possession of a chequebook.

Just to add to the mystery, a hint was dropped by another 'friend' of the alleged husband and wife. This unnamed friend came forward to tell the *Daily Mirror* that a few weeks previously Mariella had told him, 'I'm terrified. I am being hounded by British secret agents.' The friend said that Mariella was planning to write a book on espionage:

> She planned to draw upon her experiences with sixties swingers like the War Minister, John Profumo, and society osteopath Stephen Ward ... she has lived in a fantastic world for some time. She tells incredible stories about her sexual exploits and the men in her life. All of them seem to be of international importance. She also says that some people with a lot of influence want to shut her up.

39

CODENAME HENRY

The following episode in Mariella's story will only make sense if you accept that most successful fraudsters are sincere, just as most demagogues and liars are honestly intoxicated by their own dishonesty. (Further reading: *Sincerity and Authenticity*, Lionel Trilling, 1971.)

As a result of disclosures made by Mariella to her friend in West End Central police station, the Chief Constable of Kent, Barry Pain, was called upon to conduct an inquiry under section 49 of the Police Act 1964. The inquiry was based on the premise that very senior detectives had been consorting with Charlie Taylor and helping him to run 'long firm frauds' in which criminals set up shell companies, ran up large debts and loans, and then disappeared.

Mariella was the primary witness for Barry Pain and his inquiry team. But just as her evidence never appeared in the Denning Report, the contents of Mr Pain's 1,600-page report have never been disclosed.

'There was one thing that kept bothering me,' Uncle James told me. 'This Lenny character was wearing an overcoat even though it was a hot day.' In fact 1976 was the hottest summer on record, and it later transpired that this Lenny character had a tape recorder strapped to his body.

'When he came to the house he was always interested in photos and other things of me with the police,' Charlie told Steve Haywood, the reporter for *Time Out*. 'I used to tell him everything. He was an inquisitive sort of bloke.'

In February 1976 Lennie moved out of Lord Burghersh's flat in Fulham and into Charlie's hotel in Streatham, Leigham Court. Charlie's Thursday parties were in full swing. One night Viscount Colville, Tory Minister of State at the Home Office between 1972 and 1974, rocked up. Charlie had come back from his cruise round Ireland with Detective Chief Inspector Reginald Davies. When Davies found out about Leigham Court's new guest he asked Charlie to report to him on Lennie's movements. Charlie confessed he had already started to school Lennie in a 'fiddle'. Both Charlie and Lennie were borrowing vast sums of money from foreign banks and then pretending these sums were proceeds from the sale of securities on which they could claim the dollar premium. This was a sum paid by the Bank of England on cash brought back to England after the sale of foreign investments. A bank official in the Exchange Control Department was the plotters' safety net.

Charlie built his defence in court on the request from DCI Reginald Davies to frame Lennie. At no point did he realise that Lennie was going to make the same manoeuvre. Still under the impression that his girlfriend was working for an intelligence department and that her family was influential in the foreign office, he asked Charlie if he would like to become involved in selling what the Italians call *fugazzi*, fake gold medallions and half-sovereigns. The twist was that Charlie and Lennie would produce these *fugazzi* themselves. All they needed was a press.

In March 1976 information reached the Treasury that 'certain persons were planning to carry out a substantial fraud by using the dollar premium system'. In the summer of that eventful year, the former Boss of the Underworld, Billy Hill, who had once enjoyed a relationship with Eddie Chapman, introduced Charlie to a man called Terry Adams. Terry asked Charlie to get him out of trouble. He had been arrested for his part in a Heathrow Airport robbery that involved £150,000 worth of krugerrands. Charlie got in touch with DCI Bland of the Serious Crime Squad. Bland was a regular at Charlie's Thursday night parties. As well as Reg Davies, Bland was the other officer in Wickstead's sights. To help Terry Adams get out of trouble, Bland said he would contact the officer in charge of the Heathrow Airport robbery. He said that his help would cost £5,000.

The robbery had been headline news and Charlie was no doubt boasting about his contacts over an anisette at the bar. And Lennie was no doubt egging him on. Sometimes he had a girlfriend with him – a hippy blonde chick called Henrietta.

It was during the summer of 1976 that photographs and documents started disappearing from Charlie's office, only to emerge again as evidence in the Pain Enquiry into police corruption. The papers that Lennie was smuggling out were compiled and logged in a series of files organised by his girlfriend. He still did not know her name was Mariella Novotny. Under the direction of Barry Pain, Chief Constable of Kent, she was working under – and probably revelling in – the codename of Henry.

Rivalry between the two main police departments was still an issue. Of the met police, Charlie's friends were detectives. Mariella's people were the uniformed branch. Her information was going directly to the officer in charge of all uniformed policemen at New Scotland Yard.

She did a good job. Her notes contained details on aspects of my grandfather's business dealings, for which he was later to be brought to trial. There were also telephone numbers, some in code, which were direct lines to West End Central police station. There were also photographs taken at the wedding of the son of Sir Jock Wilson, Assistant Commissioner 'C', Scotland Yard. Barry Pain would have noted with interest that this high-ranking officer was on intimate terms with a fence and that his son's wedding reception was held at this man's hotel in Streatham.

With regards to Mariella's activities, the notes she made also contained information that suggested she knew about arrests before they took place. These notes were made available to Steve Haywood, the reporter from *Time Out*, who saw the files stolen from her flat by Tricky Dicky. From these notes we can draw the inference that Mariella knew that the leading lights of the Hungarian Circle would be arrested at the flat she rented from Lord Burghersh.

Let's return to my uncle James and his assessment of the situation. As far as he could see, his father was keeping him out of trouble with the police by doing 'favours' for them. James was heavily into Class-A drugs, petty crime and domestic violence, the kind of behaviour that typically surrounds addiction. Despite these distractions he was reading the moodboard of his father's life.

'I had just picked up from the chemist, and was shooting up cocaine and experiencing terrible paranoia.' We were sitting in the lobby of the Leigham Court Hotel, now a perfectly respectable guesthouse on the London to Brighton road.

'I could see police peering at me while I hid behind a palm tree. There was a party of travelling salesmen in the garden playing crazy golf. There were a couple of hippies I'd picked up crashed out on some sacks of compost. I could see officers creeping up on the greenhouse hiding behind trees, with rifles ready to shoot. Your grandad was in the office talking to Lennie. I was in love with his girlfriend – I didn't know she was Mariella. She was sitting on the terrace watching the crazy golf. She was wearing a lovely straw hat and a mini dress. I took her up to my room and we listened to Rod Stewart's "The Killing of Georgie".'

So she sucker-punched my uncle, too.

In September 1976 the detectives Pain was investigating discovered they were being informed upon. They summoned Charlie to Scotland Yard. They warned him to watch out for a woman called Henrietta. Charlie returned to the hotel and asked his son if Lennie had shown up that day.

'Has Lennie been here?'

'Yes.' James was not keen on Lennie, regarding him as a rival for his father's favours.

'When he turned up was he with a bird by the name of Henrietta or Marietta or Marie?'

James demurred. He was in love with the bird. And when Lennie was finally tracked down, he denied all knowledge of her. On 17 November 1976, acting on information supplied by Mariella via Lennie, the police arrested my grandfather. Lennie and Mariella came to the hotel at 10.30 in the morning. Lennie had with him the dies for making sovereigns and some dollars. He asked Charlie to pay Mariella £500 as part payment for the dollars. Ten minutes later the police arrived.

'He thought all along that he would be saved by his detective friends,' said Uncle James. 'But they deserted him.'

In the spring of 1977, Mariella's flat would be turned over by Tricky Dicky on the orders of a very bitter Uncle James.

When Charlie's story broke, it was considered another extraordinary saga of corruption at the highest levels. He was arrested in a police raid that smashed 'a forgery plot which could have threatened the world's gold market by flooding it with fake half sovereigns'.[34] A few weeks later he was charged alongside Leonard Knowles with conspiracy to defraud the Bank of England of £1 million by claiming false dollar premiums on non-existent investments. It was during this trial that Charlie made open accusations against his police friends and claimed that Lennie had fitted him up.

Lennie and Mariella had left Charlie's hotel minutes before it was raided by the police. During the raid, as well as dies that were to be used for manufacturing sovereigns, police found forged dollar bills. Charlie's defence barrister turned to an ancient tale – or was it pantomime? – to describe Loughton police station, the lair of the Old Grey Fox.

---

34. *Evening News*

'You've heard of Aladdin's cave?' he asked the jury. 'Well, two floors up [from the property room at Loughton police station] we had Commander Wickstead, the Old Grey Fox himself in the guise of Ebenezer. You remember Ebenezer? New lamps for old? Only this time it was new words for old, new words where old words never existed.'

In the cells at Loughton sat my grandfather. On entering the cell, Commander Wickstead ordered him to his feet.

'You know who I am?' Charlie acknowledged he did.

'You'll never come out of here again, do you know that? Your cover's blown and your police friends too.'

Charlie smiled.

'Knock that fucking grin off your face,' Wickstead said. And then, rattling off the names of two or three police officers, he said, 'You know them, don't you?' Of course you do. We know what's been happening. Just think it over and I'll see you later.'

Wickstead turned to another officer who had come into the room with him.

'Shut the door on the cunt.'

The problem for Charlie was that Bert did not seem to be interested in the gold sovereigns or the dollar premium fraud. During Pain's inquiry Wickstead had received a call from the wife of a man with whom he had dealt as a junior officer in a shooting in the East End. This man, possibly Mariella's old friend Billy Ambrose, told Wickstead that he had received an offer to set him up. Ambrose, if it was he, was being supplied with dates and places where Wickstead was alleged to have taken money.

Charlie said: 'He interviewed me three or four times about the sovs, but he was never really concerned with the case. All he was interested in was the police I'd known, especially ****.'

The gold sovereign case was tried. In his summing up Judge Grant explained his theory to the jury. 'You've seen these officers coming into court, one of them is a clean-cut young man with a great future in the police force. Would these men jeopardise their careers by telling lies?'

The jury seemed to think they would and the defendants were acquitted.

Charlie told Haywood that Lennie and Mariella had fitted him up. Lennie told Haywood that Mariella, codenamed Henry, had fitted them both up.

In January 1977 both Charlie and Lennie stood trial for the dollar premium fraud. Lennie gave Charlie a handwritten document suggesting the evidence he should give. He said that Charlie should say that DCIs Davis and Bland were involved in the fraud and had asked Charlie to finance them. Victor Durand QC, who was defending Charlie, said that Charlie was running with the hares and hunting with the hounds. He had hoped to get a large reward from the Treasury for the tip-off. Charlie denied the charge, claiming he had been acting as a police informer.

On 6 May 1978, Lennie claimed in court at the Old Bailey that he had been framed by the police because of information he passed on to Mariella Novotny, who worked for an intelligence department under the code name of Henry. He said he had been giving her information on a daily basis about police officers and their association with criminals.

'That has led to several Scotland Yard officers being suspended.' He alleged that an assistant commissioner, Jock Wilson, had been transferred to Traffic and a DCI had quit the force. DCI Reginald Davis took early retirement and became a solicitor.

When Leonard Knowles blew her cover in his statement at the Old Bailey in May 1978, Mariella was waiting to take the stand as a prosecution witness. Instead of taking the stand, she was ushered out of court. Barry Pain was protecting her cover. He had asked her to help him with enquiries into corruption at Scotland Yard. This was Operation Countryman, another report that has not seen the light of day. But Mariella's days as a paid police informant were over.

In 1978 she appeared on the London Programme on LWT. She claimed a close acquaintance with Pain and his enquiry team.

She made it known that she was involved in intelligence operations. If Ash had not already exposed her, Mariella blew the lid on her covert activities. She also revealed she was falling apart at the seams.

In October 1978, villagers in Chalford, near Stroud, were surprised to learn that one of their neighbours had in the 1960s been an 'international sex queen'. Still going under the name of Henrietta Chapman, Mariella was living with Hod in seclusion in a Gloucestershire valley when a local reporter spotted her sitting at the bar in the New Red Lion public house.

40

THE ENDANGERED *NOTORNIS*

Early retirement in Gloucestershire with an ageing and impoverished husband led to Mariella's child being taken into care by court order. This in turn led to a stint in rehab. You would think this would be it. But no, she still had some game in her. Mariella now embarked on a love affair with a female doctor she met in rehab.

On 16 November 1980, Dr Caroline Olsson revealed to the *News of the World*: 'She wanted me to be her slave, both mentally and physically. But she demanded too much from me.' This sounds about right.

Mariella had hit the headlines again. This time it was due to her first 'paymaster', Harry Alan Towers. He had been very busy since he fled America in 1961. He was still wanted by the FBI and had been working in Europe and Africa producing an endless stream of B-movies. He was around sixty years old. He had not changed much. It would be hard for a man like Harry to change since he had always looked like an ageing, well-fed accountant: greying hair, a weak chin that threatened to become a double, and the classic writer's stoop.

Appearances aside, Harry's colleagues in the film industry were aware of his wayward talents. The gossip amongst B-movie producers in Europe was that Harry was on the lam. The Spanish director Jesus Franco had collaborated with Towers on several

erotic cinematic capers. The great Hollywood actor Herbert Lom
had starred on at least five occasions. The man who had been
Napoleon and his association with Harry add to the mythology
surrounding him.

This is referenced in the novel my friend Patricia told me to
read. Javier Marías' *Thus Bad Begins* was published in Spain in
2014, by which time classified information had been released. In
the English translation, I read with interest the chapter in which
Lom confided that Towers had shown him a copy of an internal
memorandum about the Profumo Affair from Hoover himself.
I wondered if Marías had invented this anecdote or had he really
come across Herbert Lom during his work in the Spanish film
industry? I found an interview Marías gave for the *Paris Review*
in which he admitted that Jesus Franco was his uncle and he had
visited him on set several times and met Lom there. Since this was
the case, it was possible that Lom's collaboration with Towers led
to his conjectures about Towers' role in white-slave trafficking in
Kennedy's America. Whatever the case, it was perfect casting on the
part of Marías. Lom is the ideal actor to make these conjectures,
since his onscreen ability to be taken seriously is sabotaged by his
ability to be so comically sinister.

According to Marías' rendition, Hoover mentions Mariella
Novotny, adding in parentheses 'see Kennedy Brothers file'. The
file also mentions 'her pimp Alan Towers'.

'Novotny states that Towers was a Soviet agent' and that the
Soviets were collecting their proverbial *Kompromat*, says Lom.
Even within the fiction constructed by Marías lurks the possibility
that Towers is constructing his own fiction in order to impress his
showbiz friends: 'He's perfectly capable of doing that and more.'

Marías makes use of Mariella's story and features it in the same
way that he reproduces the photo in which she is accompanied
by a burly G-man. This, I guess, is the essence of the woman who
tried so hard to reinvent herself as something bigger than she was.
Despite all her efforts, she was a pawn in a larger mystery that
can never satisfactorily be resolved. As for the woman herself,

Marías poses the question: what was it about her that could cause so many high-profile men to lower their guard and risk their careers and status in order to bed her?

Apart from her resemblance to the star of Fellini's *La Dolce Vita*, Anita Ekberg, of course. The only answer I can give is the one given by Christine Keeler. As quoted at the beginning of my account, Keeler describes the 'tiny waist' and the 'Olympian proportions' of Mariella's sexual athleticism. But that's surely not the whole nine yards...

Marías' narrator ponders the photograph of Mariella in her oversized crushed-velvet bonnet. She looks thoughtful and her eyes are aslant. The FBI agent is, by contrast, predatory in his large, brooding coarseness. Marías has his narrator conclude, 'Time has covered them both with a large enough dose of unreality.'

In the course of writing his novel Marías did his due diligence. Stephen Dorrill's *Lobster* magazine and Wikipedia are quoted. His narrator puts forward the theory that the same undercover agent who attended Vic Damone's party and witnessed his Asian girlfriend's bloody showdown in the bathroom was the man who telephoned Mariella and hired her services on the day she was arrested in Harry's apartment. An interesting addition to this latter party is Harry's mother, who was apparently also present when a naked Mariella burst into Harry's study to tell him there was a policeman in her bedroom.

At this point it is worth asking the question, as Marías does:[35] what does it matter if a film producer was or wasn't involved in a sex-and-spy ring in America in the Kennedy era? And were these women vulnerable or complicit? What do we gain by finding out about them, or dwelling on them even? History is full of minor abuses and serious crimes. Perhaps we should accept, as Mariella did, that this is the way of the world. Perhaps as readers we can be assured that at least this particular 'bad' is over. As such, believing the worst to be over, are we waiting for the next 'bad' to begin?

---

35. Javier Marías, *Thus Bad Begins*

Towers surrendered to the US police in 1980 and Mariella revealed that once again she was writing a book. But this book would reveal everything, including details of her work for the secret services and a 'plot to discredit Jack Kennedy'. She told the London Programme, 'I kept a diary of all my appointments in the UN building. Believe me, it's dynamite. It's now in the hands of the CIA.' She got a fair amount of newspaper coverage but the book never appeared.

Three years later Mariella was back in London but at the wrong end of Fulham, in Parson's Green. She was living with Hod at No. 6 Dancer Road. They are starting again. It is spring equinox 1983, which can mean only one thing: pain and regret. Hod is behaving strangely – consulting horoscopes, drawing charts, and making phone calls late into the night. She tries to ignore him, having long ago realised that entering into the confines of his mind is stepping into the abyss. Besides, she has her own problems.

Where is her daughter?

She decides to go for a walk along the King's Road. It is not the same King's Road she remembers from her heyday, when her novel was published. The boutiques, The Pheasantry, where Litvinoff had held court, have given way to grungy shops. Scruffy young people loiter outside them. They ignore her but she can still feel good here, far enough away from Hod's disturbing senescence.

As she returns home, she loses herself in ecstatic reviews that she writes in her head for her forthcoming autobiography.

'A childlike state: frozen in an attitude of remembering' – Volguine's Lunar Calendar. She and Hod have returned to occult wisdom in their search for answers. Mariella turns to contemplate the old fraud. He is slouched in an armchair in front of the television. In the year since they got it, he has gained three stone in weight, just by sitting in the armchair and munching biscuits, fish fingers and Chinese takeaways.

Evenings he spends drinking. He had come to inhabit a zone in which dreams and the passive viewing of the television screen are confused. So time passes for Hod, and Mariella can see he is quite happy. But she is not. Nothing must stop her churning up the past in order to make sense of it. The fact that she is being hunted down in her pursuit of what is hidden makes her more determined. At least she thinks she is being hunted down. It could be that the truth is even worse: she is being ignored.

On 9 May 1983, the hunt turned cold. She had been feeling feverish all day. Late at night she made herself a bowl of milk pudding. Several hours later she was found face down in it. The official version is that she died of a Temazepam overdose.

'Very hard to die of an overdose,' said Jackie, 'when she'd been taking them for twenty-odd years.'

After her death, Hod confided to Stephen Dorrill that the house in Parsons Green was burgled and Mariella's papers were stolen. At her inquest, Novotny's psychiatrist, Dr Joan Gomez of Chelsea and Westminster Hospital, revealed that Mariella had a 'hysterical personality disorder'.

At her funeral in a Sussex village, men in grey suits turned up. And that was it. She died a *notornis*, the wingless bird that she had looked up in *Funk & Wagnall's* ten years before as she embarked on another restless flight. She still could not keep up with her own velocity. In the eyes of the world, this bird from Bohemia, 'a bit vulture, a bit eagle', was a world apart. In the Latin that she loved to quote, she was *immundus*. In English, this word proliferates into other meanings, loaded with fear and uncertainty. Mariella, who wanted to be on top of this world, becomes rejected by it, exorcised and 'unclean'.

AFTERWORD

As more and more stories of sexual assault have been made public in the last decade, the genre of their telling has exploded. One of the features of my narrative is the examination of the lives of both victim and perpetrator. In looking at the victim I realised we seem to focus on her past: what was she wearing? Where was she positioning herself? In other words, how was she performing her sexuality?

For the perpetrators, I saw that we consider their future prospects. Will they go to prison? Will the allegation against them affect their careers, their standing in society? We rarely ask if they will take responsibility because we know that, if they can afford it, they will hire expensive lawyers who will fudge the issue, thereby exiting the stage of their culpability.

In my reckoning we are left with the victim who is either vindicated in their exposure of sexual assault or set aside as an unreliable witness. Rarely do we lavish the attention on her, on a woman like Mariella, and ask what happens next. What happens in the post-traumatic narrative of such a life as hers?

These are the questions I tried to answer in this book. What Mariella showed me is that testaments matter; the continual rewriting of her story reveals her unconscious belief that standing witness to abuse serves a fundamental purpose: recovery of self – the self before abuse.

As a consequence of this testimony, the suffering that is somehow both sanctioned and ignored by society is mitigated by the revelation that it was always being witnessed. Mariella proves this over and over again. Strict records of abuses, her own as well as others, were being compiled contemporaneously to their commission. She left us dossiers showing wrongdoing by power brokers, the premise being that if the truth is recorded, exposed and circulated, consequences will be meted out and power will crumble.

This is the theory, anyway. The reality is that testimony does not dislodge power. Perpetrators dodge the bullets and wait for the next outrage to deflect attention. 'Thus Bad Begins.' The revolution doesn't happen, power does not collapse, the legal system is unresponsive.

Mariella died, abject and alone, stewing in her story, drowning in a confection she created to offset feelings of powerlessness. But there was something liberating in what she did: if Lord Denning would not listen to her and *Club International* cancelled her column, why should her testimony be confined to the formats that law and the press dictate?

Survivors labour under a strict code of conduct as to how they should relate their trauma: they should be pitiful and yet dignified, shocked and yet restrained, articulate and yet vulnerable. Mariella's post-traumatic narrative resorts to all the models of behaviour that are not approved by society, and then some. This is not to say that revenge, despair, acting out (by means of sado-masochistic roleplay) and the delusion that exposing the truth will secure justice work. They don't.

In the end, she went for the oldest trick in the book. She performed her abjection; she took it out on her body, holding it up for public consumption, contempt and dismay. She wore her abjection like a veil, and she danced it to the death. Every gesture told for Mariella. The last steps towards death took place on a street called Dancer Road. If her dance was macabre, at least I did not look away. I stayed with her to the end to bring her back into the story of a certain kind of world that existed in the embers of the twentieth century.

ACKNOWLEDGEMENTS

I would like to thank the Royal Literary Fund for their ongoing support and generosity, the Society of Authors for their generosity, and James Morton for his expertise.

INDEX